The Euro at Five: Ready for a Global Role?

INSTITUTE FOR INTERNATIONAL ECONOMICS

The Euro at Five: Ready for a Global Role?

Adam S. Posen, editor

Washington, DC
April 2005

Adam S. Posen, senior fellow, has been associated with the Institute since 1997. He was an economist in the International Research Function of the Federal Reserve Bank of New York from 1994 to 1997. In 1992–93 he was the Arthur D. Okun Memorial Fellow in Economic Studies at the Brookings Institution, and in 1992–93 he was a Bosch Foundation Fellow in Germany. He is the author of several works on monetary policy and political economy, including *Restoring Japan's Economic Growth* (1998), and coeditor of *Japan's Financial Crisis and Its Parallels to US Experience* (2000).

INSTITUTE FOR INTERNATIONAL ECONOMICS
1750 Massachusetts Avenue, NW
Washington, DC 20036-1903
(202) 328-9000   FAX: (202) 659-3225
www.iie.com

C. Fred Bergsten, *Director*
Valerie Norville, *Director of Publications
  and Web Development*
Edward Tureen, *Director of Marketing*

Typesetting by BMWW
Printing by Kirby Lithographic Company, Inc.

For reprints/permission to photocopy please contact the APS customer service department at Copyright Clearance Center, Inc., 222 Rosewood Drive, Danvers, MA 01923; or email requests to: info@copyright.com

Printed in the United States of America
07 06 05   5 4 3 2 1

Library of Congress Cataloging-in-Publication Data

The euro at five : ready for a global role? / Adam Posen, editor.
    p. cm.
    Includes bibliographical references and index.
    ISBN 0-88132-374-8
    1. Euro.   2. Money—European Union countries.   I. Posen, Adam Simon.
    II. Institute for International Economics (U.S.)

HG925.E97 2005
332.4'94—dc22   2004065782

The views expressed in this publication are those of the authors. This publication is part of the overall program of the Institute, as endorsed by its Board of Directors, but does not necessarily reflect the views of individual members of the Board or the Advisory Committee.

Contents

Preface

The euro celebrated the fifth anniversary of its successful launch on January 1, 1999. As the only major currency to be created in the 20th century, it now stands on the brink of becoming one of the world's two reserve currencies in the 21st century. As the signal accomplishment of European unification to date, the euro's functioning and development shape much of the agenda for ever-closer union in Europe and in turn for transatlantic relations. As the currency bearing the brunt of the US dollar's decline from its substantial overvaluation of the late 1990s, the euro's value and management will be critical to the successful adjustment of international imbalances. As a long-run competitor and collaborator with the dollar, the euro creates the potential for a bipolar international monetary system, offering unprecedented challenges and opportunities to economic policymakers.

The global role of the euro is thus a matter of pressing concern to the United States and the world economy. Yet these issues have been largely ignored as Europhobes and Europhiles focus solely on the domestic viability and benefits of eurozone membership and as American policymakers discount external—particularly European—monetary developments. However, decisions made now about the degree of cooperation between US and European monetary authorities will have lasting effects both on the international financial system and on economic growth in Europe and beyond. These decisions will be particularly important in the contexts of the sustained dollar decline and the strained political support for transatlantic partnership and globalization. With ongoing European economic underperformance, the political economy of adjustment is even more likely to react to short-term concerns with unintended implications.

In February 2004, the Institute held a conference to examine the euro's potential to fulfill its emerging global role. This book, edited by Senior Fellow Adam Posen, comprises the papers, comments, and panel discussion presented at that conference. The authors assess the progress of the euro project after five years, the implications for transatlantic relations, and the ability of a "finance G-2" to manage the transition to a bipolar monetary system. A panel of experts examines several dimensions of the financial development of the eurozone and euro-denominated transactions vis-à-vis the United States, as well as further advances required to support a strong euro, and analyze the evolution of the Stability and Growth Pact and its implications for stabilization in the eurozone and for the future of the euro. Authors also address the likely impact of the euro's role on the practical aspects of monetary and financial policy coordination among the major economies. Tommaso Padoa-Schioppa presents a view from the European Central Bank (ECB) of the euro's present and future global role, while Federal Reserve Governor Ben Bernanke offers a perspective from the Federal Reserve on the euro at five and on what to expect from Federal Reserve–ECB cooperation in the future.

One important objective of the book is to identify areas of common interest and of common vulnerability between American and European policymakers, as the euro evolves and as political resistance to international adjustment mounts in the short term. A second objective is to better inform policymakers and the American public about the euro and thereby dispel unrealistic but still all-too-common discussions on the US side of the Atlantic about whether the euro "can survive." The authors make clear that this question has long since been settled in the affirmative. The questions at hand are, What opportunities does the euro's rise present for policymakers? What might occur if these opportunities are missed?

The development of the euro and its implications for the international financial system have been of major interest to the Institute since the first pre-Maastricht proposals were made. C. Randall Henning's *Cooperating with Europe's Monetary Union* (1997) and the Institute's earlier conference volume on *Reviving the European Union* (1994) foreshadowed these questions of a bipolar monetary world. My own article "The Dollar and the Euro" in *Foreign Affairs* in 1997 was one of the first by a US economist to suggest that not only would the euro succeed but also that it would challenge the dollar. This research was part of the Institute's ongoing broader agenda on the leadership of the global economic system and on monetary regimes.

This book is part of a more recent, large-scale Institute commitment to the study of European economic performance and integration. Its initial publication was *Measuring the Costs of Protection in Europe* by Patrick Messerlin in 2001, which has become a touchstone in discussions of European structural reform. *The Benefits of Price Convergence: Speculative Calculations* by Gary C. Hufbauer, Erika Wada, and Tony Warren (2001), *Has*

Globalization Gone Far Enough? The Costs of Fragmented Markets (2004) by Scott C. Bradford and Robert Z. Lawrence, and *Transforming the European Economy* (2004) by Martin Neil Baily and Jacob F. Kirkegaard assess how much further Europe has to go to deliver all the benefits of integration to consumers.

The Institute for International Economics is a private, nonprofit institution for the study and discussion of international economic policy. Its purpose is to analyze important issues in that area and to develop and communicate practical new approaches for dealing with them. The Institute is completely nonpartisan.

The Institute is funded by a highly diversified group of philanthropic foundations, private corporations, and interested individuals. Major institutional grants are now being received from the William M. Keck Jr. Foundation, the New York Community Trust, and the Starr Foundation. About 18 percent of the Institute's resources in our latest fiscal year were provided by contributors outside the United States, including about 8 percent from Japan. Both the Euro at Five conference and this volume were made possible with a grant from the European Commission. Posen's chapter drew upon his ongoing *Germany in the World Economy* project, which is supported by a major grant from the German Marshall Fund of the United States.

The Board of Directors bears overall responsibilities for the Institute and gives general guidance and approval to its research program, including the identification of topics that are likely to become important over the medium run (one to three years), and which should be addressed by the Institute. The director, working closely with the staff and outside Advisory Committee, is responsible for the development of particular projects and makes the final decision to publish an individual study.

The Institute hopes that its studies and other activities will contribute to building a stronger foundation for international economic policy around the world. We invite readers of these publications to let us know how they think we can best accomplish this objective.

C. Fred Bergsten
Director
December 2004

Acknowledgments

This volume is based on work presented and discussed at a conference held on February 26, 2004, at the Institute for International Economics. We are grateful to all our contributing authors and discussants, particularly to those who joined us from Europe and from universities outside the Washington area, as well as to the senior American and European officials who made the time to contribute so substantively. We are also grateful to the European Commission, whose financial support made possible the publication of this volume in its current form. The volume's editor and the Institute are solely responsible for the choice of authors and topics included in (and omitted from) this study.

We would also like to thank the Delegation of the European Commission in Washington, and in particular Moreno Bertoldi, economic counselor at the delegation, for their ongoing assistance with and encouragement of our research on the European economy and transatlantic economic relations, of which this project is one example. As with all Institute books, a special debt is owed to the publications team at the Institute, led by Valerie Norville. In particular, Madona Devasahayam and Marla Banov dealt gracefully with all the travails involved in producing a multiauthor volume when the authors are distributed around the world. The authors of the individual chapters remain solely responsible for the opinions expressed and for any remaining errors in their respective contributions.

Overview: The Euro's Success Within Limits

ADAM S. POSEN

New international reserve currencies do not come along every day, or even every century. The launch of the euro, the European Union's currency (at least for 12 of the 25 current members), on January 1, 1999, was a birth long foretold. From at least the 1992 Maastricht Treaty onward, its creation was at the forefront of the overall European integration agenda, and the meeting of criteria for eurozone entry dominated macroeconomic policymaking in Western Europe. The academic and policy discussion of European Monetary Unification's (EMU's) potential advantages and disadvantages began even earlier.[1]

The tendency for many American as well as internal observers of EMU had been to be skeptical—first of the virtues of the goal of monetary integration in Europe itself; then of the project's political viability; and then of its economic sustainability, in a turn asserting that the euro was a solely

Adam S. Posen is a senior fellow at the Institute for International Economics. Daniel Gould provided multifaceted assistance in the preparation of this chapter. This overview has benefited from discussions with this volume's contributing authors, and with members of the Directorate General for Economic and Financial Affairs of the European Commission, and of the Directorates General for Monetary Policy and for Research of the European Central Bank. All views expressed here, and any errors or omissions, remain solely those of the author.

1. See Canzoneri, Grilli, and Masson (1992), De Cecco and Giovannini (1989), De Grauwe (2000), and the references therein, as well as the seminal European Commission (1990) and the Cecchini report (Cecchini 1988). Most of these studies concern how best to make EMU work, taking the goal as a given, or assessing the optimality of the European Union as a currency area.

political project.[2] Though the euro certainly has had no shortage of champions—including, beyond Euroland's borders, the economists Bergsten (1997), Eichengreen (1998), Mundell (1998), and Portes and Alogoskoufis (1991)—until recently the weight of opinion on the American side of the Atlantic has emphasized the negative if not supposedly calamitous impact of the euro on Europe.[3] As a result, the potential global role of the euro and its relationship to the dollar have been largely ignored in the United States. Why think about the implications of a currency that is deemed at best doomed to second-tier status and at worst a cause of economic weakness for its issuing area?

Only recently—as the euro passed its fifth birthday in wide usage and without a technical hitch, and went well past parity with the dollar—has sentiment changed. Increasingly, the question is being raised whether the euro might appreciate against the dollar for an extended period, be the beneficiary of substantial international portfolio adjustments, or even begin to supplant the dollar as the dominant global reserve currency.[4] One might be troubled to think that capricious nominal exchange rate movements are what drive policy discussions, and therefore be dismissive of lagging movements in economists' sentiment. Yet the United States' persistent current account deficits and its more recent fiscal erosion, which are presumed to underlie the sustained decline of the dollar against the euro since January 2002 (see figure 1.1), have given new impetus to this discussion of the euro's global role.[5] As noted by several authors of chapters in this volume, the passing of international monetary leadership from the pound to the dollar in the mid-20th century was in part driven by a series of macroeconomic policy missteps that undermined the pound's reserve status. The euro's viability in its own large economic area may not be sufficient to set it on a path to monetary leadership, but its existence now presents an alternative to which capital markets could turn should the dollar's attractiveness diminish.

The recent increase in the estimation of the euro's global prospects, however, comes without a similar leap forward of faith in European—

---

2. Notable examples of this skepticism include, on the political side, Currie, Levine, and Pearlman (1992), Walters (1990), and famously, Feldstein (1997); and on the economic side, Arestis and Sawyer (2000), De Grauwe (1996), Dornbusch (1989), Giavazzi and Spaventa (1990), and Weber (1991). Of course, there is also a well-developed, and heated, line of discussion, both political and economic, about whether or not the United Kingdom should join the eurozone, which is a separate issue.

3. See the recent essays by euroskeptics collected in Cato Institute (2004).

4. Recent examples include Chinn and Frankel (2004), Cooper (2004), Ferguson (2004), Obstfeld and Rogoff (2004), and Summers (2004).

5. The sources of and need for dollar adjustment are assessed in Bergsten and Williamson (2003, 2004).

Figure 1.1 Euro-dollar exchange rate and interest rate differential, 1992–2004

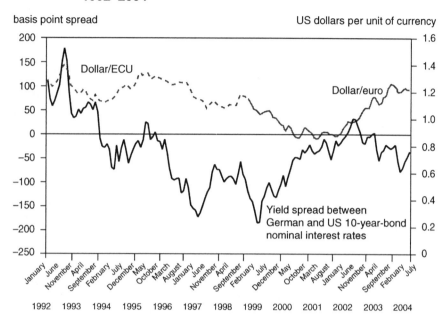

Source: International Monetary Fund, *International Financial Statistics*, November 2004.

particularly eurozone—economic performance. Most economic observers on both sides of the Atlantic are increasingly concerned about the persistent failure of the major continental economies to sustain growth and create employment.[6] Some macroeconomists caution that negative assessments of European performance should not be taken too far from the point of view of economic welfare, and that significant structural reforms are under way.[7] Even correcting for insufficient American and financial market recognition of European policy progress, however, there is little support for a marked appreciation of the euro against the dollar in the near term on the basis of productivity and growth differentials, with reforms likely to take some time to yield significant benefits. In fact, leaving American current account deficits aside (which is not entirely easy to do), the US economy retains the confidence of most economists and market participants as far stronger than most of Europe on the key measures of

6. See Baily and Kirkegaard (2004) and Sapir et al. (2004) for extensive summary assessments of the situation.

7. These would include Blanchard (2004), Gordon (2004), and Posen (forthcoming) on correcting the welfare assessment and Boyer (2003), Posen (2003), and Rogoff (2004) on the progress of reform.

growth in GDP, labor force, and productivity, and as likely to remain so in the coming decade or longer.[8]

This widespread feeling is not only a limit on the euro's rapid rise to a global role, whatever the weaknesses of the US external position, but also a critical commentary on the euro's importance to the eurozone in and of itself. When EMU was first proposed, a number of studies claimed that there would be significant direct benefits from monetary integration for the economic performance of member states. Emerson and colleagues (1992) estimated that the elimination of transaction costs from moving to a single European currency would yield direct benefits of up to 0.4 percent of the European Union's GDP; and European Commission (1996) later estimated cost savings of 1.0 percent of GDP simply from eliminating transaction costs. European Commission (1990) made the case that the reduction of nominal and real exchange rate uncertainty would lead to significant growth in intra-EU trade and investment. The International Monetary Fund (1996, 1997) explored the potential impact if the convergence programs of the EU member states to meet the criteria for euro entry, especially the reductions in general government deficits, were fulfilled, and the benefits if macroeconomic reforms and EMU served as a catalyst for further structural reform, and it came up with some very large numbers for the potential benefits.[9] Financial markets in particular were expected to benefit from the introduction of the euro; McCauley and White (1997) and the European Commission (1997) forecast a rapid deepening and liquidity increase in European bond and lending markets, and perhaps even a "decoupling" of European interest rates from those of the United States.

Although it would be difficult to determine whether these effects were realized, holding all else equal (and it would be beyond the scope of this overview chapter), there is no question that the real economic effects of EMU on the eurozone member countries have been something of a disappointment. On the one hand, though European financial markets and trade integration are far deeper today than they were before the adoption of the euro, it is doubtful how much this represents the effect of the euro on EU integration versus the broader international trends in this direction that benefited non-eurozone members as well (see the discussion in chapter 5 of this volume as well as in Mann and Meade 2002). And the eurozone's interest rates remain asymmetrically affected by US interest rates,

8. Atlantic Council (2004) and Posen (2004) are examples of such projections, although they emphasize the driving force of demographic differences between the European Union and United States.

9. A number of scenarios and conditions were presented in the IMF studies, but the main estimates were for a 0.9 percent higher annual GDP growth rate due to increased macroeconomic credibility, and an additional 3 percent higher GDP than the baseline by 2010 due to the knock-on reforms.

at least until recent times, as established by Chinn and Frankel (2003) (see the US-German interest rate differential plotted in figure 1.1).

On the other hand, the effect of EMU on price convergence and on macroeconomic discipline cannot be all that substantial, if on net there has been limited visible improvement in either of these areas (see the assessments of price convergence in Bradford and Lawrence [2004] and Rogers [2003], and of macroeconomic discipline in chapter 6 of this volume). Perhaps, EMU has proven "irrelevant" to the real growth performance of large euro zone economies, neither a harm nor a boon to them, as I forecast it would be (Posen 1998).

The euro therefore enters the second half of its first decade in something of a halfway house itself. On the purely technical functions as a currency, it has been a resounding success, with no problems in acceptance or in the payments system, as well as convergence in key eurozone interest rates. There has also been evidence indicative of stable low inflation expectations for the varied eurozone membership as a whole, and this remains an outstanding achievement of European central banking. None of the broader forecasts of economic doom or internal political conflict predicted by (mostly American) Cassandras have come to pass, and those predictions now look less credible than they ever did. European financial markets have significantly deepened and added liquidity since the euro's advent, particularly for fixed-income securities. The sheer size of the eurozone economy as well as the ongoing adjustment of the world economy to US current account deficits propel the euro toward a prominent global role.

At the same time, however, Europe's relative economic performance will fall short of the United States' for the foreseeable future, and the short-term gap is likely to be even larger. EMU and the associated convergence process have failed to induce, let alone produce, the needed transformation in European economic structures, policies, and performance. In most scenarios, a collapse in the dollar in the coming years, or even an ongoing orderly adjustment involving higher US long-term interest rates and lower net imports, will have at least as great a contractionary effect on the eurozone as it will on the US economy—even if the Asian currencies take on their share of the adjustment burden (in which case, reserve switches accruing to the euro, and their political benefits, will diminish along with the euro's share in the adjustment process). And as yet there has been little evidence of a change in global invoicing patterns from dollars to euros for traded goods transactions.

The question motivating this volume, whether the euro is ready for a global role, therefore might be better answered as the relative balance of two related assessments: What factors in the global sphere are creating opportunities and pressures for the euro to play a greater role in international financial policymaking? And does the eurozone have the internal economic wherewithal to support and take advantage of the global role about to be thrust upon its currency? To subvert an old expression regarding inflation, there are both cost-pull and demand-push factors determining the pace and extent of the euro's rise. The cost-pull factors regarding the need for international economic leadership from the eurozone, both in concert with and as a substitute for dollar-based leadership, given the costs of inaction, are discussed in chapters 3, 4, and 7 of this volume. The demand-push factors that would be driven by an increasing desire for and growth in euro-denominated assets and transactions—or rather the limitations on such an increase in demand to date—are analyzed in chapters 5, 6, and 8.

In short, the balance of assessment by the studies in this book is that the euro has been a success within limits at home, but that the eurozone economy remains sufficiently weak so that on its own merits the euro would be unlikely as yet or even for some time to challenge the dollar. The euro, however, is not judged solely on its own merits, either by markets or by the international community, but rather is judged also in relative terms against developments in the dollar zone. For the euro to avoid being thrust prematurely into a global role for which its internal structures and strengths are not yet sufficient, greater policy effort from and coordination between the eurozone and the United States are necessary. The alternative is a power vacuum in international economic leadership and increased uncertainty in global financial markets, especially in the period of internal and external adjustment that both the US and European economies face over the next several years.

The Opportunity and Need for Leadership from the Eurozone

Fred Bergsten observes (in chapter 3) that the existence of "a new global currency based on a European economy as large as that of the United States clearly indicates that the international monetary system will look very different in the 21st century" from the unipolar dollar-dominated system we have grown accustomed to in the second half of the 20th century. The eurozone has already made itself a successful role model for economic integration, attracting prospective members or peggers from throughout Eastern Europe and the Middle East and also imitators from Asia. The euro has also delivered monetary stability in the face of a long list of economic shocks, and a large initial decline against the dollar, only to rebound strongly of late.

The one concern, according to Bergsten, remains that "Europe has failed to follow up the creation of the euro with the complementary policy reforms that were widely expected and are needed to assure the [economic] success" of EMU and the EU member economies. This leaves an underlying tension between the constraints on national economic policy measures (e.g., those on fiscal policy in the Stability and Growth Pact, or SGP, discussed in chapter 6) and the national frustrations with poor economic performance—a tension that could over time put the sustainability of the euro itself at risk, despite its obvious virtues.

The potential tension of more urgent concern, according to Bergsten, is external to the eurozone and more systemic. This is the competition that the eurozone now presents to the dollar, should there be another period like the 1970s, when the United States suffered a prolonged period of very poor economic performance. This could lead to an erosion of the dollar's "global market share" given the existence of a viable alternative. The euro alternative is now viable because of the eurozone's large share of world output and trade, which is roughly comparable to that of the United States. Citing work by Barry Eichengreen and Jeffrey Frankel, Bergsten points out that size does matter for international currency purposes. The remaining constraints include the insufficient integration and depth of European financial markets (an evaluation assessed in more detail in chapter 5), as well as lagging economic performance. More important is the lack of coherent institutional representation for the eurozone in international monetary forums. Making a comparison with the emergence of the European Union "as a fully equal partner to the United States in the management of the global trading system for many years," Bergsten argues that given the eurozone's size, it will be able to mount a successful challenge to US monetary dominance only when it is able to speak with one voice on monetary issues, centralizing all decisions and negotiations in a single entity.

"Most important, US economic policy may have to foul up for the euro to . . . achieve rough parity with the dollar at the core of the international monetary system," notes Bergsten, citing the forces of inertia and incumbency (as illustrated by the lingering role of the British pound). The candidate for the cause of such a foul-up is currently all too obvious: the accumulation of international debt by the United States. An extended dollar depreciation, the natural reaction to a multiyear series of current account deficits, could "trigger important, indeed historic, systemic" changes in the current context, given the existence of the euro and the disproportionate share to date of the euro's role in dollar adjustment. A structural portfolio diversification into euros by private and official holders of dollars would mark the euro's arrival at bipolar status.

Bergsten advocates that coordination between the dollar and euro authorities, which is needed in the face of such major potential adjustments (and exchange rate swings), be extended to develop a "finance Group of Two" (G-2). The idea, first mooted in Bergsten and Koch-Weser (2003), is to get "a serious agreement on managing the floating exchange rate between the dollar and euro . . . [and] the ECB [European Central Bank] and [US Federal Reserve] could begin to collaborate more intensively on monetary policy."

Such a "finance G-2" would be informal and would not substitute for the Group of Seven (G-7) (or Group of Twenty, G-20) or for the IMF; it would provide a "steering committee" of the world's two most important currencies representing the world's two largest economic zones to make other international institutions and agenda setting work better, much as the United States and European Union lead the World Trade Organization's agenda setting. The creation of an effective finance G-2 "could play a central role in restoring harmony to overall transatlantic relations" as well.

Randal Quarles, commenting from the viewpoint of the US government, finds that "too much attention is being focused on exchange rate[s]. . . and too little on what seems. . . of far greater importance: namely, the more effective functioning of economies" with regard to growth in output and employment. Noting approvingly the European Commission's ambitious Lisbon Agenda for improved productivity and economic growth, as well as calls by national leaders for deregulation in Europe, Quarles emphasizes the G-7's role in setting an agenda for growth with specific reform goals and mutual surveillance. By implication, Quarles views both the short-term international adjustment process and the longer-term role of the euro vis-à-vis the dollar as driven by the gap in growth rates between the United States and Europe—with the burden on European economies to catch up by raising their growth rates.

Hervé Carré, speaking as a European supporter of EMU, acknowledges that he "thought that the adoption of the euro would act as a catalyst for structural reforms—and I am disappointed." Nonetheless, in Carré's estimation, the degree of monetary and capital market integration and of institutional coordination (albeit not consolidation) within the European Union—two key factors for the euro's rise to a global role cited by Bergsten—has been significant. He still views the emergence of the euro as a counterpart to the dollar as a longer-term rather than crisis-driven process, not least because of the absence of a single European public debt security (or yield curve) comparable with US Treasuries. Unlike Quarles, however, Carré does have sympathy for a finance G-2 "building on existing informal arrangements."

Edwin Truman (chapter 4) evaluates in more detail the case for improved policy coordination between the United States and the euro area, and he concludes that "a prima facie case can be made for improvement." He also offers several recommendations for how policy coordination "with and by the euro area might be improved." Under the heading of policy coordination, he considers primarily "the interaction of euro area officials with US officials but also encompasses the euro area's interaction in international forums." The current process of correction or at least temporary stabilization of the US external deficit motivates much of his case for coordination, but not all of it. EU enlargement, euro-dollar "peaceful coexistence," structural reform, and trade liberalization would all also benefit from increased coordination across the Atlantic and multilaterally with and by the euro area.

Whatever the size and speed of the US external adjustment that is under way, improved information exchange, mutual education, and analysis between the United States and the eurozone could play a constructive role in preparing for adjustments in economic policies. A sustained rebalancing of global growth will be challenging, given the contraction that almost certainly will accompany the adjustment of the US current account, both at home and abroad. Truman argues that "there is no neat separation between the short run and the longer run, nor between demand-side and supply-side policies and institutions," a separation some European officials too easily and doggedly make.

Thus, with due consideration for the uncertain effects of fiscal policy and foreign exchange market intervention on exchange rates, there will be opportunities for the G-7 to share analysis and at chosen moments take "joint action." In the background, the extended and, as Truman characterizes it, "unnatural" swing of the developing economies and the newly industrialized Asian economies into running current account surpluses has profound implications for capital flows and for the role of the IMF. A rise in US interest rates, as would be expected to accompany an adjustment of US external accounts, might well lead to new difficulties for emerging-market economies. In this area, the United States and European Union have to come to better agreement on the size and role of IMF financial assistance and crisis response.

Looking beyond the immediate adjustment process, Truman raises other potential areas for coordination. Provocatively, he asks "whether the euro area should consult with the rest of the world on the economic and financial conditions of euro area membership." The possibility of an external financial crisis is far from being ruled out for such major future euro members as Hungary and Poland, and thus the rest of the world (including the United States) has an interest in the eurozone's management of their entry process.

Given these reasons for increasing policy coordination, how can it best be achieved? Truman suggests substantive dialogue and preparation for joint action rather than the "theater" of long and vague summit communiqués, keeping such statements to verifiable commitments. He also suggests the adoption of inflation targeting by both the ECB and Federal Reserve to improve their communication about policy intentions with markets as well as with each other and their respective finance ministries. Crucially, Truman notes that "coordination with and by the euro area is an overly complicated game because often the right players are not playing." Like Bergsten, he calls for "the euro area to speak with one voice on macroeconomic matters." He adds that the European Union needs to settle its representation as either an international organization or a supranational authority, but not both (as it currently tries to have it). There are a number of steps that the United States can undertake to encourage the European Union along these lines, including how it deals with the European Union on economic matters and whom it supports in the G-7 and other similar forums. Finally, on the institutional side, Truman suggests an appropriate reorganization and consolidation of EU representation in the IMF and other international financial institutions, as well as replacing the G-7 with the G-20 for most purposes.

Richard Clarida questions whether "insufficient policy coordination to date materially contributed to the global imbalances [at present, and whether] . . . insufficient policy coordination complicate[s] the process of international adjustment that is already under way." Citing his research on the topic, Clarida argues that the US external deficits are a general equilibrium response to slower growth and relatively lacking growth prospects in Europe and elsewhere in the world—from that viewpoint, the structural and fiscal policies as well as demographic factors underlying the situation are not truly amenable to influence by policy coordination. Even on the monetary side, a common transatlantic framework for inflation targeting might lead to greater exchange rate instability, unless the required domestic commitments are made to anchor the price level.

Richard Cooper raises doubt about the need for increased euro-dollar coordination along a different line, by questioning whether the large current account deficit of the United States in fact needs to be reduced sharply. If not, many of the reasons Truman gives for coordination go away. Meanwhile, Cooper notes, there is a fundamental transatlantic divergence in views of how the world economy and macroeconomic policy work, and "it is difficult to coordinate fiscal [or exchange rate] policies when such radically different views prevail."

Cooper also observes that it is unclear—given the eurozone's strictures on macroeconomic policy and the ECB's statutory independence with regard to monetary and exchange rate policy—how policy can be coordinated, or with whom. He echoes Clarida's concern that inflation targeting without a common price-level target is likely to generate a random walk in exchange rates. Though Cooper sympathizes with Truman's call for a reallocation of European representation at the IMF, he is more doubtful of the utility and legitimacy of replacing the G-7 with the G-20, rather than updating the G-7 or going all the way to the International Monetary and Financial Committee, which "would command much greater legitimacy than the G-20."

Tommaso Padoa-Schioppa (chapter 7), a founding member of the Executive Board of the European Central Bank and long the ECB's "foreign minister," places the euro in its global context. "The end [of EMU] is to enhance economic prosperity in a stable and safe environment, and to do so both in Europe and worldwide. Indeed, in an increasingly globalized world, we cannot take a domestic perspective only." The three elements of the euro's success from this perspective, according to Padoa-Schioppa, are that, first, the euro "has brought monetary stability to an area that constitutes the world's largest trading partnership and had been for very long an area of instability"; second, the euro "has helped to anchor policies in its region, most particularly in Central and Eastern Europe"; and third, the euro contributes to global adjustment through active commitment to multilateral arrangements.

The "domestic" dimension of putting "an end to Europe as an area of monetary tensions, exchange rate crises, and macroeconomic imbalances" may be EMU's greatest achievement to date. Certainly, the experiences of intra-European depreciations upon countries exiting the Exchange Rate Mechanism, especially those of 1992–93, and their impact on economic performance and political outcomes in member states were in the forefront of European policymakers' minds in the late 1990s during the run-up to the euro's introduction. In fact, despite the divergence in the histories of eurozone members, "the eurosystem has been successful in keeping inflation and inflation expectations stable" and low. Regionally, Padoa-Schioppa reminds the American audience and others who might forget that the prospect of EU and eurozone membership has played a critical role in supporting the transition process in the former communist states to the EU's east. Though "the impressive progress in *nominal* convergence should not hide the enormous task of *real* convergence" that remains to be done, 75 million people joined the European Union in May 2004, and their economies have been integrated in trade and finance.

Turning to the global dimension, Padoa-Schioppa notes the partial progress of the euro "as the second international currency," with, for example, an explosion in the share of euro-denominated debt securities since 1999, but little change in the share of foreign exchange transactions denominated in euros from that previously denominated in deutsche marks. To enable the eurozone to play its full potential role in managing the adjustment of current large global imbalances, Padoa-Schioppa advocates that the zone pursue international cooperation through multilateral frameworks, "mainly through the Group of Seven and the IMF." While observing that the euro has borne a large appreciation since March 2002 not only against the dollar but also against the main Asian currencies, he points out that changes are required not only in exchange rates but also in growth rates. Europe has shown not only relatively low potential growth but also low actual growth falling short of that potential, and improvement on these fronts is the main contribution the Europe can make to adjustment (echoing Quarles and others from across the Atlantic). Padoa-Schioppa, however, also emphasizes the euro's role in "strengthen[ing] the multilateral character of international cooperation," and he sharply contrasts it with the persistence of unilateral dollar pegs in Asia as the global benefits of such pegs recede.

The Impact of the Euro on the Eurozone and Its Economic Performance

EMU was widely expected to transform two aspects of the eurozone economies: the integration and depth of their financial markets; and the conduct of their macroeconomic policies. On both counts, particularly the former, there has been beneficial change at least partly attributable to the euro's introduction and acceptance. The hoped-for impact remains to be achieved, however, and the state of eurozone financial markets and fiscal policy remains a hindrance to the euro's fulfilling the global role called for in chapters 3 and 4.[10]

In chapter 5, economists from both the United States and Europe, and spanning the official and academic sectors, present a multifaceted assessment of how far the eurozone's financial markets have come since 1999, and how far they still have to go to be globally competitive with those based in the United States and those based outside the zone such as the London markets. The general assessment is that factors in the nonfinancial economy—such as legal differences, obstacles to more rapid real growth, transaction costs, and institutional gaps in financial supervision—combine to keep the eurozone from achieving truly deep and integrated financial markets.

Vítor Gaspar and Philipp Hartmann of the European Central Bank bring together the results of several studies of, and a great deal of close monitoring of, the eurozone's "money market, which is the financial market closest to the implementation of monetary policy and therefore the most likely to be directly affected by the start of the single monetary policy." Money market integration is also critical to the implementation of a single monetary policy for the eurozone, given the need to transmit monetary policy in a decentralized fashion across the member economies. Assessing the degree of financial integration, Gaspar and Hartmann find that it took European money markets less than a month to "learn" how the new operational framework functioned and to eliminate most of the volatility and cross-border dispersion in overnight interest rates (despite real institutional differences and barriers between countries before EMU). The evidence of integration in the unsecured lending rates in the European money market is similarly striking—for the overnight rate, "the relevant standard deviation [of rates between lenders] was several hundred basis points in the mid-1990s . . . [declining] to somewhat above 100 basis points for most of 1998," and, by the time of the euro's launch, "converging to levels in the range of 1 to 4 basis points." Alternative measures give

---

10. One could argue that current US fiscal policy is reducing the gap in macroeconomic discipline between the United States and the eurozone by lowering US performance, but that is hardly an argument for the eurozone's capabilities or the impact of the euro itself.

similar indications of a high degree of integration of the cross-national money market in the eurozone.

Still, "the contrast between the repo [repurchase agreement] and unsecured markets [in degree of cross-national differences in interest rates] is striking"—outcomes in the important repo market are still "systematically different from those that would prevail if the network of relationships were independent of location or nationality." Gaspar and Hartmann attribute much of the difference in the repo market, as opposed to the overnight or unsecured money market, to the ongoing lack of harmonization in legal and procedural treatment of financial instruments in the eurozone countries, given the more complicated contracts and transactions involved in collateralized lending. They also note that there are still costs in the eurozone for making cross-border securities transfers that are more than tenfold what they are within countries. They conclude that "legal heterogeneity and fragmented market infrastructures provide obstacles . . . for security markets in general" and will continue to hinder the integration of bond and equity markets unless addressed.

Kristin Forbes analyzes the role of the euro's introduction in explaining the comovement of stock prices across national borders, a critical aspect of financial market integration. Given the recent surge in capital flows across borders worldwide, almost half of which were in the form of portfolio investment, one would expect a greater influence of market opinion about assets in a given currency or region upon the actual allocation of capital between regions. Forbes argues that prospects for economic growth drive the relative demand for a region's assets, mostly by determining where trade and investment expand, which in turn sets the pace for the stock market integration of that region with the rest of the world. "If investors believe that growth in Europe will recover and remain strong, earnings prospects for European companies should improve. Foreigners will seek to increase their investments in European stocks and bonds. Conversely, if growth in Europe lags that in other countries, foreign investors and Europeans will instead seek to increase investments in higher-growth regions." Given the near-term outlook for European growth, this appears to militate against an increase in investment and therefore in the integration (and influence) of European capital markets, which might be partially offset by some diversification incentives. In the long run, though, a slow growth rate in Europe would also be translated into a smaller share of global GDP and fewer incentives for central banks to hold euro-denominated reserves.

In this context, Forbes investigates "whether the introduction of the euro actually did increase stock market comovement" within the eurozone, indicating greater financial integration as a result of EMU. By examining the weekly correlation in stock market returns between France and each of the eurozone countries, both before and after the introduction of the euro, she uncovers substantial increases in the correlation after the start of 1999. Yet, repeating the same analysis for correlations between the eurozone stock markets and the US market, she finds that "for the 10 countries in the sample . . . stock market correlations with the United States increased by an average of 25 percent . . . after the introduction of the euro—greater than the 16 percent increase between the eurozone countries [market movements' correlations with those of] France." Forbes raises the possibility that relatively faster growth in the United States stimulated investment and trade across the Atlantic from Europe, while intra-European integration lagged behind.

Hélène Rey goes directly to the issue of the euro's usage internationally—the extent to which the global economy relies on euros to invoice transactions or to hold reserves. "When central banks are equally credible, market size and liquidity become very important factors in determining whether a currency is widely used by market participants around the world or not." Some researchers (including Rey) predicted before the inception of EMU that the sheer size of the eurozone would lead to more liquidity in European financial markets, thus increasing efficiency, attracting more capital inflows, and reducing the costs of portfolio substitution into the euro. Drawing on five years of data post-EMU, Rey argues that "the creation of the euro has led to spectacular developments in European financial markets, with the emergence of new markets and in most cases a significant increase in the liquidity and integration of existing markets." In particular, Rey finds that government bond markets have seen intra-eurozone interest rate spreads virtually disappear, and benchmark securities of different countries have begun to emerge. Corporate bond markets went from "almost nonexistent" prior to EMU to €150 billion of issuance in 2003, and the euro swap market has become the largest financial market in the world. Consistent with Forbes, she finds increased equity market integration as well, but not beyond the current trend in Europe and across the globe.

Yet, despite this increase in liquidity, Rey observes, "the increase in the use of the euro has been unequally distributed across markets and has been in general quite slow." Foreign exchange trading in euros has not increased post-EMU as a share of global trade, and "the share of the euro in reserves [though increasing] . . . only amounted to 18.7 percent of total reserves in 2002, compared with 64.5 percent for the dollar." Similarly, the use of the euro as an invoicing currency is somewhat higher than that for the eurozone home currencies before EMU, but it remains far from universal within Europe or comparable to the dollar's usage (with the regional exception of the new 10 members of the eurozone). The euro has "not displaced in any significant way the dollar as the currency of choice for most international transactions and as a reserve currency." Attributing this outcome to inertia in global currency arrangements and habits, Rey posits that adjustment by the United States "toward external solvency" via a substantial depreciation of the dollar could trigger lasting portfolio shifts out of the dollar into euros and other currencies.

To conclude the financial assessment, Garry Schinasi reminds readers of an often-overlooked concern: the challenges to be met by the euro zone's still evolving financial architecture. Financial infrastructure in the euro area—meaning the systems for clearing and settling transactions, exchanges for derivatives, and equities—"still has too many such systems based on national needs rather than European needs." The result, in Schinasi's characterization, is cumbersome transactions with unnecessary costs and strains on liquidity management. Similarly, financial regulation in Europe is beset by "a lack of uniformity and in fact a largely national orientation to securities regulation." Though the EU's Financial Services Action Plan, currently being implemented, is intended to achieve convergence in these regulations, it has too narrow a mandate and faces too much disagreement among national authorities to rapidly resolve the problems. Together, these divergences of infrastructure and regulation limits are "holding back market integration" in the eurozone.

Schinasi also points out significant remaining difficulties in the eurozone's approach and institutions for financial crisis prevention and resolution. Primary responsibility for banking supervision has stayed at the national level, with supervisors usually further split up by the type of financial institution covered. Though Schinasi acknowledges that US financial supervision is similarly decentralized and fragmented, and yet has performed well, he argues that there are two fundamental differences in how the eurozone and US supervision work in practice. First, "it is less obvious that national supervision in Europe would tend, as a first priority, to focus on European priorities," whereas American supervisors can be expected to show greater loyalty to the national interest than to the politics of their particular state. "In short, there is a strong risk that a propensity to protect national [financial] institutions will endure." Second, the US Federal Reserve System de facto is the "strong and unambiguous supervisor" for the core financial holding companies and the related key payment systems. Schinasi observes that "there is as yet no such supervisor in the eurozone overseeing the European equivalent of the major European financial institutions."

With regard to crisis resolution, Schinasi notes improvements in European crisis management mechanisms since the launch of the euro, "but they are still not clear enough to satisfy doubtful international market participants and other outsiders." Of particular concern is the uncertainty about how a financial crisis involving a pan-European bank, or occurring across European markets, would be handled. It is unclear who is responsible if a payments system problem originates outside the ECB-overseen TARGET system. Worse, it is ambiguous whether the ECB has the legal capacity to act as lender of last resort, whether this authority remains with the national central banks that are members of the European System of Central Banks, or whether this ambiguity opens up a spot for a European Community (i.e., elected governments') competence. Schinasi tellingly distinguishes between the useful ambiguity about the conditions under which lender-of-last-resort assistance would be appropriate and the potentially harmful ambiguity about who has the authority to decide whether to act as a lender of last resort. He is doubtful that there will be rapid progress on these issues of financial infrastructure, given the lack of a catalytic effect for the euro to date. As a result, the euro is unlikely to reach its potential as a vehicle for international finance.

Another constraint on the euro's rise to international prominence has been the underperformance of the major eurozone economies (France, Germany, and Italy), and their apparent lack of fiscal discipline, ignoring the Stability and Growth Pact in response to their recent recessions. In chapter 6, I ask "Can Rubinomics work in the eurozone?"—that is, whether Europe might experience the kind of virtuous cycle seen in the United States during the 1990s, whereby fiscal consolidation would lead to "movements toward public surplus, lower interest rates, increased private-sector investment, and economic growth—in turn further improving government balance sheets." If so, the ability of the major eurozone economies to catch up with the United States in growth, and of European monetary policy to deliver politically acceptable levels of output stabilization, would be enhanced, and so eventually would be the euro's global role. If not, the yielding of monetary sovereignty by national central banks to the ECB would make the loss of national fiscal discretion to the SGP more costly and could increase some member nations' output volatility. Larger swings of the business cycle would be expected to increase uncertainty and impede both capital inflows and economic integration. In fact, I find that the introduction of the euro (and attempts to enforce the SGP) have had no impact on the countercyclicality of eurozone members' fiscal policy compared with the pre-1999 responses of their budgets to the business cycle.

I interpret "the major eurozone economies' unwillingness to adhere to the SGP or to undertake major fiscal consolidation as more of a rational, if not optimal, response to economic realities." On the one hand, I argue that "these economies are not candidates for Rubinesque virtuous cycles, given their structural problems, as well as simply their structures." For expansionary consolidations to work, several factors are required. Interest rates must respond strongly to fiscal consolidation, which usually requires a high initial debt-to-GDP ratio and/or significant foreign-held debt. Business investment must respond strongly to interest rate reductions, which usually involve forward-looking and flexible corporations. Growth in productivity and employment must respond strongly to the increases in investment. "And, to complete the cycle, government revenue must respond strongly to the increase in growth." I argue that though these attributes did characterize the United States in the 1990s, they did not and do not characterize the large continental European economies, given their well-known structural problems. In a particularly telling example, Italy was unable to reap any structural gains in productivity or un-employment from the drop in interest rates that accompanied its entry into the eurozone. So the incentive to undertake expansionary consolidations was not there.

On the other hand, France, Germany, and Italy had the most to lose from giving up fiscal stabilization policy, because they were the places in which this policy would be most effective. I establish a strong positive correlation between a developed economy's size and its fiscal responsiveness to business cycles; I also find a strong negative correlation between developed countries' openness and their fiscal responsiveness. In short, the countries most likely to benefit from fiscal policy rather than see its impact spill abroad are the ones that use fiscal policy the most. And at least for Germany, "a eurozone–wide monetary policy is inherently less targeted toward Germany's business cycle than the Bundesbank's policy was . . . [and so] the relative worth to Germany of utilizing countercyclical fiscal policy has increased [since EMU]."

Thus, I conclude that the SGP and hopes of increased budgetary discipline more broadly will remain a dead letter for much of the euro zone membership. Need this result in a weakening of the euro, as some assert will occur, given the eroding credibility of the Maastricht commitments to bind member states and the potential increase in fiscal free riding by euro zone members? I suggest that this is unlikely. The outcome of the SGP and EMU has been no statistically significant reduction in member states' fiscal stabilization policy, not a massive increase in fiscal activism. Similarly, the members' debt levels have risen only by the deficit increases commensurate with offsetting an unusual recession of 2002–03, not by a debt issuance binge post-EMU. In any event, "because financial markets are relatively illiquid in the eurozone, the crowding-out effect [from public debt increases] should be larger than in the United States. Thus fiscal laxity in the form of ignoring the SGP should at the margin push up both interest rates and the euro. In the United States, where the economy is much more dependent upon forward-looking asset markets and flows of foreign capital, the [erosion of] confidence effect [from debt increases] is likely to dominate . . . [and] should lead to a currency weakening." The fact that a fiscal loosening arguably has opposing effects on the exchange rate on the opposite side of the Atlantic, however, is not an argument that the European fiscal-monetary mix is beneficial for eurozone members—it is instead a further example of how Euroland's structural problems have not been solved by the introduction of the euro.

Jürgen Kröger of the European Commission comments that it is difficult to compare fiscal policy effectiveness in the United States vis-à-vis Euroland. Larger European public-sector shares in GDP should mean larger automatic stabilization than in the United States, and they should also mean that fiscal activism tends to increase the size of the state and the debt. More important, "given the greater [labor market] rigidities in most

EU countries, the output costs of reducing inflation are higher . . . [and] each cycle has tended to raise the [natural] rate of unemployment, . . . [so] discretionary fiscal policy may have longer-term adverse effects on growth and employment." In any event, the reason for the European Community to have binding deficit rules, argues Kröger, is largely to fore-stall "the risk to the sound functioning of EMU, which would emerge if public debt in some (even small) member states became too high for their public finances to remain sustainable. Unsustainable public finances would likely impose hard choices on the European Central Bank's mone-tary policy, possibly threatening its prime objective of price stability."

Kröger acknowledges four "main shortcomings and weaknesses of the SGP." First, the SGP does not take into account country-specific medium-term characteristics, like differences in countries' potential growth rates, initial debt levels, size of the automatic stabilizers, and demographics. Second, "the SGP has worked asymmetrically over the cycle." Third, the impact of public finances on growth is not properly assessed. And fourth, "the enforcement of commonly agreed-on rules has become more uncer-tain." Still, Kröger argues, the implementation of more flexible fiscal rules, let alone the agreement on assessment methodology that must come first, would prove very difficult in a diverse Europe of member states. A more independent role for the European Commission in enforcing the fiscal rules would help.

In contrast, Jeffrey Frankel views the evidence (including my findings) as indicative that American economists were right in being pessimistic be-fore 1999 about two aspects of EMU and fiscal policy. "First, a permanent 3 percent ceiling on deficits, without flexibility (e.g., for recessions) would not be fully enforceable. . . . [Second], discretionary fiscal policy would be-come more, not less, necessary now that monetary independence has been lost." Frankel, however, noting the relative size and lack of openness of the US economy, asks "Why, then, did the United States pursue and achieve fiscal discipline during the 1990s?" Citing Chinn and Frankel (2003), he argues that the channel from public debt to interest rates is in-creasingly operational in Europe, as in the United States—in fact, that the "effect of the expected future change in debt [on interest rates] is . . . ac-tually stronger [in all four large countries of the eurozone] than in the United States." Meanwhile, he points out, the fiscal consolidation of the 1990s was an exception to US experience, not the rule, given the increases in public debt in the 1980s and 2000s.

Frankel suggests "that the key lies in the political economy regime that is adopted to achieve fiscal discipline." Of three regimes proposed to achieve discipline—"Starve the Beast," "Rigid Rules," and "Shared Sacri-fice"—only the third has been successful. Rigid fiscal rules, like the SGP, break when the costs of fulfilling the mandated policy become so high that they are not credible. Starve the Beast has been demonstrated empir-ically not to work; in fact, there is a negative correlation in US data between tax revenue and spending. Frankel instead advocates "shared sacrifice mechanisms," such as PAYGO and spending caps, as the means to fiscal discipline; these mechanisms "have in common budget neutrality as a criterion for future changes relative to the baseline." For Europe, Frankel suggests a formalized version of a Chilean institution, whereby an independent fiscal authority pursues a cyclically adjusted budget deficit of zero, with "responsibility to say what constitutes deviations from potential output, to compute the cyclically adjusted budget, to make forecasts, and to announce whether this year's budget satisfies the rule." This could be considered a partial echo of Kröger's calls for SGP revisions to empower the European Commission for enforcement and for emphasis on medium-term fiscal criteria.

Ben Bernanke of the Federal Reserve (chapter 8) begins an overall assessment of the euro by observing that political more than economic factors—and certainly not arguments for an optimum currency area—motivated EMU. This leads him to treat "the introduction of the euro as representing to some degree a natural experiment in monetary economics," about which he advances a hypothesis: "The most significant effects of [European] monetary unification have been felt, and will continue to be felt, in the development of European financial markets and . . . the greatest economic benefits to Europe in the long run will accrue through the improved functioning of those markets." There has been little or no expansion in trade due to the euro's adoption—among other evidence, "the share of total euro area exports destined for other members of the eurozone did not increase with introduction of the currency, as would be likely if the common currency promoted trade." As shown in Rogers (2003), the bulk of convergence in traded goods prices within Euroland occurred between 1990 and 1994, in response to the creation of the single market, and not after 1999 and the introduction of the euro. Bernanke believes that "with respect to macroeconomic stability, the common currency appears to have had both positive and negative effects," with no net result obvious from the limited experience to date. With respect to the euro's international role, he echoes Rey's findings that the dollar remains the international vehicle currency and the dominant invoicing currency for raw materials and trade.

Turning to financial markets, however, Bernanke argues that the European "common currency, with its ongoing efforts to harmonize financial regulations and institutions, has significantly reduced [financial] transaction costs. Together with lower country-specific macro risks, . . . this reduction in transaction costs has greatly improved the breadth and efficiency of European financial markets." The benefits for the euro zone of such financial development extend far beyond the direct benefits to the financial industry itself. Fixed-income markets have been the primary beneficiaries, with a remarkable convergence of sovereign debt yields, deepening of government bond markets, and enhanced liquidity and risk sharing through cross-border holdings of euro-denominated debt.

The multiplicity of sovereign issuers, given the membership of the euro-zone, Bernanke argues, puts some limit on the ability of the European government bond market to achieve the liquidity of the US Treasury market, with one sovereign issuer, but additional technical improvements—for example, developing a benchmark yield curve—could narrow the gap. "The rapid development of Europe's corporate bond market [following EMU], including a nascent high-yield market, should prove highly beneficial to European economic development." Less progress has been made in other securities markets and in banking than in fixed-income markets, but Bernanke notes that even there the single currency eliminates exchange risk, reduces transaction costs, and therefore "serves to moderate home bias in borrowing and lending, leading to larger, more liquid, and more diversified financial markets."

References

Arestis, Philip, and Malcolm Sawyer. 2000. Will the Euro Bring Economic Crisis to Europe? Economics Working Paper Archive, Washington University, Saint Louis. Photocopy (October 9). http://econwpa.wustl.edu/eprints/mac/papers/0004/0004029.abs.

Atlantic Council. 2004. *The Transatlantic Economy in 2020: A Partnership for the Future?* Policy Paper. Washington: Atlantic Council.

Baily, Martin N., and Jacob F. Kirkegaard. 2004. *Transforming the European Economy*. Washington: Institute for International Economics.

Bergsten, C. Fred. 1997. The Impact of the Euro on Exchange Rates and International Policy Cooperation. In *EMU and the International Monetary System*, ed. Paul Masson, Thomas H. Krueger, and Bart Turtelboom. Washington: International Monetary Fund.

Bergsten, C. Fred, and John Williamson, eds. 2003. *Dollar Overvaluation and the World Economy*. Washington: Institute for International Economics.

Bergsten, C. Fred, and John Williamson, eds. 2004. *Dollar Adjustment: How Far? Against What?* Washington: Institute for International Economics.

Blanchard, Olivier J. 2004. The Economic Future of Europe. *Journal of Economic Perspectives* 18, no. 4 (Fall): 3–26.

Boyer, Robert. 2003. France. In "France, Germany, and Italy Are Struggling to Recover: Who'll Come Out on Top?" *The International Economy*, Fall.

Bradford, Scott, and Robert Z. Lawrence. 2004. *Has Globalization Gone Far Enough? The Costs of Fragmented Markets*. Washington: Institute for International Economics.

Canzoneri, Matthew B., Vittorio Grilli, and Paul Masson, eds. 1992. *Establishing a Central Bank for Europe*. Cambridge, UK: Cambridge University Press.

Cato Institute. 2004. The Future of the Euro. *Cato Journal* (Special Issue) 24, nos. 1–2 (Spring/Summer).

Cecchini, Paolo. 1988. *The European Challenge 1992: The Benefits of a Single Market*. Aldershot: Gower.

Chinn, Menzie, and Jeffrey Frankel. 2003. *The Euro Area and World Interest Rates*. Working Paper 1016. Santa Cruz: Center for International Economics, University of California.

Chinn, Menzie, and Jeffrey Frankel. 2004. Will the Euro Eventually Surpass the Dollar as the Leading International Reserve Currency? Paper presented at a conference on the Group of Seven current account imbalances: sustainability and adjustment, sponsored by the National Bureau of Economic Research, Cambridge, MA (July).

Cooper, Richard. 2004. The US Deficit Is Not Only Sustainable, It Is Logical. *Financial Times*, October 31.

Currie, David, Paul Levine, and Joseph Pearlman. 1992. European Monetary Union or Hard EMS? *European Economic Review* (Elsevier) 36, no. 6: 1185–204.

De Cecco, Marcello, and Alberto Giovannini, eds. 1989. *A European Central Bank? Perspectives on Monetary Unification After Ten Years of the EMS.* Cambridge, UK: Cambridge University Press.

De Grauwe, Paul. 1996. Monetary Union and Convergence Economics. *European Economic Review* 40, nos. 3–5: 1091–101.

De Grauwe, Paul. 2000. *Economics of Monetary Union.* Oxford: Oxford University Press.

Dornbusch, Rudiger. 1989. The Dollar in the 1990s: Competitiveness and the Challenges of New Economic Blocs. In *Federal Reserve Bank of Kansas City Conference Proceedings.* Kansas City: Federal Reserve Bank of Kansas City.

Eichengreen, Barry. 1998. Will EMU Work? (In Norwegian.) In *Euroen og den norske kronens skjebne,* ed. Arne Jon Isachsen and Ole Bjorn Roste. Preliminary English version available at http://emlab.berkeley.edu/users/eichengr/policy/merrill.pdf.

Emerson, Michael, Daniel Gros, Alexander Italianer, eds. 1992. *One Market, One Money: An Evaluation of the Potential Benefits and Costs of Forming an Economic and Monetary Union.* Oxford: Oxford University Press.

European Commission. 1990. One Market, One Money. *European Economy,* no. 44 (October).

European Commission. 1996. *Economic Evaluation of the Internal Market.* European Economy, Reports and Studies 4. Brussels: European Commission.

European Commission. 1997. *External Aspects of Economic and Monetary Union.* Commission Staff Working Paper, SEC (97) 803. Brussels: European Commission.

Feldstein, Martin. 1997. The Political Economy of the European Economic and Monetary Union: Political Sources of an Economic Liability. *Journal of Economic Perspectives* 11, no. 4: 23–42.

Ferguson, Niall. 2004. The Euro as a Rival to the Dollar: Some Lessons from History. Paper presented at a conference on euro fixed income sponsored by *Euromoney,* Paris (December 9).

Giavazzi, Francesco, and Luigi Spaventa. 1990. *The "New" EMS.* CEPR Discussion Paper 369. London: Center for Economic Policy Research.

Gordon, Robert J. 2004. *Why Was Europe Left at the Station When America's Productivity Locomotive Departed?* NBER Working Paper 10661. Cambridge, MA: National Bureau of Economic Research.

IMF (International Monetary Fund). 1996. *Progress Toward EMU: Developments and Selected Issues.* IMF Staff Paper SM/96/41. Washington: International Monetary Fund.

IMF (International Monetary Fund). 1997. *World Economic Outlook* (October). Washington: International Monetary Fund.

Mann, Catherine L., and Ellen E. Meade. 2002. *Home Bias, Transaction Costs, and Prospects for the Euro: A More Detailed Analysis.* Working Paper. Washington: Institute for International Economics.

McCauley, Robert N., and William R. White. 1997. *The Euro and European Financial Markets.* BIS Working Paper 41. Basel: Bank for International Settlements.

Mundell, Robert. 1998. What the Euro Means for the Dollar and the International Monetary System. *Atlantic Economic Journal* 26, no. 3: 227–37.

Obstfeld, Maurice, and Kenneth Rogoff. 2004. *The Unsustainable US Current Account Position Revisited.* NBER Working Paper 10869. Cambridge, MA: National Bureau of Economic Research.

Portes, Richard, and George Alogoskoufis. 1991. International Costs and Benefits from EMU. In *The Economics of EMU: European Economy Special Issue* 1: 231–45.

Posen, Adam S. 1998. *Why EMU Is Irrelevant for the German Economy.* Frankfurter Volkswirtschaftliches Kolloquium, Frankfurt (June). www.iie.com/publications/wp/1999/99-5.htm.

Posen, Adam S. 2003. Germany. In "France, Germany, and Italy Are Struggling to Recover: Who'll Come Out on Top?" *The International Economy,* Fall.

Posen, Adam S. 2004. *Fleeting Equality: The Relative Size of the US and EU Economies to 2020*. US-Europe Analysis Series, Center on the United States and Europe. Washington: Brookings Institution.

Posen, Adam S. Forthcoming. *Reform in a Rich Country: Germany*. Washington: Institute for International Economics.

Rogers, John H. 2003. *Monetary Union, Price Level Convergence, and Inflation: How Close Is Europe to the United States?* International Finance Discussion Paper 740. Washington: Board of Governors of the Federal Reserve System.

Rogoff, Kenneth. 2004. Europe's Quiet Leap Forward. *Foreign Policy*, July/August.

Sapir, Andre, et al. 2004. *An Agenda for a Growing Europe: The Sapir Report*. Oxford: Oxford University Press.

Summers, Lawrence H. 2004. *The United States and the Global Adjustment Process*. Third Annual Stavros S. Niarchos Lecture. Washington: Institute for International Economics (March 23). www.iie.com/publications/papers/summers0304.htm.

Walters, Alan. 1990. Monetary Constitutions for Europe. Speech at the 28th meeting of the Mont Pelerin Society, Munich (September).

Weber, Axel A. 1991. EMU and Asymmetries and Adjustment Problems in the EMS: Some Empirical Evidence. *European Economy*, no. 44: 187–207.

2

Successes and Challenges for the Euro

GÜNTER BURGHARDT

The fifth anniversary of the introduction of the euro presents an opportunity to reflect on the successes and challenges associated with this unprecedented achievement. I am very pleased that the Institute for International Economics has published this volume on the euro at five years. In particular, Fred Bergsten has been a staunch supporter of the euro since the beginning and has never failed in his conviction that it would be a success.

For more than a decade in the run-up to the adoption of the single European currency, not many economists in the United States shared this view. Some were skeptical that Europe would actually achieve this major step (or thought that only a very small number of European Union (EU) member states would make it in). And as with the completion of the Single Market at the end of 1992, which was met by talk in the United States of a potential "fortress Europe," some Americans were wary that the single currency would make Europe more of a competitor than a partner to the United States. In retrospect, it is clear that Bergsten's analyses and insights have been vindicated and that he was right in betting on the success of the euro.

The introduction of the euro has indeed been a major historic event. It marks the achievement of full integration in the monetary field for 12 of the present 15 member states of the European Union. The mere existence of national currencies was the last barrier to fully achieving the single European market and the ultimate step in reaping all of its rewards. The sin-

Günter Burghardt is the head of the Delegation of the European Commission to the United States.

gle currency has had real economic benefits for the countries that adopted it. A preliminary study by the European Commission indicates that trade within the euro area accelerated by 14 percent during the 1999–2002 period, while trade between euro area member states and the other three EU countries increased by only 9 percent.

If an underlying rationale for the Economic and Monetary Union was economic, the deepest reason for such a move was profoundly political and aimed at involving all European citizens in the process of European integration. As has been pointed out by former European Commission president Jacques Delors, whose *Memoirs* have just been published, the introduction of the euro has created "the perception of an emerging European identity." The euro is the most visible example of the European Union's "finalité politique" and contributes decisively to making the process of unification irreversible. The euro has also become part of daily life for more than 300 million citizens since the introduction of euro notes and coins on January 1, 2002, and it serves as a yardstick for the public to measure how far the integration process has come in only 50 years.

The biggest ever enlargement of the European Union took place on May 1, 2004. Enlargement from 15 to 25 members increased the European Union's population by 20 percent (to more than 450 million people), while its GDP has grown by only 5 percent. This implies that at the moment of enlargement, the prosperity gap will increase by about 20 percent, twice as much as the income disparities increased when Greece, Portugal, and Spain entered the European Union in the 1980s. To foster growth so that these disparities may narrow over time will be a formidable challenge for Europe, a challenge that is bigger than those we had to face in previous enlargements and that will absorb a significant amount of EU budgetary resources in the years to come. But it is a challenge that can produce a very large reward.

Enlargement is in fact an unprecedented economic opportunity that, economists agree, will bring significant benefits to both old and new EU members. It will promote competition and favor a more efficient allocation of resources within the European Single Market. The new member states have performed particularly well in the past three years; despite the global slowdown, their GDP has grown at a rate close to 3 percent. But they still have a large untapped growth potential. This has been well understood by European—and also American—investors, who have significantly increased their presence in these countries ahead of their accession, correctly anticipating the economic opportunities for these countries in an enlarged internal market.

By joining the European Union, the acceding countries also become members of the Economic and Monetary Union. They are committed to eventually adopting the euro, and steps are being taken in that direction. But accession to the European Union does not mean automatic adoption of the euro. Specific criteria must be met first, as laid out in the Maastricht Treaty. The new members will continue on a path of economic restructuring and economic and policy convergence as part of the process of getting in shape for the euro—a process that is guided and encouraged by the European Commission and other EU institutions. I am reasonably confident that by the end of the decade, the euro will have replaced the national currency in a number of them.

Institutionally, the introduction of the euro is so far the most important example of structured cooperation inside the European Union. This method allows countries that want deeper integration to move forward when the Maastricht Treaty criteria are met, and this method will also gain more prominence within the enlarged European Union. The draft Constitution presented by the European Convention last year provides for the development of such a method of integration. Despite the fact that it has not yet been possible to conclude negotiations among member states on a Constitutional Treaty, I remain optimistic about the chances for the treaty to be approved this year. The euro, enlargement, and the Constitutional Treaty would then become the three landmarks of a new phase of European political and economic integration that will enhance stability and prosperity within Europe and strengthen Europe's voice in the world.

Having set this context, I turn to the main topic of this volume: whether the euro is ready for a global role. In the five years the euro has been in place, it has established itself as a key currency on the international scene and as an alternative to the dollar. There are four criteria to assess the international role of a currency: (1) the share of the currency in global foreign reserves, (2) the share of bonds issued in the currency, (3) the share of demand for money market instruments denominated in the currency, and (4) the number of countries using the currency for trade transactions with foreign partners.

With regard to the first criterion, the share of the euro in global foreign exchange reserves increased from less than 15 percent in 1999 to almost 19 percent in 2002—still a long way from the dollar's share in reserves (about 65 percent in 2002), but growing steadily. On the second criterion, following the introduction of the euro, there was a surge in euro-denominated bond and note issues. At the end of 1998, the outstanding amount of bonds and notes denominated in the legacy currencies of the euro accounted for barely 28 percent of world issues, compared with 45 percent for dollar-denominated bonds and notes. By mid-2003, the gap had become relatively small; the share of issues in dollars had fallen to 43 percent, while the euro's share had increased to 41 percent.

Turning to the third criterion, the share of demand for money market instruments denominated in euros rose even more dramatically, from just above 17 percent to 46 percent, overcoming the share of issues in dollars, which declined from 58 percent in 1998 to 30 percent in mid-2003. Finally, with regard to the fourth criterion, more than 50 countries now operate managed exchange rate arrangements that include the euro as a reference currency, either alone or with other reserve currencies. All four criteria seem to indicate a strong and increasing confidence in the euro as a key international currency.

The introduction of the single currency has had a fundamental impact on the European financial sector, as a catalyst for European financial integration and restructuring, and for the expansion of the financial market itself. The European Union is committed to the completion of a single market in financial services by 2005, a formidable task but one that the European Union is on its way to achieving. The EU-US financial services dialogue adds another promising area for cooperation to the transatlantic agenda. The EU has already modernized and unified its rules on prospectuses and created a single European patent, for example, and it is working toward a "single passport for investment services" to facilitate investment while protecting the investor. According to a European Commission study, an integrated European capital market could in the long run raise the level of GDP in the European Union by more than 1 percent—a boost EU economies could undoubtedly use.

The impact of the euro is being felt deep and wide, within the euro area and the European Union but also outside Europe's borders. The growing international role of the euro, including its profound impact on the financial sector, make it highly worthy of attention on the US side of the Atlantic.

3

The Euro and the Dollar: Toward a "Finance G-2"?

C. FRED BERGSTEN

In March 1997, my lead-off paper for the IMF's major conference on European monetary unification and the international monetary system began with the following paragraph:

> The creation of the euro will be the most important development in the evolution of the international monetary system since the widespread adoption of flexible exchange rates in the early 1970s. It will almost certainly be the most important development for the monetary (as opposed to adjustment) dimension of the system since the dollar succeeded sterling as the world's top currency during the interwar period. (Bergsten 1997b, 17)

Nobel Laureate Robert Mundell used very similar words a year later when he offered his own outlook for the pending new currency:

> The introduction of the euro will represent the most dramatic change in the international monetary system since President Nixon took the dollar off gold in 1971 [and since] the era of flexible exchange rates began . . . the euro is likely to challenge the position of the dollar [and hence] this may be the most important event in the history of the international monetary system since the dollar took over from the pound the role of dominant currency in World War I. (Robert Mundell, "The Case for the Euro—I and II," *Wall Street Journal*, March 24 and 25, 1998, A22)

The spectacular success of the euro during its first five years provides strong support for these predictions (which were of course virtually alone among those of American economists at the time). *The advent of a new glo-*

C. Fred Bergsten is the director of the Institute for International Economics.

bal currency based on a European economy as large as that of the United States clearly indicates that the international monetary system will look very different in the 21st century than it did in the dollar-dominated world of the 20th century or the sterling-dominated world of the 19th century. Euroland and the United States need to create a new "Group of Two" (G-2) mechanism to manage the dramatic change in their bilateral monetary relationship implied by this development and to exercise the cooperative leadership of the global monetary system for which they will now be jointly responsible.[1]

Current events underline the need for such new institutional arrangements. The euro has appreciated by more than 50 percent against the dollar from its lows of late 2000, and many observers believe that it will rise by at least another 10 to 20 percent. Anxieties are rising rapidly in many European quarters as a result, and the issue was at the top of the agenda of the meeting of Group of Seven (G-7) ministers of finance and governors of central banks in Boca Raton on February 7, 2004.

There is no agreement between Europe and the United States, however, on even the most fundamental elements needed to address the current situation in a constructive manner: the appropriate level or at least range within which the dollar-euro rate should settle, the mechanisms (sterilized intervention? changes in monetary policy? changes in fiscal policy? structural reforms?) for achieving and sustaining that rate or range, the implications thereof for economic and monetary policy in the two regions, and the impact on the rest of the world.

There are no institutional arrangements through which Euroland and the United States meet to address these issues together. As far as is known publicly, there have been no discussions on the need for such institutional arrangements, let alone on the substantive issues that would require agreement as a basis for fashioning cooperative policy responses to the problems identified here, either immediately with respect to the currencies' fluctuations or over the longer run with respect to the advent of a bipolar monetary system.

The Euro at Five

The first five years of the euro itself have been a spectacular success. Price stability has been maintained in previously low-inflation countries and remarkably achieved in member countries that were formerly prone to rapid price increases. The European Central Bank (ECB) has seamlessly succeeded the Bundesbank as the guardian of European stability. Nominal in-

---

1. The overall "G-2" concept is developed and described in Bergsten and Koch-Weser (2004). Short versions can be found in C. Fred Bergsten, "The Transatlantic Century," *Washington Post*, April 30, 2002; C. Fred Bergsten and Caio Koch-Weser, "Restoring the Transatlantic Alliance," *Financial Times*, October 6, 2003, 13.

terest rates are about 250 basis points below the weighted average of the predecessor currencies. The physical euro was introduced without a hitch. The euro became the leading currency for denomination of international bond issues in its very first year. The initial depreciation of the currency has now been replaced by appreciation to and beyond its initial starting point. The launch of the euro probably represents the most successful episode in the entire history of the European integration movement.

Countries throughout the world are expressing their admiration for the euro by seeking to join or emulate it. Virtually all the new members that will enter the European Union shortly wish to join the eurozone as well as soon as possible. Some of these countries, and a few others, have already "euroized" by adopting the euro as their domestic money or pegging to it. And being motivated at least partly by the success of the euro, many countries in Asia aspire to eventually create an "Asian currency unit" à la euro, and the South American countries have similarly considered a "Mercosur currency unit."

All this has occurred despite a series of external shocks that could have easily derailed a more fragile monetary innovation. The global economy experienced its first recession in a decade. A bubble burst in financial markets around the world. The events of September 11, 2001, and two subsequent wars roiled the security environment. The exchange rate of the euro against the dollar dropped by more than 30 percent in less than two years and then appreciated by an even larger magnitude.

To be sure, there have been some glitches during this startup period. The ECB's communication of its policy actions and intentions has not always been as clear as desirable. The decision to create the new currency three years before its physical introduction was possible generated confusion and probably contributed at least partially to the unnecessary depreciation (Sinn and Westermann 2001). Three members of the European Union, most notably the United Kingdom, have so far declined to join the common currency. And monetary policy should have been eased much more rapidly to respond to the turndown in European growth in the period 2001–03 (Mussa 2003).

Most important, Europe has failed to follow up the creation of the euro with the complementary policy reforms that were widely expected and that are needed to ensure the success of the overall Economic and Monetary Union (EMU) and its members' economies. The creation of the common currency of course meant that the participating countries gave up two major national policy instruments: monetary policy and exchange rate policy. The adoption of the Stability and Growth Pact eliminated much of discretionary national fiscal policy as well. Moreover, currency unions (e.g., the United States) work effectively only if they possess the requisite internal adjustment devices, mainly via market mechanisms but assisted by governmental policies if necessary, notably regarding labor mobility and capital transfers from "surplus" to "deficit" regions.

Europe, at the national and/or regional levels, thus needed to implement a series of reforms to complement the creation of the euro and to capitalize on its potential for strengthening the region's growth and international competitiveness. Most of the needed changes are structural, relating to labor and capital markets but also to competition policies and the excessive intrusion of the state into numerous areas of the economy (Baily and Kirkegaard 2004, Posen forthcoming). Reform of the Stability and Growth Pact, which has proven far too rigid in the face of economic downturn or even prolonged stagnation, is also urgently required (as discussed in Adam Posen's chapter in this volume).

Even the most ardent supporters of the euro, both inside and outside Europe, have been severely disappointed by Euroland's failure to adopt the needed reforms. Much of the case for creating the common currency in fact hinged on the application in this case of Europe's traditional "bicycle theory," where one set of reforms led inexorably to follow-on reforms that would sustain the progress of the overall integration strategy. There has of course been some progress, and a number of countries are now pursuing at least initial steps in the needed direction. But much more is needed and, after five years, inadequate follow-on has been achieved.

Hence the Euroland economy is the most notable laggard in the entire world recovery. It has trailed even Japan in growth terms since the start of 2003. Its longer-run outlook remains cloudy. *The sustainability of the euro itself could even be at risk, due to the combination of sluggish economic performance and growing frustration with the constraints on national action imposed by monetary union, unless the requisite reforms are achieved before the currency's first decade is concluded.* This risk could even grow over time as the original rationale for the euro (and the entire European integration movement), the overarching security imperative of avoiding renewed conflict between France and Germany, recedes ever further into history and becomes at best a distant memory for current generations.

The overall verdict on the great European monetary experiment at age five is thus mixed. The common currency itself, as noted, has been a spectacular success. The surrounding policy environment, however, has not evolved nearly as rapidly as had been hoped nor nearly as fully as will be essential to successfully complete the process of Economic and Monetary Union. This uneven outcome clouds the outlook for the future international role of Euroland and thus its ability to develop, with the United States, an informal "G-2" steering committee to effectively manage both the bilateral dollar-euro relationship and the international monetary system more broadly.

The Euro in the World Economy

This mixed verdict on the EMU of course affects the international role of the euro. On the plus side, global acceptance of the new currency has already produced a bipolar international financial market (Draghi and Pozen 2004). The ECB's joint intervention with the Federal Reserve in the currency markets in September 2000 (and subsequent unilateral intervention) stopped the excessive depreciation of the euro and laid the foundation for its subsequent rebound. Again in cooperation with the Fed, the ECB injected substantial liquidity into financial markets in the wake of the terrorist attacks on September 11 and helped avoid any excessive spillover effect from those events. The international progress of the euro and ECB per se thus mirrors their impressive "domestic" record.

At the systemic level, and for all the complexities injected into the usual discussions of this topic, the fundamental issue surrounding the potential "struggle for dominance" between the dollar and the euro is quite simple.[2] The basic reason for the supremacy of the dollar during the past half century or more is that it had no competition. No other economy even came close to the size of the United States. Hence no currency could acquire the network externalities, economies of scale and scope, and public goods benefits necessary to rival the dollar at the global level. A largely similar situation for the United Kingdom explains the pound's dominance in the nineteenth century.

The clearest evidence for this conclusion is the fact that the dollar reigned supreme despite prolonged periods of very poor economic performance by the United States:

- The US economy grew very slowly for two full decades, from the early 1970s through the early 1990s, and its productivity growth was especially mediocre (running at 1 percent or less a year).

- It experienced high inflation for almost a decade, from 1973 through 1981, including three years of double-digit price increases.

- It has run large external deficits for most of the past 23 years, including two periods when those deficits were rising at clearly unsustainable rates (1982–87 and 1998–2003), and has become by far the world's largest debtor country (with a negative net international investment position of perhaps $3 trillion at the end of 2003).

The dollar did experience significant erosion of its global market share in the late 1970s and early 1980s. Moreover, its weakness and instability provided crucial impetus to the first effective efforts to create a European alternative, culminating in the European Monetary System in 1979. However, the dollar's share of global finance stabilized again in the 1990s and remained far above that of any other national money.

The overwhelming reason for the dollar's dominance is that the United States remained far larger, especially in terms of GDP but also in trade and

---

2. The following paragraphs are largely drawn from Bergsten (2002).

other size variables, than any other currency-issuing economy. Increasingly reinforced by incumbency advantages (see below), the dollar remained preponderant and attained a share of currency markets about four times as great as its share of world output and trade. The deutsche mark was the world's second key currency for most of the postwar period but never attained a market share greater than one-fourth that of the dollar; this was quite logical because the economy of the former West Germany was about one-fourth the size of the United States (and, as Chancellor Helmut Schmidt constantly reminded us, its geographical size was approximately equal to the state of Oregon). Japan, whose economy at one point grew to be more than half as large as America's, never realized anything like that portion of world finance because of the underdevelopment of its financial markets (as amply demonstrated during the decade-long crisis from which it may only now be emerging).

Econometric evidence verifies the central importance of size for international currency purposes. Eichengreen and Frankel (1996) concluded that a rise of 1 percentage point in a key currency country's share of world product (measured at purchasing power parity) is associated with a rise of 1.33 percentage points in that currency's share of central bank reserves. In a more sophisticated version of those estimates, which attempted to account for historical inertia (see below) as well as economic size, Eichengreen (1997) found consistent if modestly smaller effects: The rise of a currency's share in global reserves that derived from a rise of 1 percentage point in its country's share of global output (at purchasing power parity) is 0.9 percentage point, about two-thirds as much as in the prior calculation. The central importance of size was clearly validated.

The present Euroland is 20 to 30 percent smaller than the United States in total output and about 25 percent higher in its share of world trade. For all practical purposes, the two currency areas are close enough to be regarded as rough equivalents. The expansion of the eurozone to include all 15 members of the current European Union would take the numbers modestly (10–20 percent) above the United States in output. And the inclusion of the 10 new EU members would add at least another 10 percent or so to Euroland's output superiority (as well as bringing its population to about two-thirds greater than that of the United States).

In short, *it is clear that the euro provides the first real competition for the dollar since the latter's ascent to global currency dominance*. The most interesting questions relate to the time period and adjustment path over which that competition will play out and what its systemic consequences will be.

First, Euroland will need to further integrate its money and capital markets to realize the full international potential of its new currency (Portes and Rey 1998). The superiority of the American financial markets and those of the United Kingdom during the period of the pound's dominance were key elements in their global monetary leadership. The negative case of Japan is also instructive; its failure to modernize its financial markets, despite repeated calls for such reform and even announcements of programs to do so (such as Prime Minister Ryutaro Hashimoto's "big bang" in 1996), undercut any possibility that the yen might have come to play a major international role.

The European financial markets, galvanized both directly and indirectly by the euro itself, have already made impressive strides (Danthine, Giavazzi, and von Thadden 2000). However, national rivalries have impeded cross-border mergers of both banks and equity markets. No single benchmark security, or yield curve, has developed to rival the US Treasury bill and other US government assets. The pace at which Euroland overcomes these shortcomings will be a major factor in the timing of the euro's rise in international asset allocation. Entry of the United Kingdom into Euroland would presumably accelerate the process.

Second, Europe will need to get its act together institutionally. The European Union has been a fully equal partner to the United States in the management of the global trading system for many years. Cooperation between the members of this "trade G-2" was thus a necessary condition for the successful launch and completion of each of the major multilateral trade agreements of the postwar period (and again with the launch of the Doha Round in November 2001). Europe was able to successfully challenge the previous dominance of the United States in the trading system for two reasons. One, as with finance, was the rough equivalence of its trade volume (and, though less important here, of its total output) with the United States. The other, and of crucial importance, was Europe's early decision to centralize virtually all trade policy decisions and negotiations in a single entity (in this case, the European Commission in Brussels).

A somewhat parallel situation exists on the monetary and macroeconomic front. On most of the relevant objective criteria, Europe already equals the United States. But Europe still speaks with a multiplicity, even a cacophony, of voices on these issues. Hence it dissipates much of the potential for realizing a key international role for the euro.

Macroeconomic and monetary issues are qualitatively different from trade policy issues because markets dominate most outcomes on the former whereas intergovernmental activities by definition dominate the latter. Hence European institutional cohesiveness will not ensure a rapid rise in the international position of the euro. But organizational reforms that enable the countries making up Euroland to act together and speak with a single voice will probably be an essential prerequisite of full European equivalence with the United States à la trade (Henning 1997, 2000, 2003).

Third, the international role of the euro would obviously be strengthened if Europe were to improve its economic performance. Euroland has already achieved convincing price stability, but the achievement of dynamic growth may also be necessary for the euro to effectively challenge the dollar (Kawai 1997). Whether or not that is true, international interest in the euro will surely rise. This will set in motion a self-reinforcing cycle of euro appreciation and increased portfolio diversification into euros by both private and official holders—but only if Euroland countries are able to both overcome their continuing structural impediments and find a way to employ more expansionary macroeconomic policies. For example, the eurozone members should recognize that the ECB ought to attach importance to output as well as stability goals and/or adopt more flexible guidelines for government budgets than those in the present Stability and Growth Pact.

Fourth, and perhaps most important, US economic policy may have to foul up for the euro to realize its potential to achieve rough parity with the dollar at the core of the international monetary system. Inertia is so strong in financial affairs that it may be impossible to dislodge an incumbent unless that incumbent essentially abdicates (Bergsten 1996). The pound maintained a central international role for at least a half-century after the United States had surpassed the United Kingdom's level of GDP. That role faded only due to the shock of World War I (during which the United Kingdom's trade and investment were disrupted and it had to sell off many of its foreign assets) and its own major economic mismanagement in the 1920s (a persistent macroeconomic slump, the pound's overvaluation, creeping protectionism, and a variety of capital controls) (Eichengreen 1997).

An interesting thought experiment is to ask what would have happened to the international role of the dollar in the late 1970s and early 1980s if the euro (or any other realistic competitor for the dollar) had existed at that time. That was a period when US inflation hit double digits, when US economic growth was mediocre, and when the United States started running huge external deficits and shifted from being the world's largest creditor country to its largest debtor. Even without such a competitor, the global market share of the dollar dropped substantially. European monetary integration was galvanized. Replication of such a period of poor US economic performance, which is certainly possible if not inevitable, might be a necessary condition for the euro to realize its underlying potential—whatever the Europeans do themselves to ensure, or even accelerate, the process.

Are there any foreseeable developments that could represent such a repetition of recent history? Here I would again join Robert Mundell and quote from his writings on the eve of euro creation in 1998:

> It would be a mistake to ignore [the fact that] in the last 15 years US current account deficits have turned the US from the world's biggest creditor to its biggest debtor. . . . The low-saving high-debt problems will one day come home to roost. . . . There will come a time when the pileup of international indebtedness makes reliance on the dollar as the world's only main currency untenable. . . . The fact that the bulk of international reserves is held in dollars makes the currency a sitting duck in a currency crisis. . . . Sole reliance on the dollar as the main reserve,

invoice and intervention currency presents risks that are no longer necessary. (Robert Mundell, "The Case for the Euro—I and II," *Wall Street Journal*, March 24 and 25, 1998, A22)

The United States' international debt and deficit problems have of course become much greater during the past six years since Mundell wrote those words. In 2003, the US current account deficit reached $550 billion, or about 5 percent of GDP. This took it well into the traditional "danger zone" in which the Organization for Economic Cooperation and Development's member countries, including the United States on three previous occasions in the postwar period, are forced to adjust (Mann 1999; Freund 2000). The net international investment position of the United States probably approached negative $3 trillion at the end of 2003 and could hit 40 to 50 percent of GDP within the next few years (Mann 1999, updated 2001).

Hence the dollar is now undergoing a substantial depreciation. Major dollar depreciations are nothing new; they have occurred about once a decade since the advent of generalized currency convertibility in the postwar period (in 1971–73, 1978–79, 1985–87, and 1994–95 to the dollar's all-time lows against the deutsche mark and yen). The current depreciation, however, is taking place in a very different world: one that includes the euro, the first potential competitor for global status that the dollar has faced throughout its period of currency hegemony.

This fall of the dollar could thus trigger important, indeed historic, systemic as well as market and macroeconomic effects, especially because the decline of the dollar is producing a proportionately much greater rise in the euro (because many of America's major trading partners, such as Mexico and China, are unable or unwilling to accept substantial appreciation of their currencies against the dollar). This substantial and prolonged strengthening of the euro could at some point begin to trigger the inevitable structural portfolio diversification into euros by both private and official holders, which I and others earlier estimated at between $500 billion and $1 trillion (Bergsten 1997b). That shift would mark the arrival of the euro as a major competitor for the dollar.

Such a scenario might indeed trigger the far-reaching systemic implications hypothesized at the outset of this chapter. Mundell in fact concluded that the euro "could present problems in the transition . . . magnified by the likelihood of a massive diversification into euro-denominated deposits. Both the EU and the US would need to take strong defensive action to ease the transition [but] it is unlikely that bilateral handling of the problem would be amicable" (Robert Mundell, "The Case for the Euro—I and II," *Wall Street Journal*, March 24 and 25, 1998, A22; see also Bergsten 2001). The next big problem facing the "international financial architecture" may thus center on the countries and currencies at its core, the United States and the European Union, rather than on the emerging market economies and their currencies as during the past decade.

A "Finance G-2" to the Rescue?

At the very minimum, the key finance and monetary authorities of Euroland and the United States need to create a new consultative arrangement to monitor the evolution of the dollar-euro exchange rate and to be prepared to recommend contingency plans to their governments if market movements become disorderly and/or overshoot. Part of the initial task of the group would of course be to define these key concepts ("disorderly," "overshoot") in the current context. It is simply inadequate for these officials, as at present, to get together sporadically around G-7 or other broader meetings—which are also complicated by the presence of other countries that are less relevant (e.g., Canada and even Japan) as well as by the absence of countries that *are* relevant (e.g., China and sometimes South Korea). A detailed agenda is suggested in Edwin Truman's chapter in this volume.

The more interesting and controversial question is whether such a consultative exercise should go further and develop a new "G-2 monetary regime." At some point, it will almost certainly be necessary for the G-2 members to decide on at least a very wide range within which they are prepared to see their currencies fluctuate. They in essence agreed to a floor for the euro in September 2000 and could at some early point approach a level at which they would seek to set a ceiling. The United States and Japanese authorities essentially reached agreement on such a range in the past decade when they intervened to check the yen's appreciation in 1995 and its depreciation in 1998. In retrospect, the three boundaries set under these implied ranges in the past permitted substantial overshooting in both directions and should presumably be significantly narrowed in the future.

A serious agreement on managing the floating exchange rate between the dollar and euro, even within very wide margins, would of course eventually require agreement on means for implementing that management. Sterilized intervention and even jawboning have now been demonstrated to represent additional policy instruments (Evans and Lyons 2003, Fratzscher 2004) and would represent initial lines of defense. The ECB and Fed could begin to collaborate more intensively on monetary policy. Meaningful cooperation on fiscal and broader economic policies will probably have to await substantially greater consolidation of the decision-making process within Euroland, however, perhaps as a result of the constitutional convention that is now in progress across the European Union.

A "finance G-2" would be wholly informal and would probably never even be publicly announced. Far from substituting for the G-7 or the IMF, one of its chief goals would be to make those bodies work better. As the group of players that is relevant to the effective management of the international monetary system increases, now to include China and a number of other Asian countries, the need for a small informal steering committee à la G-2 of course increases.

It would be difficult for other countries to criticize the G-2 for providing such a steering committee. The dollar and euro stand leagues above all other currencies in the international monetary system. Their underlying economies are by far the largest in the world. China may need to be added to the group in a decade or so, if its economy continues to expand rapidly and its currency attains the global status that has always eluded the yen, but a finance G-2 would appear politically legitimate as well as economically essential for at least the foreseeable future.

The European Union and the United States both have major interests in constructing and implementing a finance G-2. Euroland was quite anxious about the decline of its currency in 2000 and is already extremely anxious about the present appreciation. It surely recognizes that the process could go much further—simply as a result of continued dollar decline, especially if the Asians continue to resist increases in the value of their own currencies; additionally if the inevitable portfolio diversification into euros gets under way in earnest; and even more so if their productivity and economic growth accelerate appreciably and enhance the appeal of their asset markets. A decision by China or Japan to shift a substantial portion of its official reserves from dollars to euros would in and of itself trigger sympathetic moves of private portfolios and dramatically intensify the currency problem from a European perspective.

American reactions have been similar. The dollar's overvaluation and a soaring trade deficit were widely tolerated when the economy was booming in the late 1990s but became a major source of concern and criticism with the slowdown after 2000 (Baily 2002). Nor would the United States now welcome a free fall of the dollar any more than it did in 1987, when it attempted to call a halt to the Plaza-induced depreciation with the Louvre stabilization effort. More fundamentally, as noted above, the existence of the euro as a credible alternative to the dollar means that the United States may be unable to finance its future external deficits—and hence its budget deficits as well—nearly as painlessly as in the past.

A finance G-2 would of course contribute substantially to a broader evolution of systematic economic cooperation between the European Union and the United States. Such a structure would in turn help both regions overcome their most fundamental foreign policy problems: the tendency of the United States to pursue unilateral strategies and the tendency of Europe to ignore its external responsibilities because of its intensive internal agenda. A *finance* G-2 (whether or not part of a broader G-2) would constantly remind the United States that unilateralism is not an option for it in the economic domain, even in the financial component thereof, where dollar supremacy has prevailed for so long. It would constantly remind Europe that its external affairs need to be managed carefully. It *will inevitably become a necessary feature of the international monetary policy of both and thus a central element of the global monetary system of the 21st century.*

Moreover, the creation of an effective G-2 across a number of economic issues (including but ranging well beyond finance, per Bergsten and Koch-Weser 2004) could play a central role in restoring harmony to overall transatlantic relations. Relations between the United States and much of Europe remain tense, in the wake of the sharp disagreements that preceded the Iraq war, and their security dimension seems unlikely to produce reconciliation any time soon. New economic initiatives are thus the most likely route to patching up the overall relationship and could bring major foreign policy as well as economic benefits (Bergsten 2004).

References

Baily, Martin N. 2002. Persistent Dollar Swings and the US Economy. In *Dollar Overvaluation and the World Economy*, ed. C. Fred Bergsten and John Williamson. Washington: Institute for International Economics.

Baily, Martin N., and Jacob Kirkegaard. 2004. *A Transformation of the European Economy.* Washington: Institute for International Economics.

Bergsten, C. Fred. 1996. *Dilemmas of the Dollar: The Economics and Politics of United States International Monetary Policy,* 2d ed. Armonk, NY: M. E. Sharpe.

Bergsten, C. Fred. 1997a. The Dollar and the Euro. *Foreign Affairs* 76, no. 4: 83–95.

Bergsten, C. Fred. 1997b. The Impact of the Euro on Exchange Rates and International Policy Coordination. In *EMU and the International Monetary System,* ed. Paul R. Masson, Thomas H. Krueger, and Bart G. Turtelboom. Washington: International Monetary Fund.

Bergsten, C. Fred. 2001. America's Two-Front Economic Conflict. *Foreign Affairs* 80, no. 2: 16–27.

Bergsten, C. Fred. 2002. The Euro Versus the Dollar: Will There Be a Struggle for Dominance? *Journal of Policy Modeling* 24, no 4: 307–14.

Bergsten, C. Fred. 2004. Foreign Economic Policy for the Next President. *Foreign Affairs* 83, no. 2: 88–101.

Bergsten, C. Fred, and Caio Koch-Weser. 2004. The G-2: A New Conceptual Basis and Operating Modality for Transatlantic Economic Relations. In *From Alliance to Coalitions—The Future of Transatlantic Relations,* ed. Werner Weidenfeld, Caio Koch-Weser, C. Fred Bergsten, Walther Stützle, and John Hamre. Frankfurt: Bertelsmann Foundation.

Danthine, Jean-Pierre, Francesco Giavazzi, and Ernst-Ludwig von Thadden. 2000. *European Financial Markets After EMU: A First Assessment.* NBER Working Paper 8044. Cambridge, MA: National Bureau of Economic Research.

Draghi, Mario, and Robert Pozen. 2004. US-EU Regulatory Convergence: Capital Markets Issues. In *From Alliance to Coalitions—The Future of Transatlantic Relations,* ed. Werner Weidenfeld, Caio Koch-Weser, C. Fred Bergsten, Walther Stützle, and John Hamre. Frankfurt: Bertelsmann Foundation.

Eichengreen, Barry. 1997. Comments on Bergsten. In *EMU and the International Monetary System,* ed. Paul R. Masson, Thomas H. Krueger, and Bart G. Turtelboom. Washington: International Monetary Fund.

Eichengreen, Barry, and Jeffrey Frankel. 1996. The SDR, Reserve Currencies, and the Future of the International Monetary System. In *The Future of the SDR in Light of Changes in the International Financial System,* ed. Michael Mussa, James D. Boughton, and Peter Isard. Washington: International Monetary Fund.

Evans, Martin D. D., and Richard K. Lyons. 2003. Are Different-Currency Assets Imperfect Substitutes? In *Exchange Rate Economics: Where Do We Stand?* ed. Paul De Grauwe. Cambridge, MA: MIT Press.

Fratzscher, Marcel. 2004. *Communication and Exchange Rate Policy.* ECB Working Paper Series 363. Frankfurt: European Central Bank.

Freund, Caroline. 2000. *Current Account Adjustment in Industrialized Countries.* International Finance Division Working Papers, 2000-692. Washington: Federal Reserve Board.

Henning, C. Randall. 1997. *Cooperating with Europe's Monetary Union.* POLICY ANALYSES IN INTERNATIONAL ECONOMICS 49. Washington: Institute for International Economics.

Henning, C. Randall. 2000. *Transatlantic Perspectives on the Euro.* Washington: Brookings Institution Press and European Community Studies Association.

Henning, C. Randall. 2003. Transatlantic Economic and Monetary Relations. Paper presented at a conference on transatlantic relations between Europe and the United States sponsored by Calouste Gulbenkian Foundation, Lisbon, October 21–22.

Kawai, Masahiro. 1997. Comments on Bergsten and on Alogouskoufis and Portes. In *EMU and the International Monetary System,* ed. Paul R. Masson, Thomas H. Krueger, and Bart G. Turtelboom. Washington: International Monetary Fund.

Mann, Catherine L. 1999. *Is the US Trade Deficit Sustainable?* Washington: Institute for International Economics.

Mann, Catherine L. 2001. Perspectives on the US Current Account Deficit and Sustainability. *Journal of Economic Perspectives* (summer).

Mussa, Michael. 2003. A Global Growth Rebound: How Strong for How Long? Presentation at the Global Economic Prospects conference sponsored by the Institute for International Economics, Washington, September 9.

Portes, Richard, and Hélène Rey. 1998. Euro vs. Dollar. *Economic Policy,* April 26: 306–43.

Posen, Adam. Forthcoming. *Germany: Reform in a Rich Country.* Washington: Institute for International Economics.

Sinn, Hans-Werner, and Frank Westermann. 2001. *Why Has the Euro Been Falling? An Investigation into the Determinants of the Exchange Rate.* NBER Working Paper 8352. Cambridge, MA: National Bureau of Economic Research.

Comment

RANDAL QUARLES

Having been asked to discuss the stimulating chapter by Fred Bergsten on the past and future of the euro, my reaction was that too much attention is being focused on exchange rate policy coordination mechanisms and attempts to define appropriate exchange rates and too little on what seems to me of far greater importance: namely, the more effective functioning of economies in the interests of sustained stronger growth and higher employment.[1]

Bergsten himself gets into this when he notes the disappointments connected with the European Union's efforts to achieve the admirable goals of the Lisbon Agenda, including in particular the limited progress in adopting structural reforms to provide greater incentives for investment and for both job creation and willingness to take jobs. As the chapter notes, "Europe has failed to follow up the creation of the euro with the complementary policy reforms that were widely expected and that are needed to ensure the success of the overall Economic and Monetary Union." Even accounting for the recent economic slump, the trend in the euro area has been toward declining long-term growth rates. Consensus forecasts for average growth in the euro area for the next 10 years have declined from 2.8 to 2.2 percent during the past three years. Though the explanation includes the slower growth of the working-age population, that is only part of the story.

European leadership has recognized the long-term problems it must confront, and the European Union itself put forward the goal at Lisbon of

Randal Quarles is the assistant secretary for international affairs at the US Treasury.

1. I should say at the outset that I do not plan to comment on currencies.

becoming the most competitive and dynamic economy in the world by 2010. This is a challenge that the United States relishes, and its policymakers no doubt would be happy to see Europe—and other areas—grow faster, create more jobs, achieve the higher productivity growth that will expand real incomes, and in general provide a more dynamic contribution to the world economy.

So far, though, identifying and agreeing on a goal has not been enough to ensure progress. The European Union still faces a number of challenges on the path to meeting its Lisbon objectives, and the European Commission has warned that the European Union may fail to reach them. Early in 2004, Commission president Romano Prodi said that member states were in danger of missing midterm targets, and productivity and employment growth were still contributing too little to European growth. The Commission has put its finger on the major problems: low employment ratios (especially among men 55 to 64 years of age), inadequate use of information and communication technologies, and lagging investment in research and development.

The European Commission's own findings show a clear path to higher productivity: lowering regulation, increasing expenditures on research and development, completing the integration of markets and promoting competition, and reforming financial services so that capital markets can respond to these policies by directing finance to dynamic, employment-producing enterprises.

The recent announcement in Berlin by Prime Minister Tony Blair, Chancellor Gerhard Schröder, and President Jacques Chirac calling for decreased regulation and support for more state-led investment, sincere as it is, seems to indicate part of the problem as well as part of the solution. So long as the underlying assumption that state activity is the solution to every economic problem governs European thinking about growth, it will be hard to achieve the freedom for individual economic action and competition that will promote innovation, adoption of technological improvements, and higher investment.

Using a database from the Organization for Economic Cooperation and Development, Alesina et al. (2003) have reaffirmed the relationship between investment levels and the extent of deregulation. They found that the greatest effect on investment can be had from deregulation in areas such as financial services and retail and wholesale trade, where progress has been made but more can be done. This accords with the European Commission's own work showing that productivity differences in service sectors such as those that use information and communication technologies account for much of the gap between US and EU productivity growth in the past 10 years.

In my view, the vigorous pursuit of growth-oriented policies is critical, and the Group of Seven (G-7) has made an Agenda for Growth the key theme for its 2004 process. By specifying individual reform goals and using a process of mutual surveillance and support, the G-7 hopes to lay the groundwork for stronger growth in all seven economies, including the United States.

Coming back to the issue of policy coordination, I am not sure quite what Bergsten has in mind or what deficiencies he sees more generally. Whether it is a matter of discussion of exchange rates, monetary and fiscal policy, or anything else, the G-7 has very extensive and mostly informal processes of discussion. The G-7 ministers and central bank governors meet at least three times a year. The G-7 deputies meet many times more than that. That remarkable Washington invention—the telephone—is used frequently for consultations. Officials travel a lot. And there are many other forums: the Bank for International Settlements meetings, the Financial Stability Forum, the Group of Twenty, United States–EU summits, and so on.

In today's world, no country can set global economic policies all by itself or only with one or two others. A continual process of informal discussion and contact provides the best means for understanding the interaction of national policies around the globe and greater sensitivity to each country's concerns. I have a particular concern that a formal "Group of Two" could fail to take appropriate account of financial developments in other important economic areas—not only the other G-7 members, but also some of the large and fast-growing economies that are acquiring real weight in the international financial system.

In the end, I think our current informal processes are working as well as they can in a world of diverse perspectives. The most important contribution any country can make is to improve its own economy's performance—to raise growth, employment, and standards of living for all its residents. The better an economy functions individually, the more positive a contribution it can make to the global economy.

Reference

Alesina, Alberto, Silvia Ardagna, Giuseppe Nicoletti, and Fabio Schiantarelli. 2003. Regulation and Investment. NBER Working Paper 9560. Cambridge, MA: National Bureau of Economic Research.

Comment

HERVÉ CARRÉ

Fred Bergsten's chapter includes both a careful assessment and thought-provoking propositions. The first part of his chapter, "The Euro at Five," is a particularly well-balanced assessment of what has been achieved with the new currency. I cannot but agree with the statement that "the first five years of the euro have been a spectacular success" and that "even the most ardent supporters of the euro, both inside and outside Europe, have been severely disappointed by Euroland's failure to adopt the needed reforms." Being one of these supporters, I have nothing to add. I thought that the adoption of the euro would act as a catalyst for structural reforms—and I am disappointed.

So I direct my remarks to the second part of the chapter, which focuses on the euro and the world economy. It rightly states that the euro provides the first real competition for the dollar, and it raises four issues, which I will address in turn.

First, *for the euro to realize its potential, there is a need to further integrate money and capital markets.* I fully agree, but it is useful to point out that the pace of financial integration has accelerated with the adoption of the euro. Deeper integration is reflected in more homogeneous markets, a wave of consolidation among intermediaries and exchanges, and the emergence of new products and techniques. Market operators have adopted more pan-European strategies and policymakers have responded by assigning a high political priority to the completion of the internal market for finan-

Hervé Carré is the minister for financial affairs at the Delegation of the European Commission to the United States. The views expressed are those of the author and do not necessarily reflect the views of the European Commission.

cial services. They are committed to implementing the Financial Services Action Plan (FSAP)—a package of policy initiatives aimed at improving the functioning of the EU financial system—by 2005. As a matter of fact, the money and derivatives markets are already highly integrated, and the bond markets are deeper and more homogeneous, with higher issuance volumes and a sharp rise in corporate bond issuance. But, despite a growing internationalization of equity issuance, more mergers and acquisitions across borders, and consolidation of formal stock exchanges, equity markets are still fragmented. Posttrading infrastructure is slowly being transformed—still offering limited scope for cross-border trading.

Finally, while consolidation among financial intermediaries has taken place mainly within national boundaries, cross-border mergers show an increasing trend. The objective of a single financial market remains to be achieved, but significant progress has been made, and the deadline for the implementation of FSAP by 2005 is expected to be met.

The second issue raised by Bergsten's chapter is *the need for the European Union to get its act together institutionally*. It is clear that the Economic and Monetary Union (EMU) project is still in the making as regards the external side. The European Community Treaty sets out procedures to deal with the international aspects of the EMU, and since 1999 practical arrangements have been devised for the internal coordination of external positions. The Eurogroup and the Ecofin have devoted much work to establishing common positions and common understandings on a wide range of issues. Although this allows the euro area to start playing a role commensurate with its financial and economic weight, it needs to be complemented by further progress on external representation. A single European voice is long overdue, as Bergsten points out.

The third issue is *the need for the European Union to improve its economic performance*. This is much needed, and I can only agree, but I would introduce a nuance into Bergsten's assessment. The slow growth in the euro area is mainly due to the lack of structural reform or, to be more accurate, to the slow adoption of the much-needed structural reforms in implementing the Lisbon Agenda. I really think that the macroeconomic policy of the past five years has been broadly appropriate.

I have stronger reservations about the fourth issue—that *for the euro to realize its potential to achieve rough parity with the dollar at the core of the international monetary system, the United States may have to foul up*. Although a crisis scenario cannot be excluded, it is not likely. Increased portfolio diversification into euros by both private and official holders will certainly take place over time, but this will be a long-term development. It will also be a market-driven development, which can occur only when the euro-denominated financial markets are as wide, deep, and resilient as the dollar-denominated markets. Furthermore, there is a practical obstacle to such a crisis scenario: US Treasury notes, the preferred asset of official holders, have no equivalent in the euro-denominated markets. Government bonds in the euro area will still be issued by 12 agencies with different borrowing requirements, issuance strategies, and instruments.

However, over time, the euro will become an alternative to the dollar, and this has systemic implications for international monetary relations. With no past experience in the management of a multipolar monetary system, the proposal to set up a "finance Group of Two" (G-2) made in Bergsten's chapter is particularly relevant. There is a strong economic case to set up an informal finance G-2 along the lines sketched out in the chapter. Such an arrangement is already working informally in many areas. The chapter mentions the trade area, obviously, and the cooperation between the European Central Bank and the US Federal Reserve. I would also add financial markets, where an informal ongoing dialogue has already proved quite successful, and more recently a structural policy dialogue.

The question is how to develop this method to cover exchange rate development and, more generally, fiscal and macroeconomic policies. Obviously the difficulty comes from the EU side, from the present inability of the euro area to get its act together. Unfortunately, under existing circumstances, there is no short-term answer to this governance problem in the euro area. Even the draft Constitutional Treaty that is now being discussed does not provide a solution to the problem.

To conclude, I would like to stress how stimulating Bergsten's chapter was. As he reported, Europe is facing two major challenges:

- completing the Lisbon Agenda in time, and

- getting its act together on the external aspects.

I agree with most of the chapter, and I particularly welcome the suggestion to construct and implement a finance G-2, building on existing informal arrangements. Let us hope that this proposition will be as successful as the ideas Fred Bergsten developed in March 1997!

4

The Euro and Prospects for Policy Coordination

EDWIN M. TRUMAN

This chapter is divided into two sections. In the first, longer section, I evaluate the case for improved policy coordination with and by the euro area, which is the principal focus of the chapter. I review 10 topics and conclude that a prima facie case can be made for improvement. In the second section, I put forward 6 recommendations for how policy coordination with and by the euro area might be improved. Before moving on to substance, I cover some preliminaries.

What do I mean by policy coordination? In general, I prefer a broad concept including information exchange, dialogue and shared analysis, common objectives, joint action, and endorsement of current policies (Truman 2004a, 268). However, it is useful to try to distinguish which type of policy coordination one is talking about, which I have tried to do in the first section of the chapter.

What do I mean by policy coordination by and with the euro area? There is considerable policy coordination by and with the euro area today—with central institutions like the European Central Bank (ECB), with the European Commission in Brussels, and with officials in capitals of the various European countries. The issue considered here is whether more can and should be done. I am deliberately vague in the first section

Edwin M. Truman is a senior fellow at the Institute for International Economics. He is grateful for the comments by Richard H. Clarida and Richard N. Cooper on an earlier version of this chapter. He is also grateful for comments from his colleagues William R. Cline, C. Randall Henning, and Catherine L. Mann and from Peter B. Kenen. He also thanks Fabrizio Iacobellis for excellent research assistance in preparing this chapter.

of the chapter on the issue of the structure of the coordination process on the European side. However, in this context, policy coordination is intended to apply principally to the interaction of euro area officials with US officials but also encompasses the euro area's interaction in international forums such as Group of Seven (G-7) meetings, G-7 and Group of Eight (G-8) summits, Group of Twenty (G-20) meetings, and various meetings at or associated with the International Monetary Fund (e.g., its International Monetary and Financial Committee). It is a considerable complexity, at a minimum, that the euro area is not the same as the European Union, and I return to this issue in the second section of the chapter under the heading "Getting the Right Players on the Field."

The Case for Improved Policy Coordination with the Euro Area

The global economy has just emerged from an extended slowdown that followed a period of uneven global growth punctuated by a rash of external financial crises directly affecting countries in Latin America, Asia, and Europe (treating Russia as part of Europe for these purposes). For much of this period, the US dollar was strengthening or was very strong, ultimately casting a shadow over the early years of full European Monetary Union with the birth of the euro. That strength was associated with a dramatic rise in US productivity and economic growth, but also with the emergence of an oversized current account deficit and rapid further deterioration of the US net international investment position. It now may be that the US external deficit is in the early stage of correction or at least temporary stabilization.

This judgment provides the background for the first 6 of the 10 topics for policy coordination with and by the euro area that are examined below: external adjustment, rebalancing the global economy, global growth, fiscal policies, intervention strategy, and the IMF and global capital flows. I also consider four other topics: EU enlargement, euro-dollar peaceful coexistence, structural reform, and trade issues.

External Adjustment

The US current account deficit reached 4.2 percent of GDP in 2000, surpassing its previous maximum of 3.4 percent in 1987, and it has remained, or is projected to remain, at that level or above through at least 2005. The deficit narrowed a bit in 2001 under the influence of the US recession but widened to 4.6 percent in 2002 and 4.9 percent in 2003. Meanwhile, the weighted-average foreign exchange value of the dollar on the broad Federal Reserve index declined in real terms by about 13 percent from February 2002 through February 2004; the decline against the currencies of the major industrial countries more than accounted for the decline in the broad index.[1]

The explanations for the dollar's rise are as numerous as those of the dollar's decline. Debates about whether either its rise or its fall is good for the United States or the global economy, similarly, have failed to reach a consensus. It is very difficult to prove anything in this area in the absence of robust models of exchange rate determination. It is also very difficult to prove how large an adjustment of the US current account position may be under way. Estimates range from a couple of percentage points of GDP, from the current 5 to 3 percent, to more than 5 percent of GDP, enough to push the US balance on goods and services—which was 4.5 percent of GDP in 2003—into surplus and begin paying down the US net external debt.

Interestingly, both explanations can be supported by the productivity story about the behavior of the US economy during the past decade. Rosenberg (2003) justifies a smaller adjustment, down to 3–4 percent of GDP on the basis that the extraordinary surge in US productivity will continue and the global economy should and will continue to accumulate net claims on the United States. Erceg (2002), conversely, reminds us that in the face of a productivity shock that ultimately dies out, an economy has to repay the external debt that it accumulated while the productivity shock was under way, which means that the country must run trade surpluses.[2] In this connection, it is important to recall that if the United States is to stabilize its net international investment position relative to GDP, it might have to be running a surplus on trade in goods and services sufficient to cover its net income payments, currently approximately zero, but likely to move into negative territory once dollar interest rates return to neutral, plus net transfer payments, currently running about 0.5 percent

---

1. Over the two-year period, the real decline against the major currencies (Australia, Canada, euro area, Japan, Sweden, Switzerland, and the United Kingdom) was 23 percent on average while the dollar rose 2 percent on average against the currencies of 19 other important trading partners. Much of the increase is attributable to the dollar's nominal appreciation against the Mexican peso of 21 percent over the period, and its substantial appreciations against other Latin American currencies included in the index: the Argentine peso, the Brazilian real, and the Venezuelan bolivar.

2. The Erceg simulations, using an optimization model that takes account of intertemporal budget constraints, support the view that the dollar's appreciation was induced by the relative acceleration of US productivity in the second half of the 1990s. Hunt and Rebucci (2003) use a similar model and obtain a similar result for an asymmetric productivity shock to the United States; they also note that to explain fully the dollar's appreciation, their model requires a temporary but persistent decline in the perceived riskiness of US assets—in other words, a dash of irrational exuberance.

of GDP.[3] Stabilization of the US net international investment position as a share of GDP does not involve any paying down of US net indebtedness.[4]

However, Dooley, Folkerts-Landau, and Garber (2004) opine that a US current account deficit of less than 3 percent of GDP is "manageable." Mann (2003), looking at shares of the global portfolio of equities, has made an estimate that a deficit between 2.4 and 3.6 percent of GDP as of 2005 would be sustainable. Richard Cooper ("America is Saving Enough," *Financial Times*, February 20, 2004, 13) has argued that from the vantage point of the United States the case is weak for deliberately reducing US reliance on net savings from abroad in the form of large current account deficits. The United States is benefiting from the net inflow of foreign savings because it is adding to net investment, which importantly embodies technological advances, and enables the United States to absorb more goods and services than we produce, living beyond our means. From a global perspective, the issues are: How long will the rest of the world be content to send substantial amounts of their net saving annually to the United States? And how disruptive to global prosperity is an eventual US external adjustment process likely to be?

One does not have to rely on sophisticated macroeconomic models to conclude that US external adjustment may well be under way. Federal Reserve Board governor Donald Kohn (2004, 4) goes no further than the analysis of former Federal Reserve Board staff member Caroline Freund (2000) to conclude "when the deficit approached this magnitude [5 percent of GDP] in the past, markets had generally already begun to adjust to reduce it."

Federal Reserve Board chairman Alan Greenspan (2003, 3; 2004a, 4) is slightly more cautious:

> There is no simple measure by which to judge the sustainability of either a string of current account deficits or their consequence, a significant buildup in external claims that need to be serviced. Financing comes from receipts from exports, earnings on assets, and, if available, funds borrowed from foreigners. In the end, it will likely be the reluctance of foreign country residents to accumulate additional debt and equity claims against US residents that will serve as the restraint on the size of tolerable global imbalances in the global arena.

---

3. Assuming a normal nominal growth rate of US GDP of 6 percent, stabilizing the US net international investment position at the level of 25 percent of GDP that prevailed at the end of 2002 would be accomplished with a current account deficit of 1.5 percent of GDP. If US net income payments were 0.5 percent of GDP and net transfer payments were also 0.5 percent of GDP, the United States could have a small trade deficit of 0.5 percent of GDP, compared with its recent deficit of 4.5 percent of GDP. However, if, as would be likely, net income payments were to rise to 1 percent of GDP or higher, the United States would have to move into trade surplus.

4. Dollar depreciation does have a positive effect on US net international indebtedness as a share of GDP by increasing the dollar value of foreign-currency-denominated assets, which are more substantial than foreign-currency-denominated liabilities.

However, he too cites Freund as providing evidence that the point will arrive when this adjustment process will be fully under way. Neither Kohn nor Greenspan offers a view on the extent of possible adjustment in the US external accounts, when it will come, or if it is coming, but both are sanguine about the process.

Issing (2003, 5) is less sanguine than Kohn and Greenspan about the US external adjustment process. He is concerned about a disorderly adjustment process: "The current level of the US current account deficit is in the longer run unsustainable and an adjustment will eventually occur, whether actively supported by macroeconomic policies or not. The question is only whether it will happen in an orderly fashion." However, he does not define what he means by orderly. Presumably he means a process that is not disruptive to global economic growth and financial markets. He argues that the risk of a disorderly adjustment is increased the longer the flow imbalances exist and the larger they are because the required adjustment back to more reasonable levels would be larger. He also argues implicitly that the US current account deficit was the result of an inefficient allocation of world savings associated with euphoria over the US "new economy," which unreasonably boosted expected returns in the United States and resulted in "hot" portfolio flows partly induced by accounting irregularities at US companies.[5]

Issing does not express a view on the size of the needed adjustment in US external accounts, but he implicitly aligns himself with an IMF view that a US current account deficit of about 2 percent of GDP would be consistent with equilibrium in the saving-investment balance, which is his preferred analytical framework.[6] He suggests that there may need to be a

---

5. Issing seems to ignore the fact that the German DAX stock market index declined 68 percent from its recent (monthly average) peak in February 2000 to its trough in March 2003, and the UK *Financial Times* 100 (FT100) declined by 48 percent from its peak in December 1999 to its low in March 2003, while the US Standard & Poor's (S&P) 500 declined by 46 percent from its peak in August 2000 to its low in September 2002. Since their recent troughs through February 2004, the DAX has recovered 53 percent of its decline, the FT100 65 percent, and the S&P 500 75 percent. Moreover, the incidence of accounting and corporate governance scandals has been high in Europe as well as in the United States; witness the cases of Adecco, Ahold, Credit Lyonnais, Kirsch Media, Parmalat, Shell, and Vivendi. Irrational exuberance, artificially induced or not, was not confined to the United States. It may have continued longer or still be present in the United States because of excessively easy monetary policy, but that is another debate into which Issing did not enter. He did argue implicitly (*Wall Street Journal*, February 18, 2004) that the Bundesbank-ECB monetary policy framework with its emphasis on monetary and credit developments contributes "to limiting the emergence of unsustainable developments in asset prices" compared with other monetary policy frameworks. His argument is not supported by the data cited above.

6. Issing does not provide a source for the IMF view that he cites. It most likely is Isard et al. (2001), which estimates a saving-investment norm for the United States in 2003 of about 1.75 percent of GDP of net capital inflow. IMF (2002) can be read as supporting a view that a correction of 2 percent of GDP down to 3 percent of GDP is likely to be in the cards,

further adjustment in the US private saving-investment balance, but he is confident (Issing 2003, 8): "A considerably larger correction will be necessary for the public saving-investment balance, with the current [US] fiscal stance certainly not sustainable in the long run. Such a correction will in all likelihood imply lower growth for a long time." His basic message (2003, 5) is to get on with it, and the sooner the better: "By supporting an adjustment sooner rather than later policy-makers could, in principle, help to ensure such a gradual and orderly adjustment, while at the same time possibly contributing to a more efficient use of global savings and safeguarding the global trading system by limiting protectionist pressures."

It is not clear through what mechanism Issing thinks the narrowing of the US savings-investment balance will be translated into a narrowing of the US current account imbalance. Though slower US growth might play a role, and without denying that a significant ex post adjustment of savings and investment would be observed, one would think that substantial and rapid US external adjustment would be associated with substantial and rapid downward adjustment of the dollar. ECB president Jean-Claude Trichet has already decried the early-January 2004 movements of the dollar as "brutal" (*Financial Times*, January 13, 1).

US external adjustment may be under way. It could well involve a substantial further adjustment of exchange rates. The adjustment might be closer to 5 percent of GDP than 2 percent of GDP. A larger adjustment, which I think is more likely, can be based on the influence of the Erceg long-run equilibrium condition, a judgment that the cyclically adjusted US current account deficit is larger than the actual deficit,[7] and the observation that external adjustment processes generally overshoot.

My views, however, are not germane to the question at hand: Is there a case for the policy coordination with the euro area to try to understand and if necessary to adjust economic policies to help manage the inevitable adjustment process or to establish whether it is inevitable? As part of that policy coordination, the euro area and its partners might want to consider how large the adjustment is likely to be, through what channels it is likely to occur, and how the euro area and other policies should react. Thus, the policy coordination process by and with the euro area should include improved information exchange, dialogue and mutual education, and analysis. On the basis of that analysis, it is possible that policy coordination could progress to the establishment of common objectives and joint action

---

because that has been the historical pattern for industrial countries with large current account deficits. The same source can be read as implying a correction of closer to 4.5 percent of GDP down to 0.5 percent of GDP to stabilize the US international investment position as a ratio of GDP at its 1990–98 average.

7. This judgment is based on an assumption that the US output gap is likely to be closed, but that the probability that the output gaps in the euro area or Japan will be closed is substantially lower.

to achieve those objectives. The basic issues—size, channels, and policy adjustments—inform the next five topics.

Rebalancing the Global Economy

Even if the adjustment of the US external deficit during the next couple of years turns out to be unsubstantial—say, less than 2 percentage points of GDP—it will be the first step in an important rebalancing of the global economy, because the growth of the world economy cannot rely indefinitely on the further expansion of the US external deficit.[8] By assumption, even if the US external adjustment does no more than stabilize at 4 to 5 percent of GDP for the foreseeable future, the US deficit will no longer be providing a demand stimulus to the global economy.

If the US external adjustment is substantial, say, closer to 5 percentage points of GDP, the deflationary impact will have to fall on all regions of the world. To date most of the impact has been felt, at least directly, by other industrial countries: the euro area, other countries in Europe, Japan, Australia, Canada, and New Zealand.

The G-7 agreed in Dubai in September 2002 that this unbalanced process had continued far enough: "We emphasize that more flexibility in exchange rates is desirable for major countries or economic areas to promote smooth and widespread adjustment in the international financial system, based on market mechanisms." The language was convoluted, no doubt reflecting the contorted drafting by committee that was involved. However, the language broke fresh ground in embracing exchange rate flexibility, something that the Europeans and Japanese had resisted in the past, and in seeking to broaden the international adjustment process.

The G-7 communiqué issued in Boca Raton, Florida, on February 7, 2004, was substantially similar. It did offer a sop to the Europeans by including the tired phrasing "excess volatility and disorderly movements in exchange rates are undesirable for economic growth," terms that have been used and undefined in similar communications for three decades. The G-7 also clarified its call for exchange rate flexibility by confining it redundantly to those that lack such flexibility. The new G-7 statement changed nothing, certainly nothing fundamental with respect to economic and financial policies.

---

8. In general, it is inappropriate to look at bilateral trade balances. However, changes in those balances are indicative of the direct effects on the rest of the world of changes in a particular country's overall trade balance. In the recession year of 1991, the US deficit on goods and services was 0.5 percent of GDP, its lowest point since the mid-1970s. In that year, the US trade surplus with the EU was $17 billion, compared with a deficit of $86 billion at an annual rate in the first three quarters of 2003. The swing in the bilateral balance with the European Union accounts for more than a fifth of the $470 billion deterioration in the US deficit during the period.

It was a tactical mistake to link exchange rate adjustment to market mechanisms because that appeared to rule out a one-time upward adjustment of the Chinese renminbi. It was an even greater travesty or tragedy (take your pick) for the International Monetary Fund to abdicate its responsibility and not speak out on the question of the need for exchange rate adjustments and flexibility by emerging-market economies at the same time that it was expressing concern about the US current account deficit and the level of foreign exchange reserves in Asia (IMF 2002, 2003a).

This does appear to be an area where further policy coordination with the euro area could be fruitful. Again, in the first instance, improved policy coordination would involve information exchanges and dialogue backed by economic analysis. It could later mature into the development of common objectives and joint actions.

Global Growth

The adjustment of the US external accounts, when it occurs, will be accompanied by slower global growth; the only question is how much slower. US growth will be lower in the short run because US interest rates will have to rise to choke off the growth of consumption and investment demand and replace it with increased export demand, unless the US economy is not already at full employment, which it most likely will be by late 2005 when these adjustments are likely to begin to kick in. The lower investment will reduce US potential growth over the longer run because of the slower growth rate of the capital stock; the extent of the reduction will depend in large part on whether there is a concomitant narrowing of the US fiscal deficit.

At the same time, growth abroad will be adversely affected in the short run by the need to offset the removal of up to $500 billion (4.5 percent of US GDP) in net stimulus to the world economy, roughly 2 percent of non-US global GDP of $25 trillion, at current exchange rates. No doubt policies will respond, with a lag, and economies will adjust slowly on the supply side, but for a period of three to five years while the US external adjustment is under way, growth outside the United States will be lower than it otherwise would be.

These prospects raise issues about policy adjustments in the short and longer runs. With respect to European economic policy or at least the ECB's policy, if Issing's view is representative, the view appears to be that nothing needs to be done in the short run to facilitate global adjustment. Issing argues that there are no major imbalances in the euro area constraining growth; the real structural problem in Europe is that potential growth is too low; and Europe (and Japan) need to avoid being hoodwinked—as they were in the late 1980s, for example, in the Louvre Accord—into adopting misguided policies to expand domestic demand.

Issing also rejects the view that strong growth in domestic demand in the United States in the late 1990s had anything to do with saving the rest of the world, especially Europe, from stagnation and recession. He is right that strong US growth was largely spontaneous, with a supporting role played by a responsible fiscal policy and a neutral monetary policy in the United States. But the simple fact is that from 1998 to 2000 the growth of US domestic demand was more than three-quarters of a percentage point higher than the growth of real GDP. From 2000 to 2002, during the birth of the euro, the growth of US real GDP annually exceeded the growth of domestic demand by more than half a percentage point on average. The euro area was in stagnation from 2001 to 2003, and without the pull of its external sector, it most likely would have experienced a recession.

In 1999 (Truman 1999b), I argued that appropriate structural reforms in Europe should improve the investment climate and stimulate investment, thereby narrowing the savings-investment imbalance in Europe and boosting growth in the euro area, which would be in the US interest as well. Five years later, we can wish more had been done. The G-7 Agenda for Growth issued in Dubai in September 2003 emphasized supply-side policies but also made a tepid bow in the direction of the role of macroeconomic demand-side policies in the global adjustment process: "Higher economic growth through the G7 will redress global imbalances that arise inter alia from uneven growth within the G7." Such statements suggest that the policy coordination process with the euro area has a lot to address with respect both to future policies as well as learning the lessons of the past.

Turning to longer-run policies, as the chapter in this volume by Adam Posen and the work of Baily and Kirkegaard (2004) demonstrate, there is no neat separation between the short run and the longer run, nor between demand-side and supply-side policies and institutions. The G-7—in its Dubai Agenda for Growth, and reverting back to the G-7 in the late 1980s—links the two: "Working as a group we intend to do regular supply-side surveillance, benchmarking proposals and reviewing results. This will complement our ongoing demand-side surveillance and mutually encourage progress toward pro-growth policies."

One can ask whether the US commitment in Dubai to tort reform will have much of a supply-side impact, but both demand-side and supply-side issues at least are on the table. For the euro area, they include reform of the Stability and Growth Pact, reorientation of the monetary policy framework of the ECB in the direction of greater clarity and more emphasis on short-term growth, proemployment labor market reforms, and product market and competition reforms. For all the mature industrial economies, these policies are linked to the impending demographic overhang of elderly people as well as to immigration policies.

Thus, issues of global growth in the long run as well as the short run would appear to provide more than ample opportunity for improved policy coordination with and by the euro area. That policy coordination could take the form of the establishment of common objectives as well as agreements on joint action designed to support and sustain global growth.

Fiscal Policies

The lack of agreement within the euro area as well as within the United States on the role of fiscal policies in promoting growth and external adjustment is palpable. We have already noted the debate within the euro area about the Stability and Growth Pact. In the United States a similar debate rages, including about the external risks associated with profligate fiscal policies (see Rubin, Orszag, and Sinai 2004 for a recent example).

The current European view appears to be that the United States should act now to reduce its fiscal deficit and slow its growth in order to reduce its external deficits and slow the depreciation of the dollar. Japan's finance minister Sadakazu Tanigaki, as reported in the *Financial Times* of January 15, 2004, expressed a similar view; he called upon the United States to repair its trade and fiscal deficits because concern about them is driving the dollar lower on exchange markets.

It is worth remembering that macroeconomic relationships between changes in fiscal positions and exchange rates are not well understood. For example, during the second half of the 1990s, the US fiscal position swung into surplus, the dollar appreciated, and US external deficits widened. However, from 1993 to 1995, when the US fiscal position improved by 1.5 percentage points of GDP on a nominal and structural basis (OECD calculation, December 2002), the dollar depreciated by more than 5 percent on a real effective basis (Federal Reserve Board staff Broad Index) from the fourth quarter of 1993 to the second quarter of 1995, and the federal funds rate rose by 300 basis points in nominal terms and only slightly less in real terms.

Again, it appears that the euro area has the scope for constructive policy coordination on fiscal issues, which matter not just for the euro area but also for the rest of the world, especially against the background of the apparent incipient adjustment process for US external accounts. That policy coordination should start with extensive dialogue and shared analysis of the role of fiscal policy in the euro area as well as the United States and other industrial economies. On the basis of that shared analysis, joint and supportive action might be developed.

Foreign Exchange Market Intervention

Once a substantial adjustment of the US external position gets under way, it is likely to involve significant further adjustments in exchange rates. In that context, the question that will arise is whether foreign exchange market intervention should be one of the instruments used to attempt to manage the adjustment process. In my view (Truman 2003b, 262–63), exchange market intervention has definite limits as a policy instrument. Its effectiveness is uncertain and imprecise, and therefore it is at best a blunt or blunted instrument. It is more appropriately best used as a supplement to other more fundamental economic policies. As the Japanese have demonstrated by their actions during the past several years, exchange market intervention with respect to the major currencies is an easily discredited instrument that rapidly loses its effectiveness as the result of overuse unconnected with other policies. This is not to say that foreign exchange market intervention is an instrument never to be used. Moreover, I confidently predict that it will be used at some point by both the euro area and the United States during the period of adjustment of the US external balance that is likely to unfold over the next several years.

The challenge facing the euro area and the process of policy coordination by and with the euro area is to choose those moments wisely. Choosing them involves reaching a collective judgment about such matters as the likely extent of US external adjustment, how much has already occurred, and whether other more fundamental policies are likely to be supportive of that adjustment and exchange rate stability—for example, that ECB monetary policy is not tightening when there is a desire to depreciate the euro.[9]

The experience during the period 1985–88 is instructive in this regard. Foreign exchange market intervention had very little to do with the decline of the dollar starting in February or March 1985. The famous Plaza Accord, to the extent that it hurried the dollar along its descent, involved very little actual exchange market intervention, only oral intervention. The dollar's decline generally was regarded as orderly through 1986, but US and other authorities became nervous about its decline in early 1987.

This nervousness led to the Louvre Accord. The best efforts of the Federal Reserve Board staff failed to convince Federal Reserve Chairman Paul Volcker and the US Treasury that the dollar had a long way to go if it was to accomplish the scale of current account adjustment that we felt was under way. Thus, the G-7 minus Italy undertook in February 1987 to halt the dollar's decline with both oral and market intervention.

However, the dollar's decline continued right through the G-7's "Telephone Communiqué" of December 22, 1987, following the October stock market crash. The dollar did not reach its low on a real weighted-average basis until the second quarter of 1988, 10 percent below its level in the first quarter of 1987. It is also interesting to note that the Plaza and Louvre

---

9. This is a demanding condition. I have calculated (Truman 2003b, 258) that in half of the years from 1981 to 2002 the stance of US monetary policy was inconsistent with bringing the foreign exchange value of the dollar back to its average value for the entire period.

Accords contained US commitments, which were not kept, to reduce the US budget deficit, and the Telephone Communiqué was not agreed on until Congress had passed a two-year, $76 billion deficit reduction package as part of the budget summit that was held in the wake of the stock market crash.[10]

In the late 1980s, heavy intervention by Europe, the United States, and Japan conspired to give use of the policy instrument a bad reputation. It is possible that since 1995, the last period of substantial coordinated intervention, there has been too little use of the instrument. It is also possible that coordination with the euro area will again lead to premature and ineffectual foreign exchange market intervention by the United States and Europe. It is even possible that events will unfold—for example, another stock market crash—would justify such intervention on the basis of disorderly market considerations. However, let us hope that the underlying policy coordination is better informed than it was in the late 1980s and any intervention more effective. Certainly this is an appropriate topic for coordination by and with the euro area. The policy coordination would involve dialogue and shared analysis that could lead to joint action. I do not believe that it should involve the establishment of common exchange rate objectives.

Global Capital Flows and the International Monetary Fund

One of the major counterparts to the accelerated enlargement of the US current account deficit during the past decade has been the swing of the combined current account position of the developing countries and the newly industrialized Asian economies. They moved from a combined deficit of $72.8 billion in 1995–97 to a combined surplus of $124.9 billion in 2000–03, accounting for just over half of the $362.7 increase in the US current account deficit.[11] It has been unnatural for these countries to run current account surpluses, or at least surpluses that are so large for so long. They reasonably can be expected to be part of the solution to the global problem of the US current account adjustment, as was discussed above, moving from a position of net capital exporters back to a position of net capital importers.

In this context, the additional issue for consideration for policy coordination with and by the euro area is the associated adjustments in international capital flows and the consequent implications for the role of the

---

10. A similar package, which amounted to about 1.5 percent of GDP in 1987–88, today would be about $175 billion.

11. These data are from the September 2003 IMF *World Economic Outlook*. The corresponding enlargement of the total global discrepancy accounted for another 30 percent of the increase in the US deficit, which helps explain the attitude of the other advanced countries: "Why must all the [statistical] burden of adjustment be borne by us?"

IMF vis-à-vis emerging-market economies. Gross international capital flows are a magnified manifestation of net international capital flows. The Institute of International Finance (IIF) estimates that in 2003 its grouping of emerging-market economies ran a collective current account surplus of $91 billion, accompanied by $188 billion in net private capital inflows and $259 billion in reserve increases (IIF 2004). However, these numbers, even the net private capital flows, obscure much larger gross flows, especially given that the different categories of private capital flows are netted across those economies receiving net inflows and those economies producing net outflows.

It is notable that the IIF (2004, 1) commented that its modest further projected pickup in net private capital flows to emerging-market economies in 2004 to $196 billion came with "a risk that the pickup in flows into relatively risky assets has pushed valuations to levels that are not commensurate with underlying fundamentals." Regardless of the riskiness of the investments, larger gross flows in the context of smaller current account surpluses, or even deficits, which implies a change in the sign on net flows, will no doubt be accompanied by a resumption of financial difficulties in emerging-market economies after a period of relative quiescence without new problems.[12]

Moreover, as the IIF also notes in passing, one can reasonably expect that the narrowing of the US current account deficit will be accompanied by a substantial adjustment in US dollar short-term interest rates during the next two years of at least 250 basis points just to bring their level back to neutral.[13] The last time the world witnessed such an adjustment was in 1994, and some commentators (Roubini and Setser 2004) cite the Federal Reserve's removal of monetary stimulus as a factor contributing to the Mexican financial crisis of 1994–95.[14] Again, it is reasonable to expect new financial difficulties in emerging-market economies.

As a consequence, the IMF will be back in the center of international financial debates. It may or may not have adequate financial resources to deal effectively with the new problems. The US administration has decided to put its mouth where its money is not and has effectively vetoed an in-

---

12. Of course the problems of Argentina, Turkey, and Uruguay are still with us, but they date from financial flows of the late 1990s, not post-2000.

13. The federal funds rate is currently 1 percent and inflation is between 1 and 2 percent, depending on the measure used. A normal, neutral level of the real federal funds rate is around 2 percent, which suggests that the funds rate will have to rise by at least 250 basis points even if there is no increase in the US inflation rate.

14. In retrospect, the start of the Federal Reserve's monetary policy adjustment in 1994 was delayed too long. The increase in the nominal federal funds rate was 300 basis points and the increase in the real federal funds rate was 250 basis points, moving the stance of monetary policy from ease through neutral to restraint without a pause. In fact, the macroeconomic effects on the US economy of the Mexican crisis meant that the tightening was reinforced and did not have to be extended further during 1995.

crease in IMF quotas in connection with the Twelfth General Review of IMF quotas that was concluded in early 2003 (IMF 2003b). The US administration took this position to limit the resources that the IMF could devote to financial rescue operations at the same time the United States was voting for ever larger rescue operations (Roubini and Setser 2004, chapter 4).

The authorities in several European countries disagreed strongly with the way the IMF and the United States addressed the Mexican financial crisis in 1994–95, treating it as a liquidity crisis and providing a large financial package to meet the threat. That disagreement contributed to the much more cautious IMF response to the Asian financial crises of 1997–98. One consequence in the postcrisis period was the policies of many Asian countries to build up their foreign exchange reserves as a defensive reaction to the prospect of future crises on the understanding that financing from the IMF would not be available. In the process, those countries have contributed to the large US current account deficits of recent years and the substantial increase in US net international indebtedness. Today, the basic issues of the scale of IMF financial assistance, the balance of financing and adjustment, and the role of external private-sector financing in crisis management remain unresolved.

Thus, a case can be made for improved policy coordination by and with the euro area in the period ahead in connection with issues involving both the size and role of the International Monetary Fund against the background of the probable resumption of emerging-market financial crises. That policy coordination would involve a better dialogue on the underlying issues and the possible establishment of common objectives.

EU Enlargement

Not all potential topics for policy coordination with and by the euro area concern the evolution of US external accounts and its implications for the global economy. One potential candidate topic involves EU enlargement—not whether it should have happened in May 2004, which might earlier have been a matter for political dialogue, but how it is happening. Of particular interest and concern are the applications of the various accession countries to join the euro area. What is the timetable? What are the associated economic and financial conditions and exchange rate arrangements?

Kenen and Meade (2003) have written on this important subject. They counsel that the exchange rate requirements should not be too rigid; for example, the requirement that the applicant members belong to the Exchange Rate Mechanism (ERM) II arrangement with narrow 2.25 percent bands is misguided. They also argue that the economic conditions should not be too strictly defined; for example, price stability should not be defined relative to the three euro area national jurisdictions with the lowest inflation rate when some of these jurisdictions are flirting with deflation. Finally, they advise that the larger accession countries should not rush the process of joining the euro area.

With respect to policy coordination with and by the euro area, the question is whether the euro area should consult with the rest of the world on the economic and financial conditions of euro area membership—for example, with the IMF and the G-7—or whether the euro area should treat the subject as an internal matter, as has been the case in the past. If history is any guide, the answer is that it is time to turn over a new leaf. The Europeans made a hash of such matters in 1992–93 with modest, but nontrivial, adverse implications for the international financial system; see Truman (2002). More controversially, but also more relevant, a strong case can be made that a major mistake was made on January 1, 1999, in not devaluing the deutsche mark as it entered the euro.

Given the IMF's abdication of responsibility recently with respect to exchange rate policies in Asia, one should not hold one's breath that the IMF will become involved in choices about transitional exchange rate arrangements in Europe; but that does not mean that the IMF's posture would be correct. Moreover, should the Europeans, including the euro applicant countries, once again make the wrong choices along the way, the risk would be a regional financial crisis that could have financial and economic implications extending beyond Europe.

Consider Hungary and Poland. Both are experiencing relatively slow growth, both have large budget and current deficits of close to or more than 5 percent of GDP, and both have government debt ratios of more than 50 percent of GDP and external debt ratios of more than 40 percent of GDP—and we can be confident that both ratios are understated. Both countries have moderate amounts of foreign exchange reserves equal to about twice their short-term external debts, but those reserves could be dissipated quickly in the solitary defense of a rigid exchange rate peg by each country if it is forced to join the ERM II with narrow 2.25 percent margins in order to qualify for joining the euro area. Hungary's short-term interest rate is close to double digits in nominal terms and quite high in real terms, with consumer price inflation in the 5 to 6 percent range. Poland has low inflation and moderate nominal interest rates, but its new monetary council is under pressure to cut interest rates further to stimulate the economy.

Can anyone be confident that either country will avoid an external financial crisis during the next five years or that a crisis in one country would not spread to other euro applicant countries? Are such risks the basis for international policy coordination by and with the euro area? I would say yes. Therefore, the case for improving policy coordination by and with the euro area on this topic would involve stepped-up exchanges of information, enhanced dialogue, and possible endorsement of the plan of action put forward by the Europeans.

Peaceful Coexistence Between the Euro and the Dollar

Some observers in the United States (e.g., Bergsten 1997) have projected that the euro is likely to emerge as a rival to the dollar as an international currency.[15] One has the impression that some in Europe, long envious of the reserve role of the dollar and more recently the international role of the dollar and the supposed benefits that the dollar's roles convey to the US economy, were expecting that in January 1999 each citizen of the euro area would receive a windfall gain from the birth of the euro.

Alan Greenspan recently has offered a more balanced view of the dollar's role. He acknowledges (2004a, 4) that "the United States has been rare in its ability to finance its external deficit in a reserve currency. This ability has presumably enlarged the capability of the United States relative to most of our trading partners to incur foreign debt." Noting that less than 10 percent of US foreign liabilities are currently denominated in nondollar currencies, he neglects to note that someone somewhere must be bearing the associated foreign exchange risk. He comments, "To have your currency chosen as a store of value is both a blessing and a curse." On the side of the blessing, he presumes, are somewhat lower interest rates, though one could question the quantitative significance of this effect if not the sign. On the side of the curse, he reminds us that during three decades following World War II the British economy was under severe pressure, in part, associated with the liquidation of pound sterling balances. Moreover, these were largely official balances. Therefore, their runoff was potentially easier to handle than a private-sector runoff of dollar-denominated assets would be for the United States.

As long as the United States keeps its economic house in order, including the flexibility and accessibility of its financial markets, I doubt the euro will rise to challenge the dollar as an international currency. This is assuming that the United States corrects its current fiscal excesses before they become serious. Fundamentally, I agree with Eichengreen (1997), who argues that the dollar's international role is a function of the economic vitality of the US economy and the avoidance of irresponsible policies, along with a heavy dose of inertia.[16]

I define (Truman 1999a) an international currency as one that is widely used as an international unit of account, a means of payment, and a store of value by nonresidents exclusively, for example, as issuers of securities

---

15. I am more skeptical; see Truman (1999a). The Conference Board (2004) finds that foreign direct investors report that the introduction of the euro has had less of an impact on global business than they might have expected.

16. Bergsten (1997) fully accepted the view that US macroeconomic policy errors might be necessary to accelerate the decline of the dollar's reserve role.

as well as investors and as sellers of goods and services as well as buyers.[17] Fundamentally, two international currencies would be inefficient and contrary to the rationale for having an international currency. It would be like giving international airline pilots who now universally communicate in English the option of communicating, or not communicating as the case might be, in their own languages.[18] The emergence of the euro as a significant international currency is not likely to happen. The euro's role in the immediate European environment may continue to expand, especially in connection with economic and financial activities involving on one side residents of the euro area, but this is not the same as becoming an international currency according to my definition.[19]

However, what if this judgment is mistaken? Would that not make the peaceful coexistence of the euro and the dollar an appropriate topic for policy coordination by and with the euro area?

Greenspan's recollection of the pressures on the British economy associated with the postwar decline in the role of the pound should remind us not only that they were painful for the British but also that they were painful for the rest of the international monetary system, first, by inhibiting the adjustment of the dollar's value and, later, some would argue by hastening it. The pound's role declined in the context of three international agreements with respect to managing the reduction in sterling balances. The third sterling balances agreement was associated in 1976 with one of the last IMF lending arrangements in support of an adjustment program by an industrial country. If the United States and the dollar were to get to that stage, the current hand-wringing and debates about the dol-

---

17. It is important to appreciate that the choice of an international currency today is made by the private sector via market forces, not by the public sector by government decisions or fiat. The dollar's private international role is much more important than its reserve role; at the end of 2002, foreign official assets in the United States were only 16 percent of total foreign holdings of portfolio claims on the United States. In their recent provocative paper on the revived Bretton Woods system, Dooley, Folkerts-Landau, and Garber (2003) draw an implicit connection between reserve currencies and international currencies. Whereas managing the former might prove to be difficult, managing the latter would be substantially more so. Moreover, the inertia of monetary authorities with respect to the currency denomination of their substantial reserve holdings (an inertia that is reinforced by self-interest when their holdings are large) is considerably larger than the inertia of the private sector. The reserve role of the dollar will be the last to go for the same reason that the US monetary authorities will be the last to reduce their official gold holdings substantially.

18. This is more clearly a sound argument with respect to the unit-of-account and means-of-payment roles for an international currency than the store-of-value role. In the last case, diversification arguments can be invoked in the name of the individual investor if not of the stability of the system as a whole.

19. The Conference Board (2004) reports that the US dollar is the currency most commonly used in business transactions, even for firms based outside the United States.

lar and the adjustment of the US external accounts would fade into relative insignificance.[20]

Given the political prominence of this issue and the focus upon it by commentators and the financial press, a strong case can be made for improved policy coordination with and by the euro area to address the matter. It should at least involve extensive dialogue and analysis. It could involve joint action. For example, Henning (2000) has suggested that US and European authorities should forswear official competition with respect to the international roles of their currencies, leaving decisions to private actors and monetary authorities in other areas without coercion or lobbying. Any competition would be limited to the liberalization of capital markets and to efforts, which could be jointly coordinated (see below), to make them more efficient.

Structural Reform

The G-7 in Dubai launched an initiative, as part of its Agenda for Growth, that is largely focused on the supply side of G-7 economies: "structural policies that increase flexibility and raise productivity growth and employment." Does this initiative suggest that structural policies are ripe for international policy coordination with the euro area? With all due respect to the good intentions of the G-7, there is not much mileage in policy coordination in this area. Moreover, the G-7's intentions may not have been so good; it may just have been interested in creating a diversion.

Notwithstanding the basic case for continuous structural change in modern market economies, a point eloquently stressed in Baily and Kirkegaard (2004), the case for cross-border policy coordination in this area is weak. The basic reasons are that there are limited spillovers across national boundaries from most structural reforms and that the immediate benefits are limited. Consider the range of issues identified as upcoming reform plans in the G-7 Progress Report on its Agenda for Growth issued in Boca Raton. The United States lists, along with tort reform, lifetime and retirement savings accounts, reducing the structural budget deficit (which some would classify as a demand-side measure), and affordable health care. The United Kingdom lists reductions in enterprise regulatory requirements, while Italy lists pension and corporate tax reform.[21]

---

20. See Bergsten (1997) and Henning (2000) for some of the issues involved, although they tend to focus on winding down the dollar's narrower reserve role rather than the dollar's broader role as an international currency.

21. None of these areas rises to the level of a structural reform that has substantial external spillovers. The leading example in this area is the US commitment at the Bonn Economic Summit in 1978 to decontrol its petroleum market, but the rarity of such examples suggests that it is the exception that proves the rule.

Experience has shown that policy coordination in practice is most likely useful when it is ad hoc, the benefits are relatively immediate, and they are generally available. Any cross-border payoffs from structural reforms are long term, such as, for example, a higher potential rate of growth for the national and the global economy. Policy coordination in the structural area qualifies principally as policy endorsement.

In the fall of 1987, US Treasury secretary James Baker proposed the introduction of structural indicators into the multilateral surveillance process, and this new element was reflected in the communiqué from the Toronto Summit in 1988. The IMF struggled with how to implement this suggestion, but in the end decided it was too complex. The countries were too diverse to provide much hope that this type of device would promote Baker's laudable objective that focused at the time on the liberalization of labor markets. (See Boughton 2001, chapter 4, for an account of this episode.)

The OECD has labored in this vineyard with increasing intensity during the past 20 years. Its most recent impressive effort, OECD (2003), masterfully demonstrates the links between structural reforms and economic growth in member countries, drawing on an impressive array of both in-house and external research. The idea, as in the G-7 Growth Agenda announced at Dubai, is to draw upon this research and develop a scorecard for use in multilateral surveillance exercises conducted at the OECD. However, as detailed in Baily and Kirkegaard (2004), because many of the labor market and product market reforms that are desirable today in Europe are very country specific in their content, there is little scope for policy coordination at the level of the euro area as a whole. It is not enough to call for or agree upon the need for structural reforms in these areas; broad agreement on diagnosis is one thing, but agreement on appropriate policy action is more problematic.

Policy coordination in this area offers some benefits: the exchange of information, the potential for solid analysis, and the articulation and endorsement of shared objectives and best practices (even if they are not always shared by domestic populations). However, that is pretty thin gruel.

One broad exception to this generalization is structural policies with respect to institutional harmonization, which do have spillovers across national borders. An example is capital standards for financial institutions that promote financial stability and a level playing field. Another example, cited by Fred Bergsten and Caio Koch-Weser in the *Financial Times* (October 6, 2003), is regulatory convergence in the area of accounting standards. The US-EU Financial Market Dialogue now covers many of these topics, including accounting standards, integration of equity markets, management of pension investments, and supervision of financial conglomerates. These examples are more about policy harmonization by and with the euro area, but they also potentially involve the establishment of common objectives and the coordination of policy actions, and they do have positive spillover effects. Another narrower exception might be the link between labor market reform in the European Union and restrictions or limits on migration that will be applied to new EU members, which would involve improved information exchange and dialogue.

Trade Policy

A final area where benefits might be reaped from policy coordination by and with the euro area is trade policy. The world knows that the European Union has a number of active policy disputes in the trade area, and with the United States in particular. Moreover, the European Union has a strong interest in promoting successful multilateral (Doha Round) negotiations. Cooperation is essential if progress is to be made in any of these areas.

However, there is no dearth of forums for cooperation by the European Union in the trade area with respect to information exchanges, dialogue, common objectives, or joint action. As pointed out by Bergsten and Koch-Weser in the *Financial Times* article cited above, a process of informal policy coordination has existed between the European Union and the United States in the trade area for many years with respect to bilateral, and also multilateral, trade issues. Problems remain, but not because of a lack of US or euro area attention to the underlying issues through a wide range of channels.

Improving Policy Coordination with and by the Euro Area

The preceding discussion made the positive case for improved policy coordination in its various dimensions with and by the euro area on at least 8 of the 10 topics considered. Six were linked in whole or in part to the prospect of substantial adjustment in the US external accounts, but 2 involve other matters. Eight topics make up a more than adequate agenda for policy coordination with and by the euro area, and others could be added.

The basic case having been made for increased policy coordination with and by the euro area, the question is how such policy coordination might be improved. I offer six suggestions.

Substance over Theater

The bias in most policy coordination processes is to prefer theater to substance. The objective is to make sure that you get a headline from a meeting, even if the topic has been inadequately prepared and there is little intention of following up. However, a second bias in policy coordination processes tends to militate against the first: a preference for long communiqués when it would be preferable to say only what is worth saying and is new, and if nothing is worth saying or new, to be quiet. This suggests the need for great care in expanding euro area policy coordination.

Former Federal Reserve governor Laurence Meyer tells a story (2004) about one of the first international meetings that he attended as part of a US delegation. He was surprised that at the delegation meeting before he left Washington, the staff produced a draft of the communiqué that was expected to come out of the meeting. In part, this phenomenon reflected conscientious staff work, but the problem was that the coverage of any real substance in the communiqué could only be drafted after some part of the meeting had occurred. If it all could have been drafted in advance, there would have been no reason to have the meeting, which is one reason the emphasis often shifts from substance to theater. This suggests a balance in policy coordination between substance, theater, and boredom.

The topics reviewed in the first section of this chapter are too important to be trivialized by an excess of theater or unnecessary verbiage involving platitudes with respect to common objectives or vapid endorsements of current policies. If policy coordination by and with the euro area is to be improved, it should focus as much as possible on issues of substance principally involving dialogue, shared analysis, and joint action. When a statement is issued that involves policy commitments, they should be explicit and verifiable.[22]

Mutual Education

Consistent with my first suggestion for improving policy coordination with and by the euro area, the policy coordination process—whatever the forum or the outcome—should place as much emphasis as possible on mutual education as a central aspect of dialogue and a necessary condition for establishing common objectives and agreeing on joint action.

Most of the topics outlined in the first section of this chapter involve issues about which there is genuine disagreement among authorities, in part, because of real disagreement about goals or the lack of a common analytical framework at the technical level. For example, how large a current account adjustment is necessary for the United States or the world? What is the best way to go about achieving it? What should be the respective roles of monetary, fiscal, and other policies in the process? What will be the likely implications for the global economy? What role can or should exchange market intervention play in managing the process? How best to achieve global balance in the context of a substantial adjustment of the US external accounts? What are the likely implications for capital flows to emerging-market economies as a consequence of US external adjustment? What should be the role of the IMF in any external financial crises that may follow? What is the link between growth policies and external adjustment? What is the best framework for thinking about fiscal

---

22. See Truman (2004a) for an elaboration of this argument.

policies, including countercyclical policies, automatic stabilizers, and medium-term fiscal objectives? What are the chances that the process of enlarging the euro area will have adverse implications for global financial and economic stability? What role should the IMF play in the euro area enlargement process? What are the implications of a world with two major international currencies? If we are headed for such a world, what is the best way of managing the transition process?

These are all important questions that can be, and in some cases have been, subjected to analytical treatment. To the extent that policymakers differ in their views of those analytical treatments or in their nonanalytical biases, an effort should be made to sort out those differences. This is likely to be a research-intensive process, but it is also likely to be the only way to achieve improved policy coordination. The euro area can take a lead in this mutual education process. It is an open question, which I touch on below, whether it is organized or equipped to do so.

Monetary Policy Framework

I have written about the contribution of the monetary policy frameworks of the three major economies (the euro area, the United States, and Japan) to international economic policy coordination. My conclusion (Truman 2003a) is that the adoption of inflation targeting as the framework for the conduct and evaluation of monetary policy by the ECB, the Federal Reserve, and the Bank of Japan would make a substantive contribution to improving Group of Three policy coordination.

First, the adoption of inflation targeting in the euro area and the United States would improve communication about policy intentions with markets. The empirical evidence suggests that this would improve economic performance, producing higher and less variable growth and lower and more stable inflation. Today, in the case of the ECB, the markets are thoroughly confused by the ECB's revised definition of price stability as inflation less than but close to 2 percent. The ECB has a long-run inflation goal of something between 1.75 and 2 percent, but the operational implications of that goal for current policy are opaque. In the case of the Federal Reserve, we learned during the period 2003–04 that it has developed a concern about deflation, but as to what level of increase in any particular measure of price inflation is too low or high, the market has been left to guess.

Second, the adoption of inflation targeting in the euro area and the United States would force the central bankers in their dialogues with each other and their dialogues with their finance ministry colleagues to be more frank about their policy objectives and how they intend to achieve them. This, in turn, would facilitate better analysis of their respective policies and the compatibility of those policies with the achievement of common objectives.

Third, I would hope that the adoption of inflation targeting by the ECB would improve policy performance, in particular average growth, because the ECB would choose a target closer to 2.5 percent, plus or minus 1 percent, rather than one of less than 2 percent. However, this has to do with the implementation of inflation targeting, not with the framework itself. Nevertheless, the framework, with its forward-looking emphasis, should also contribute to more proactive policymaking by the ECB. Moreover, the statistical analysis presented in Truman (2003a) suggests that economic performance (higher and less variable growth along with lower and less variable inflation) is likely to be enhanced by the adoption of inflation targeting regardless of the target chosen.[23]

I have proposed concrete steps by which the Federal Reserve and the ECB could adopt inflation targeting as a framework for their respective policies by themselves in a manner consistent with their current mandates and how they go about their business. The two central banks could use a bit of nudging to move to adopt inflation targeting and ex post blessing once they have done so. In the euro area, this might help to bury the hatchet between the monetary and the fiscal authorities.

In the United States, Alan Greenspan is regarded as a skeptic about inflation targeting. His recent speech on risk and uncertainty in monetary policy (2004b) has been similarly interpreted. Recently he has been more open to the framework than he had been previously. The softening of his position on this issue may reflect his exposure to my own analysis, but I suspect that the cumulative writings of Ben Bernanke (for example, Bernanke 2003) have been more influential. However, the evolution of Greenspan's position indirectly illustrates the basic point about the importance of mutual education in the success of the policy coordination process. An educational process has shaped US official thinking about inflation targeting. It follows that there is scope for mutual education by and with the euro area.

Getting the Right Players on the Field

Policy coordination with and by euro area is an overly complicated game because often the right players are not playing. To address this problem,

---

23. Clarida, in his comment on this chapter, notes that for inflation targeting to lead to exchange rate stability, formally a stationary exchange rate, the framework should target the price level rather than an inflation rate. Cooper, in his comment, suggests that exchange rate stability would be enhanced if the ECB and the Federal Reserve merely targeted a common price index. However, a common target, say 2 percent, is not the same as a common index; there are substantial differences between US and EU price indexes (Truman 2003a, 100). Moreover, one should expect only a limited contribution to exchange rate stability from the adoption of inflation targeting by the Group of Three economies, largely because during the past decade differences in inflation rates have not provided much guidance with respect to exchange rate movements; see Truman (2003a, 163).

several steps are necessary, mostly involving the euro area itself but also those seeking to coordinate with the euro area or with which the euro area is seeking to coordinate.

First, the euro area will have to speak internationally with one voice on macroeconomic matters. For example, currently the ECB represents the European monetary authorities at portions of G-7 meetings of finance ministers and central bank governors. At the remainder of the meeting, the heads of the national central banks of France, Germany, and Italy join the meeting and the president of the ECB leaves. Moreover, there is no representative of the European fiscal authorities at these meetings because there is no euro area fiscal authority. The cure for this problem lies partly in Europe and partly elsewhere.

In Europe, it is desirable for the European project to get its act together and decide (1) who is in and who is out of the euro area and (2) what the euro area is. In this chapter, I have generally treated the euro area as if it were the same as the European Union. However, we know it is not. For many aspects of potential policy coordination, this lack of congruence may be a problem for both the euro area and its potential partners. For example, the role of exchange rates in the adjustment of US external accounts involves not only the euro-dollar relationship but also the euro-pound relationship.

The issue of who is in and who is out of the euro area principally involves the United Kingdom. The United Kingdom attends Ecofin meetings, is not a participant in the euro area, but is a full-fledged member of the G-7.

Once membership in the euro area is settled, or even if it is not, the basic issue is whether the European Union is an international organization or a supranational authority. Currently the Europeans want to have it both ways, and their interlocutors want to as well. For example, leaders of the European Commission sit down with leaders of the World Bank and IMF as international organizations to discuss financial assistance to the Balkans. At the same time, the European Commission is a member of the Financial Action Task Force on anti–money laundering along with most EU members. Is it there as an international organization or a supranational authority?

From the standpoint of interlocutors with the euro area, and of the United States in particular, they have a stake in how Europe evolves. In my view, US policy should push in the direction of encouraging the Europeans to get on with the construction of their own internal playing field.[24] Con-

___

24. In Truman (1997), I warned of the potential dangers of the EU project spending too long in a halfway house. My views on this subject appear to be similar to those of Henning (2000), who argues that the United States would be best served by streamlined EU decision making on economic issues accompanied by qualified majority voting (rather than consensus decision making) and substantially increased transparency.

versely, the United States recently, over the past decade or so, has preferred to preserve the option of divide and conquer with respect to its dealings with European authorities on some economic matters. That choice complicates meaningful policy coordination. For example, the Federal Reserve now deals principally with the ECB, but the US Treasury prefers to deal with the finance ministries of France, Germany, Italy, and the United Kingdom, which in turn complicates internal US policy coordination.

The United States has some leverage in this matter. For example, it could move to sunset the participation of the United Kingdom in G-7 meetings. As the UK economy shrinks in relative importance in the global economy, the rationale for including its representatives separately from the representatives of the euro area in international meetings also will shrink. The United States could also favor sunsetting participation of representatives of national euro area central banks in the G-7 process, along with the Bank of England.

The United States could also take steps to put the right players from its own team on the playing field when dealing with the euro area on economic matters. For historical reasons, including the fact that the European Union started out as an international organization motivated primarily by political considerations, US-EU summit meetings are handled primarily by the US Department of State. When it comes to economic matters, representatives of the State Department see their historical role as a way finally to get a seat at the economic policy table. The problem is that their presence, including their organization of such meetings, means that the right people, actual policymakers, are not at the meetings. Even if they are at the meetings, the meetings are underprepared and the potential for meaningful policy coordination is limited to a sideshow at best. They are detached from substance and have limited potential for mutual education.

Finally, coming back to the euro area itself, the role of the ECB needs to be clarified. The institution needs to be integrated better into the euro area policy process. The ECB has been endowed with the highest degree of goal independence of any central bank in modern history, enshrined in the Maastricht amendments to the Treaty of Rome. The treaty requires the ECB to support the general economic policies of the European Community, including "a harmonious and balanced development of economic activities, sustainable and noninflationary growth respecting the environment, a high degree of convergence in economic performance, a high level of employment and social protection, the raising of the standard of living and quality of life, and economic and social cohesion and solidarity among Member States." The treaty also leaves it to the ECB to decide how best to accomplish this, and the ECB has decided that achieving its definition of price stability is the only thing that it can do or publicly admit that it can do.

Presumably, the political authorities in the euro area have a bit of leverage over the ECB and its policy orientation when they make appointments to its governing board. They could require new appointees to take a different attitude toward the ECB's mandate. As was noted above, the adoption of inflation targeting as the ECB's monetary framework might aid in this process as well as make it more attractive for the United Kingdom and Sweden to join the euro area because they are comfortable using inflation targeting as their frameworks for the conduct and implementation of monetary policy.

Institutional Representation

As part of the process of institutional consolidation sketched above, the euro area should also take steps to rationalize its representation in international economic and financial bodies. Such steps have been considered within the European Union and euro area, but to date little progress has been made.[25]

EU representation on the IMF Executive Board is a prime example. Currently, EU members appoint or play a major role in electing 10 of the 24 members of the board. Nationals from these countries are 7 of the 24 executive directors and 8 of the 24 alternate executive directors. They not only directly control 32 percent of IMF votes, but they also potentially control an additional 12.5 percent of the votes of nonmembers of the European Union as of May 2004.[26] The decision-making process in the IMF Executive Board is primarily one of consensus, in which the number of bodies in the room is important because each of them speaks on important matters. Currently that process is distorted. European voices are heard much too often and tend to distort the consensus.

To remedy this situation, the EU countries should first agree to drop from their IMF Executive Board constituencies all countries that are not members of the European Union. This would reduce the number of EU first-row or second-row chairs below 10. Second, the EU countries should progressively consolidate their chairs into one appointed chair.[27] This consolidation would leave open the two other appointed chairs for China

---

25. Henning (1997) addressed this issue and concluded that the European Union should strike a bargain with the United States in which (1) the members of the European Union would establish common positions on IMF issues, (2) the EU quota in the IMF would be adjusted downward by eliminating intra-area trade and setting it equal to the US quota, (3) quotas of other IMF members would be increased commensurately, and (4) the IMF headquarters would remain in Washington. Kenen (2004) also addresses the issue of consolidation of EU representation in the IMF.

26. The 10 EU accession countries have 2.1 percent of the votes.

27. Representation of the ECB on the IMF Executive Board could be achieved by having the alternate executive director come from the ECB.

and Canada, on the basis of current quotas.[28] As a consequence, the size of the Executive Board could be shrunk back toward its original 20, and the door would be opened for representation of a broader set of countries on the board.

Again, this is an area where the United States has some leverage. As long as the IMF Executive Board is larger than the 20 seats mandated in the IMF Articles of Agreement, a vote is required every two years to maintain its size. That vote requires an 85 percent majority, which means US support is required to maintain the current 24 seats. Reducing the number of European seats on the IMF Executive Board and related bodies, allocating some of them to countries in other areas of the world, and reducing the total number of seats in the process would provide many political benefits as well as contribute to better policy coordination. It would also demonstrate euro area leadership.

Replace the G-7 with the G-20

Many of the topics for policy coordination by and with the euro area involve issues that extend beyond the purview of a US-EU Group of Two or the G-7 to the other major economic and financial players in the world, such as China, India, Mexico, Brazil, and South Africa.

If the euro area and the United States were to act jointly to disband the G-7/G-8 and move many of their policy coordination discussions at the level of finance ministers and central bank governors to the Group of Twenty,[29] this would be a major constructive step in rationalizing the institutions of international economic cooperation. It would reduce the number of international meetings. It would recognize the changing shape of the global economy. It would utilize a forum that was established in 1999 but has not yet taken on much responsibility. The G-20 involves central bankers in addition to representatives of finance ministries, which is

---

28. The five members of the IMF with the largest quotas appoint executive directors and their alternates. Currently those five are the United States, Japan, Germany, France, and the United Kingdom. If in the future the European Union were consolidated into one seat, and treating the euro area as the same as the EU, its collective quota would be reduced under most quota formulas by excluding intra-EU trade. A decline in the size of the EU quota would reduce the resources available to the IMF. Presumably, some of the Asian countries, which now consider themselves underrepresented in the IMF, would stand ready to compensate for the shortfall.

29. In addition to the G-7 countries (Canada, France, Germany, Italy, Japan, the United Kingdom, and the United States), the G-20 includes Argentina, Australia, Brazil, China, India, Indonesia, Mexico, Russia, Saudi Arabia, South Africa, South Korea, Turkey, and the European Union, represented by the president of the ECB and the finance minister of the country holding the presidency of the EU if it is not a European G-7 country.

useful in an era of an increasing number of independent central banks, with respect to information exchange, dialogue, and mutual education as well as agreements on common objectives and joint actions.

My presumption is that economic summits eventually would be converted to G-20 affairs as well; that conversion is already under way with special invited guests at most recent summits.[30] With the G-20 as the new standard for summit meetings and meetings of finance ministers and central bank governors, this might facilitate other adjustments in institutional representation, including in due course collapsing the G-20 into the Group of Sixteen, concentrating EU representation in one pair, rather than the current five pairs, which would make room for adding other countries. In this manner, the development of the G-20 would follow the development of the Group of Ten in the 1960s as a grouping of the major countries responsible for the stability of the international economy and financial system and including both countries in deficit as well as countries in surplus, net debtors as well as net creditors. The IMF's International Monetary and Financial Committee includes as members many of the G-20 countries, but they are constrained to represent the views of their constituencies and as a result there is very limited scope for uninhibited interchange.

In the interests of mutual education, the G-20 should be strengthened through the use of ad hoc working groups to supplement the current structure that involves meetings at the level of ministers and governors and their deputies. This would help to increase the ratio of substance to theater. No doubt the United States and the euro area would continue to take the lead in guiding the work of the G-20, but the process would be more inclusive and more relevant. Enhancing the role of the G-20 would not preclude, and it probably would necessitate, an increase in informal policy coordination between the United States and the euro area, as an informal Group of Two.

Conclusion

This chapter has demonstrated the scope and need for increased policy coordination with and by the euro area, primarily with respect to topics linked to US external adjustment, but in other areas as well. I have outlined guidelines and concrete steps that could be taken by the euro area and its principal interlocutor, the United States, to facilitate improved policy coordination.

I am under no illusion that any of my suggestions will be implemented in the short term, but the need for improved policy coordination by and

---

30. The G-7 started as meetings of the Group of Five (G-5) in 1973 and generally included central bank governors after the first meeting. The G-5 did not meet at the level of heads of state or government until 1975.

with the euro area will remain and most likely increase over the years, especially if the euro and the European project prosper. Europe has long been a free rider with respect to the post–World War II institutions of international economic and financial cooperation. More often than not, the perspective of Europeans has been a short-run national perspective—what is in the immediate interests of their country, or occasionally region, rather than of the system as a whole. Alternatively, the European perspective has been to be against what the United States has proposed or advocated. It is time that Europe started pulling its full weight, especially if the euro is to emerge during the next 5 or 10 years as a major international currency.

References

Baily, Martin Neil, and Jacob Funk Kirkegaard. 2004. *A Transformation of the European Economy*. Washington: Institute for International Economics.

Bergsten, C. Fred. 1997. The Impact of the Euro on Exchange Rates and International Policy Cooperation. In *EMU and the International Monetary System*, ed. Paul R. Masson, Thomas H. Krueger, and Bart G. Turtelboom. Washington: International Monetary Fund.

Bernanke, Ben S. 2003. A Perspective on Inflation Targeting. Remarks at the Annual Washington Conference of the National Association of Business Economists, March 25. Board of Governors of the Federal Reserve System. Photocopy.

Boughton, James M. 2001. *Silent Revolution: The International Monetary Fund 1979–1989*. Washington: International Monetary Fund.

Conference Board. 2004. *Global Exchange Rates: Do They Affect Investment?* New York: Conference Board.

Dooley, Michael P., David Folkerts-Landau, and Peter Garber. 2003. *An Essay on the Revived Bretton Woods System*. NBER Working Paper 9971. Cambridge, MA: National Bureau of Economic Research.

Dooley, Michael P., David Folkerts-Landau, and Peter Garber. 2004. *The Cosmic Risk: An Essay on Global Imbalances and Treasuries*. Frankfurt: Deutsche Bank Global Markets Research.

Eichengreen, Barry. 1997. Comment on Bergsten's "The Impact of the Euro on Exchange Rates and International Policy Cooperation." In *EMU and the International Monetary System*, ed. Paul R. Masson, Thomas H. Krueger, and Bart G. Turtelboom. Washington: International Monetary Fund.

Erceg, Christopher. 2002. The Effects of the US Productivity Acceleration on the External Sector. Division of International Finance, Board of Governors of the Federal Reserve System, Washington. Photocopy (November 18).

Freund, Caroline. 2000. *Current Account Adjustment in Industrial Countries*. International Finance Discussion Paper 692. Washington: Federal Reserve System.

Greenspan, Alan. 2003. Remarks on the Current Account at the Cato Institute. Federal Reserve System, Washington. Photocopy (November 20).

Greenspan, Alan. 2004a. Remarks on Globalization at the Bundesbank Lecture, Berlin. Federal Reserve System, Washington. Photocopy (January 13).

Greenspan, Alan. 2004b. Remarks on Risk and Uncertainty in Monetary Policy at the Meetings of the American Economic Association, San Diego. Federal Reserve System, Washington. Photocopy (January 5).

Henning, C. Randall. 1997. *Cooperating with Europe's Monetary Union*. POLICY ANALYSES IN INTERNATIONAL ECONOMICS 49. Washington: Institute for International Economics.

Henning, C. Randall. 2000. US-EU Relations After the Inception of the Monetary Union: Cooperation or Rivalry? In *Transatlantic Perspectives on the Euro*, ed. Randall Henning and Pier Carlo Padoan. Pittsburgh: European Community Studies Association, and Washington: Brookings Institution Press.

Hunt, Benjamin, and Alessandro Rebucci. 2003. *The US Dollar and the Trade Deficit: What Accounts for the Late 1990s?* IMF Working Paper WP/03/194. Washington: International Monetary Fund.

IIF (Institute of International Finance). 2004. *Capital Flows to Emerging Market Economies*. Washington: Institute of International Finance.

IMF (International Monetary Fund). 2002. How Worrisome Are External Imbalances? In *World Economic Outlook*, September. Washington: International Monetary Fund.

IMF (International Monetary Fund). 2003a. Are Foreign Exchange Reserves in Asia too High? In *World Economic Outlook*, September. Washington: International Monetary Fund.

IMF (International Monetary Fund). 2003b. *IMF Executive Board Recommends to Governors Conclusion of Quota Review*. Public Information Notice 03/02. Washington: International Monetary Fund.

Isard, Peter, Hamid Faruqee, G. Russel Kincaid, and Martin Fetherston. 2001. *Methodology for Current Account and Exchange Rate Assessments*. Occasional Paper 209. Washington: International Monetary Fund.

Issing, Otmar. 2003. Europe and the US: Partners and Competitors—New Paths for the Future. Remarks at German-British Forum, London. European Central Bank, Frankfurt. Photocopy (October 28).

Kenen, Peter B. 2004. Transatlantic Relations and the Global Economy. Princeton University. Photocopy (January).

Kenen, Peter B., and Ellen E. Meade. 2003. *EU Accession and the Euro: Close Together or Far Apart?* International Economics Policy Brief PB03-9. Washington: Institute for International Economics.

Kohn, Donald L. 2004. Remarks on the United States in the World Economy at the Federal Reserve Bank of Atlanta. Federal Reserve System, Washington. Photocopy (January 7).

Mann, Catherine L. 2003. How Long the Strong Dollar? In *Dollar Overvaluation and the World Economy*, ed. C. Fred Bergsten and John Williamson. Washington: Institute for International Economics.

Meyer, Laurence H. 2004. *A Term at the Fed: An Insider's View*. New York: Harper Business.

OECD (Organization for Economic Cooperation and Development). 2003. *The Policy Agenda for Growth: An Overview of the Sources of Economic Growth in OECD Countries*. Paris: OECD.

Rosenberg, Michael R. 2003. The Dollar's Equilibrium Exchange Rate: A Market View. In *Dollar Overvaluation and the World Economy*, ed. C. Fred Bergsten and John Williamson. Washington: Institute for International Economics.

Roubini, Nouriel, and Brad Setser. 2004. *Bailouts or Bail-ins? Responding to Financial Crises in Emerging Markets*. Washington: Institute for International Economics.

Rubin, Robert E., Peter R. Orszag, and Allen Sinai. 2004. Sustained Budget Deficits: Longer-Run U.S. Economic Performance and the Risk of Financial and Fiscal Disarray. Paper presented at the American Economics Association–North American Economics and Finance Association Joint Session, San Diego, January 4.

Truman, Edwin M. 1997. Remarks at Roundtable on Lessons of European Monetary Integration for the International Monetary System. In *EMU and the International Monetary System*, ed. Paul R. Masson, Thomas H. Krueger, and Bart G. Turtelboom. Washington: International Monetary Fund.

Truman, Edwin M. 1999a. The Evolution of the International Financial System. Remarks at the Institute for International Monetary Affairs Eighth Symposium, Tokyo, December 6.

Truman, Edwin M. 1999b. The Single Currency and Europe's Role in the World Economy. Remarks to the World Affairs Council, US Treasury, Washington, April 6.

Truman, Edwin M. 2002. Economic Policy and Exchange Rate Regimes: What Have We Learned since Black Wednesday? Paper presented at European Monetary Symposium, London School of Economics, London, September 16.

Truman, Edwin M. 2004. A Critical Review of Coordination Efforts in the Past. In *Macroeconomic Policies in the World Economy*, ed. Horst Siebert. Berlin: Springer-Verlag.

Truman, Edwin M. 2003a. *Inflation Targeting in the World Economy*. Washington: Institute for International Economics.

Truman, Edwin M. 2003b. The Limits of Exchange Market Intervention. In *Dollar Overvaluation and the World Economy*, ed. C. Fred Bergsten and John Williamson. Washington: Institute for International Economics.

Comment

RICHARD H. CLARIDA

In his fine chapter, Edwin Truman raises 10 issues pertaining to the subject of policy coordination "with and by" the euro area. The chapter makes six policy recommendations and many provocative and thought-provoking observations in between. One senses a certain liberation of spirit and a desire on Truman's part not to quibble or qualify. After years of "speaking his mind" in offering private counsel at the highest levels of government, he now can "write his mind," and this makes the chapter a lot of fun to read.

The chapter offers a useful and timely organizing principle for discussing policy coordination and focuses on the issues of international imbalances and the process of international adjustment. I might have chosen a slightly different issue: Has insufficient policy coordination to date materially contributed to the global imbalances, which are the focus of much of the chapter's first section? Does insufficient policy coordination complicate the process of international adjustment that is already under way? I think the answer to these questions is probably "no."

On the real side, rebalancing the global economy has to do with global growth, fiscal policies, and structural reform. On the financial side, international adjustment has to do with foreign exchange intervention and with capital flows and the IMF.

Eliminating or even scaling back the US current account deficit will exert a material drag on global growth. Indeed, I have argued that the US current account deficit is a global general equilibrium outcome that reflects a deficit of growth and growth prospects in the rest of the world as

Richard H. Clarida is the C. Lowell Harriss Professor of Economics at Columbia University.

well as a postbubble excess supply of global saving relative to profitable investment opportunities. Given plentiful global supply (for goods if not commodities), global demand outside the United States must rise. I applaud the chapter's emphasis on structural reforms as contributing to both the present demand and future supply side. However, I share with the chapter a skepticism that "there is not much mileage in policy coordination" in the area of "structural policies that increase flexibility and raise productivity growth and employment."

Obviously, a major issue of policy coordination within Europe is the Stability and Growth Pact (SGP). In reality, I think that little can feasibly be achieved to coordinate US and European fiscal policies over the business cycle. In the medium term, fiscal consolidation is called for in the United States. However, it is hard for me to see how the pace or magnitude of this could be influenced by feasible paths for European fiscal policy—especially because the SGP puts pressure for fiscal consolidation in Europe as well.

With regard to foreign exchange market intervention, I share Truman's view that intervention "has definite limits" as a policy instrument. However, I also note that the evidence suggests that publicly coordinated interventions are most likely to succeed. Thus, although there is a possible benefit to coordination, it is only at the margins of a "limited" policy.

With regard to the issue of international capital flows, the main argument here is to improve coordination within the structures of an existing institution, the IMF. Global adjustment will require reduced net outflows from emerging-market countries and perhaps large net inflows to some (and certainly increased gross flows). As global interest rates inevitably rise, so do risks of emerging-market debt-service problems. I think it is at best an open question whether or not previous crises were exacerbated by insufficient policy coordination between the United States and the euro area. As I understand it, many in Europe wish to strictly limit IMF packages except under truly exceptional circumstances. It is not clear that a better coordinated process would produce "better" IMF packages, but it could well produce fewer smaller packages more promptly. Although a potentially better long-run equilibrium, it could in fact produce worse near-term outcomes if capital flows reflect the existing ad hoc regime.

Truman's recent book (Truman 2003) has made a persuasive case for explicit Group of Three inflation targeting. He argues that this would offer better communication with markets, more honest dialogue with finance ministries, and faster average eurozone growth.

However, coordination is not commitment. In my research with Mark Gertler and Jordi Gali (2002), we work out the theory of inflation targeting in a two-country Nash noncooperative game, showing that inflation targeting is optimal and can be implemented with a forward-looking Taylor rule. This requires the exchange rate to be flexible and not anchored. Under this policy, the exchange rate is nonstationary. In general, there are gains to cooperation, and inflation targeting in the form of a modified Taylor rule with weight on home and foreign inflation is optimal. This rule requires a flexible and nonanchored exchange rate, and it implies a nonstationary exchange rate. Under commitment, even without cooperation, an anchored and stationary exchange rate can be achieved. This is because commitment will require price-level targeting, not just inflation targeting.

References

Clarida, R., M. Gertler, and J. Gali. 2002. A Simple Framework for International Monetary Policy Analysis. *Journal of Monetary Economics* 49: 879–904.
Truman, Edwin. 2003. *Inflation Targeting in the World Economy*. Washington: Institute for International Economics.

Comment

RICHARD N. COOPER

Edwin Truman discusses the possible desirability of policy coordination between the European Union and the United States under 10 headings, and he supports 8; he also makes 6 proposals for improving the structure and process of international economic cooperation. I cannot comment on all of them, and I agree with many of his suggestions, so I will be selective and emphasize areas of disagreement, or at least doubts.

For a start, I find it helpful to distinguish clearly among the possible modes of economic cooperation, which range from the simple exchange of accurate information (data and policy), through analysis of current circumstances, advance notice on upcoming changes in policy (with explanations), occasional coordinated changes in policy or joint action, to routinized joint action and harmonization of policy. Many of these different forms of cooperation can be found in Truman's chapter, but he is not entirely clear about what should actually be done under each of his headings.

Several of Truman's suggestions for policy coordination arise from his clearly stated assumption of the need to reduce sharply—by 2 to 5 percent of GDP—the large current account deficit of the United States. My guess, in contrast, is that on the 10th anniversary of the euro, 5 years from now, we will still have a large US current account deficit—perhaps not 5 percent of GDP, but running several hundred billion dollars and still a dominant feature of the world economy, as it is today. With the special exception of 1991, the United States has run a current account deficit since 1982, and it has generally exceeded $100 billion since 1984. For complex reasons

Richard N. Cooper is Maurits C. Boas Professor of Economics at Harvard University and chairman of the Advisory Committee of the Institute for International Economics.

involving demography, habits formed at low income levels followed by rapid growth, risky political and legal environments, and imperfect national capital markets, the rest of the world has savings in excess of acceptable investment opportunities, and the United States (along with Britain and Australia) and the world's poorest countries alone show a willingness to absorb these savings on an ongoing basis, the latter because of foreign aid grants. I do not believe this condition will change soon or quickly, so to try to reduce greatly the US deficit would put tremendous and unnecessary contractionary pressure on the world economy.

Active and socially useful cooperation on policies requires that the cooperating parties have a similar (and approximately accurate) view of how the world economy works and a shared view of objectives. The first condition is not met in the domain of macroeconomic policy, and the second is met only at a high level of generality: Everyone favors growth with low inflation and low unemployment. For example, my impression is that the consensus view among American economists is that fiscal stimulus (a reduction in taxes or an increase in expenditures) will increase GDP in normal circumstances. My impression is that the consensus among German economists is that a fiscal stimulus will not increase GDP and indeed may reduce it. It is difficult to coordinate fiscal policies when such radically different views prevail. It is logically possible that both consensuses are correct, domestically; but to coordinate policy usefully and effectively we would need shared views on that point.

Europeans, I believe, have gotten themselves into a serious bind, both substantively and procedurally, with respect to macroeconomic management. In the Economic and Monetary Union (EMU), "price stability" is the primary and so far the sole objective of European Central Bank (ECB) policy. Under the Stability and Growth Pact, budget deficits cannot exceed, except in exceptional circumstances, 3 percent of GDP. These are highly constraining conditions. Indeed, the usual instruments of macroeconomic policy—monetary, fiscal, and exchange rate policy—are in practice denied or severely limited to EU member states, and can be used for the EMU as a whole only to pursue price stability, ignoring entirely the other influences that monetary and exchange rate policy can have on an economy. There is little under these constraints that can be coordinated with the United States—or any other country or group.

Procedurally, the ECB alone decides on monetary policy and exchange rate intervention; it can neither solicit nor accept advice from member governments. How can it "coordinate" anything—unless the prohibition on advice does not apply to foreign governments! It is unclear who is in charge of exchange rate policy, as opposed to intervention; the practical result is that no one is in charge.

Truman points out that there is some US ambivalence toward a unifying Europe, and he suggests that the US government sometimes exploits the capacity to "divide and rule." Though not denying that claim with respect to some individual officials, I suggest that the US practice of going to national European capitals rather than to Brussels in many instances is driven by a desire to get something done, sometimes urgently, rather than to "divide and rule," because only in national capitals has it been possible to get decisions. Thirty years ago, Henry Kissinger famously asked what "European" number he should call in the event of a foreign policy crisis. Europe provided a response, 28 years later, in the form of Xavier Solana—although even today he has almost no authority to make decisions. Yet in the area of macroeconomics there is still no Xavier Solana, one person who can speak authoritatively (even if noncommittally) for Europe.

Europe has been integrating for half a century. Much progress has been made, slowly, but much remains to be done. Europeans cannot agree on what is the unfinished business because they cannot agree on a desired destination. At the present pace, another 50 years may be required to "complete" Europe, whatever that may mean. In the meantime, how can Europe coordinate macroeconomic policy with the United States? Perhaps only a crisis will speed up the process. I favor government by foresight, rather than government by crisis. But too few governments show great foresight. The Maastricht Treaty of 1992 is directed to the problem of the 1980s, inflation, not to the problems of the early 21st century. It may be that a strong further appreciation of the euro could provide the jolt necessary to provoke the necessary substantive and procedural changes in European macroeconomic policy.

Truman urges the ECB, and on the Federal Reserve, to set explicit inflation targets. I am not enthusiastic about inflation targeting for these two large economies, unless the target is a *common* price index, which I would also urge on Japan, as a stepping stone to much tighter management of exchange rates—ultimately a single currency. As Richard Clarida points out in his comment on Truman's chapter, independent inflation targeting leads to a random walk in exchange rates. An exception is when the same target is used and is achieved.

The US approach to "anchoring" monetary policy is to empower a committee of people with diverse but sensible views to argue about how best to achieve the many objectives they have been given and make a practical decision every six weeks, subject to close public and especially congressional scrutiny. The Federal Reserve, it should be noted, is independent of the president, in that he or his executive branch leaders cannot instruct it on monetary policy, but it is not independent of the political process, having been chartered by simple legislation, which could be changed through the normal legislative process. The Federal Reserve thus must continually earn its independence, like the Bundesbank (whose primary objective was, artfully, "stability of the currency," not "price stability") but unlike the ECB.

Given the primary objective of price stability, it would be difficult, I believe, for the ECB to target inflation at a rate other than zero, which would be undesirable. The ECB's official formulation, "less than two percent," I assume was a fudge to reconcile its statutory charge with practical considerations. The ECB is apparently satisfied that an inflation rate close to 2 percent is "low and stable" and satisfies the requirement to achieve price stability, even though after a decade a 2 percent inflation rate would leave the measured price level 22 percent higher than it was initially. But could the ECB legally set a target of 2.5 percent (up 28 percent in a decade), as Truman suggests, or 3.0 percent, which could arguably still be called "low and stable"?

Truman makes several suggestions to improve the structure and procedures for international economic cooperation. One of them involves consolidating European seats on the board of the International Monetary Fund, which now number 8 out of 24, not counting Russia. This could surely be done within the current IMF Articles of Agreement; but the ECB could not be seated formally on the Executive Board without an amendment to the Articles, because only states can join (unlike the World Trade Organization, which also allows entities other than states as members).

Truman urges substituting the Group of Twenty (G-20), at the ministerial level, for the current Group of Seven and Group of Eight (G-7/G-8) meetings. The G-20 first convened in 1999, following the Asian financial crises. No doubt considerable thought was given to the selection of countries, but I am not aware that there was a formal rule beyond an emphasis on emerging markets and some attempt at geographical dispersion. Its legitimacy is open to question. Apart from India and, arguably, Indonesia, it does not include any of the world's poorest countries.

At the time it was formed, the G-7 encompassed the seven largest countries of the world, in terms of both GNP and foreign trade; and all were democracies, with the leaders able to appreciate the problems for sensible policy sometimes posed by electoral politics. A Group of Five summit was created initially, at French initiative, to coordinate action to overcome the world recession of 1975. These were the countries with enough economic weight to make a difference if they coordinated their policies; and except for President Gerald Ford, all the heads of government had been ministers of finance. Ford evidently liked the meeting, because he convened a second one the following year, at which Canada and Italy were added.

Thus a precedent was set that has endured for nearly 30 years. The G-7 is outdated in terms of GNP and trade, now that China exceeds Canada and Italy in both. But the criteria for expanding the G-7 are unclear. One could create a club of countries whose GDP exceeds $500 billion; in 2004, that would add China, Spain, Mexico, Brazil, India, and South Korea, in that order. All but China are democracies. If on political grounds it was thought necessary to add an Arab country and a sub-Saharan African country, they should probably be Egypt and Nigeria, the most populous representatives of which Nigeria formally is democratic. With the G-7, that would bring the total to 15, and to 12 if the 4 Euroland countries could designate a single representative.

As the number grows, it is more difficult for the participants to have a serious conversation, as opposed to making preset statements. The G-20 almost certainly exceeds this limit of viability. But if the committee is to become that large, it might as well be the International Monetary and Financial Committee, which includes 24 principals, all ministers, representing most of the countries of the world following the constituencies of the IMF's Executive Board—which, according to Truman, could and should be cut back to its statutory size of 20. I believe that would command much greater legitimacy than the G-20.

5

The Euro and Financial Markets

The Euro and Money Markets: Lessons for European Financial Integration

VÍTOR GASPAR and PHILIPP HARTMANN

The financial landscape of Europe has been evolving rapidly in the past 20 years. The introduction of the euro and the inception of the single monetary policy on January 1, 1999, accelerated the pace of change. However, it is clear that many driving factors foster transformation in the European financial system, including the Single Market Program, technological developments, financial innovation, globalization, liberalization, increased competition, and deregulation (for a brief review, see Gaspar, Hartmann, and Sleijpen 2003, chap. 1).

The financial system is a key element determining the functioning and the performance of modern economies. It may be defined as the set of markets and institutions (intermediaries) through which households, firms, and governments channel available savings to investment opportunities (financing), carry out transactions (payments and settlements), and take relevant information into account (production of information, screening, and monitoring). The financial system is of key importance for the intertemporal allocation of resources, the allocation of risk, and the production of information. It is therefore not surprising to see a link between growth and finance associated with greater efficiency in the allocation of capital and, more generally, in the functioning of markets (see Hartmann et al. [2003] and Baele et al. [2004] for further references).

Vítor Gaspar is director-general research and Philipp Hartmann is head of the financial research division at the European Central Bank. The views expressed are the authors' own and do not necessarily reflect those of the European Central Bank or the Eurosystem.

One important aspect of this transformation is financial integration. By removing segmentation across national borders, financial integration is expected to lead to increased sophistication in financial instruments, increased liquidity, and stronger competition. The European Central Bank (ECB) is interested in European financial integration. Its interest is shown by the theme chosen for its Second Central Banking Conference, "The Transformation of the European Financial System" (see Gaspar, Hartmann, and Sleijpen 2003), by the publication of a *Monthly Bulletin* article (ECB 2003), and, more recently, by the release of an Occasional Paper (Baele et al. 2004).[1]

A complete assessment of the state and prospects of financial integration in the euro area would require covering money, bond, equity, loan, and derivatives markets. It would also require covering a broad set of institutions, including banks, investment companies, mutual and pension funds, and insurance firms. It would further require a particular focus on clearing and settlement infrastructures. This chapter has a more modest aim: to focus on the money market, which is the financial market closest to the implementation of monetary policy and therefore the most likely to be directly affected by the start of the single monetary policy.

This chapter shows that after the introduction of the euro and the inception of the single monetary policy on January 1, 1999, the money market in the euro area integrated smoothly and rapidly. There are, however, different segments of the money market. For example, it is possible to distinguish between the market for unsecured interbank deposits and the repurchase agreement (repo) market. These two markets are characterized, according to some indicators, by persistently different degrees of market integration. This contrast will allow some reflections on the nature of remaining barriers to full financial integration in the euro area in general.

The Importance of Money Market Integration for Monetary Policy

The Eurosystem implements monetary policy through the money market. Its operational framework is predicated on a well-functioning money market, requiring only a limited presence of the monetary authority. The Eurosystem's operational framework is based on three key elements. First, reserve requirements, with an averaging provision over the reserve maintenance period, allow banks to spread out the impact of liquidity

---

1. In this paper, Baele et al. systematically review the available evidence on quantitative indicators of the integration of money, sovereign bonds, corporate bonds, equity, and credit markets in the euro area. The paper is required reading for anyone who wants a complete review of research on financial integration in the euro area.

shocks over time and thereby help to contain volatility in overnight interest rates. Required reserves (together with the net effect of so-called autonomous liquidity factors) also create a structural liquidity shortage for the banking system as a whole, ensuring that the central bank will be regularly required to supply liquidity to the system.

The second key element is standing facilities. The Eurosystem provides two such facilities, a marginal lending facility and a deposit facility. Both are used on the initiative of commercial banks. The two standing facilities define a corridor (or band) for overnight rates.[2] The third key element, open market operations, is used to control liquidity conditions in the market. In its regular main refinancing operations, the Eurosystem uses repos, supplying liquidity by buying assets under a repo or granting loans against adequate collateral.[3] Money market integration is therefore crucial for the implementation of the single monetary policy because it provides the locus for the first step in the monetary policy transmission mechanism.

Gaspar, Perez-Quiros, and Sicilia (2001) document the story of what they call the "learning period" in the money market. This period is identified with the three weeks after the introduction of the euro. More precisely, it covers the period from January 4 to 21, 1999. They argue that the introduction of the new operational framework proceeded remarkably smoothly. If one focuses on volatility or cross-bank dispersion in overnight interest rates, the effects found are much smaller than the effects associated with recurring events such as the end of a reserve maintenance period.

This finding is all the more surprising because national money markets, before the start of the single monetary policy, displayed important distinctive features (as surveyed, e.g., in Escrivá and Fagan 1996). Gaspar, Perez-Quiros, and Sicilia (2001) also look at the dispersion of interest rates across banks. For this purpose, they use the interest rates obtained by the major European banks when they lend funds in the overnight market. In particular, each data point represents the average interest rate charged in that day by each lending bank. The dataset was provided by the European Banking Federation (EBF) and is the one used to compute the time series for the Euro Overnight Index Average (EONIA), which is based on data from a panel of more than 50 banks. It is important to emphasize that observations in the EBF database correspond to actual trades. They show that at the very beginning of the single monetary policy, that is, during the first business week of 1999, some banks reporting to the EONIA panel lent at rates above the marginal lending facility. On January 5, 1999, the dif-

---

2. See Woodford (2003) for a general description of the functioning of such a system and Hartmann, Manna, and Manzanares (2001) for a broad discussion of how the operational framework of the Eurosystem relates to the euro money market.

3. See ECB (2004a, 2004b) for detailed official descriptions of operational procedures and their relation to monetary policy.

ference was about 25 basis points. The dispersion of rates reported subsequently narrowed to low levels.

During the period from January 4 to 21, 1999, the corridor defined by the two standing facilities was temporarily narrowed to 50 basis points, which limited the volatility that might have been associated with the transition to the new regime. When the corridor was widened to its normal size, the market rate (measured by the EONIA rate) remained stable and close to the Eurosystem's main refinancing operations rate of 3 percent. The dispersion of rates across banks was also already much lower on January 22.

However, Gaspar, Perez-Quiros, and Sicilia (2001) provide evidence showing that the transition was not, strictly speaking, instantaneous and that learning did take place. They identify a number of inefficiencies and other forms of abnormal behavior during the first days of the month—for example, the above-mentioned trading at rates significantly higher than the marginal lending facility on January 5. However, they also show that banks have adapted quickly and easily to the new environment.

Money Market Integration in the Euro Area: Two Different Sides of the Same Coin

Focusing on intercountry differences, Baele et al. (2004) document the integration of money markets in the euro area, using the cross-sectional standard deviation of unsecured lending rates, among the 12 average country rates.[4] They also use data from the EONIA panel of banks referred to above.

Figures 5.1, 5.2, and 5.3 respectively plot the results for overnight, 1-month, and 12-month maturities.

Focusing on the overnight rate, the relevant standard deviation was several hundred basis points in the mid-1990s. It has then reduced, very gradually, starting in 1996, to somewhat above 100 basis points for most of 1998. Toward the end of the year, the standard deviation declined sharply, converging to levels in the range of 1 to 4 basis points. It confirms the existence of a well-integrated market across countries. The almost complete disappearance of cross-country differences after the start of the single monetary policy was also documented earlier by Santillan, Bayle, and Thygesen (2000), who found that cross-border differences had been reduced to a 2- to 4-basis-point range, and by Hartmann, Manna, and Manzanares (2001, figure 4), who plotted intraday overnight rates quoted

---

4. There were 11 average country rates before Greece joined the euro area in 2001. The period before 1999 is added to provide a benchmark for comparison. It is clear, however, that the presence of exchange rate risk prior to 1999 allowed for decoupling of national money market rates. In any case, the convergence of economic developments and policies and the increased credibility of convergence toward monetary union led to a gradual narrowing of interest rate differentials.

**Figure 5.1 Cross-sectional standard deviation of the average
lending rates for overnight maturities among euro area
countries** (30-day moving average)

1994–2003

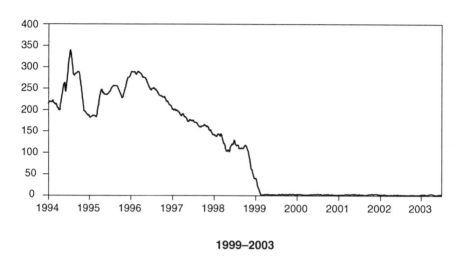

1999–2003

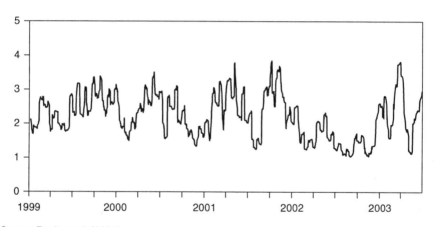

Source: Baele et al. (2004).

by brokers located in different euro area countries. Integration is also suggested by the sharp increase in cross-border unsecured interbank lending between euro area countries at the time of the introduction of the euro, as documented, for example, by Hartmann, Maddaloni, and Manganelli (2003, figure 7).

Gaspar, Perez-Quiros, and Rodriguez-Mendizabal (2004) also look at the cross-sectional dispersion of the EONIA overnight rate. They charac-

Figure 5.2 Cross-sectional standard deviation of unsecured lending rates for 1-month maturities among euro area countries (30-day moving average)

1994–2003

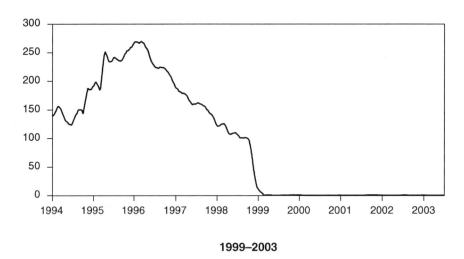

1999–2003

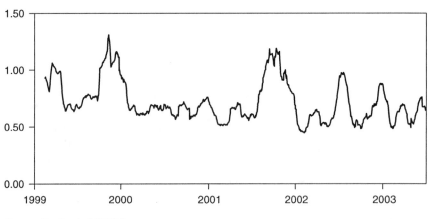

Source: Baele et al. (2004).

terize the distribution of rates across contributing banks and study how it evolves over time. Baele et al. (2004) look instead at the *difference* between the cross-country EONIA rate deviations and the corresponding measure within a country. Specifically, they compute the ratio between the average cross-country EONIA rate deviations and the average within-country deviations. The data from Baele et al. (2004) are plotted as figure 5.4.

**Figure 5.3 Cross-sectional standard deviation of unsecured
lending rates for 12-month maturities among euro area
countries** (30-day moving average)

1994–2003

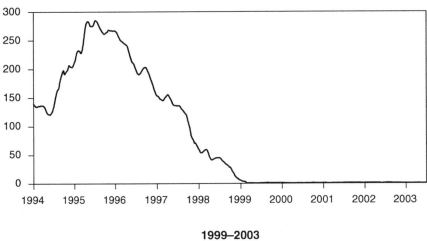

1999–2003

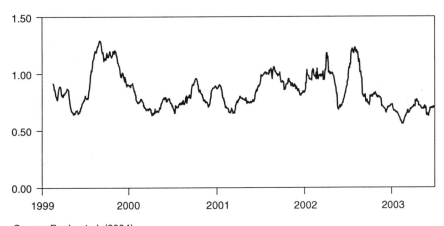

Source: Baele et al. (2004).

Baele et al. argue that one should expect the ratio to be close to 1 if the market is strongly integrated. Interestingly, figure 5.4 does indeed show that the ratio remained quite close to 1 throughout the 1999–2003 period, with some registered values below unity. These results are consistent with a very high degree of cross-country integration of the overnight money market.

Figure 5.4 Ratio between average cross-country Euro Overnight Index Average (EONIA) rate deviations and average within-country deviations (30-day moving average)

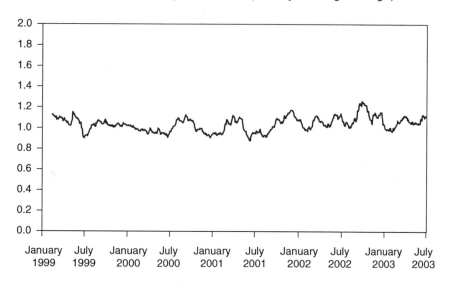

Source: Baele et al. (2004).

In order to interpret these results, it is useful to recall that liquidity distribution in the euro area follows a two-tiered structure (see, e.g., Santillan, Bayle, and Thygesen 2000; Freixas and Holthausen 2001; Ewerhart et al. 2004). The idea is that cross-border trading occurs predominantly among large banks, with smaller banks concentrating on their respective national markets. The interest rates, reported in the EONIA panel, refer to actual lending rates for operations of the contributing banks. As was stressed above, the EONIA sample includes the major European banks. In the light of the two-tiered-structure hypothesis, differences between the deviation within and across countries would measure the relative density of the network of relationships in the money market. If the ratio were consistently close to 1, that would suggest outcomes equivalent to those that would be found if the network of relationships were independent from location. In such a case, conditions prevailing in the different national segments are equivalent and the market is fully integrated.

Building on their findings, reported above, Baele et al. (2004) go further and contrast the developments in the unsecured market with developments registered in the repo market. Long time-series data on repos, comparable to the ones from EONIA for the unsecured market, do not exist. Therefore it is not possible to produce the exact analogues of figures 5.1 through 5.4 from repo markets.

Figure 5.5 Cross-sectional standard deviation of one-month repo rates among euro area countries (30-day moving average)

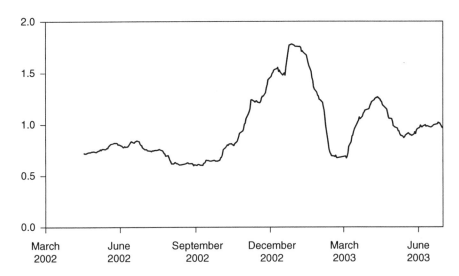

Source: Baele et al. (2004).

From early 2002 on, it is possible to rely on the panel contributing to the so-called Eurepo indices relating to repurchase agreements denominated in euro. The Eurepo indices allow for comparability across countries because the collateral used is standardized and the risk characteristics of banks are similar.[5] Figure 5.5 shows that the degree of integration across countries is very high. Standard deviations range from 0.5 to 2 basis points.

The interesting insight from Baele et al. (2004) was, however, that it is possible to learn more by focusing on the *difference* between the corresponding ratios between the average cross-country interest rate deviations and the average within-country deviations (see figure 5.6).

The point of interest here is that the ratio is significantly and persistently above 1 for the repo market measure. Before going further, it is important to recall that we are focusing on a ratio with a few basis points in the numerator and the denominator. Deviations of only a few basis points still reveal a generally efficient and well-integrated market. Nevertheless, the contrast between the repo and unsecured markets is striking. Recall-

---

5. The Eurepo panel is compiled by the European Banking Federation. The number of contributing banks is about 40. The characteristics of the panel are similar to those of the EONIA.

Figure 5.6 Ratios between average cross-country interest rate deviations and within-country deviations

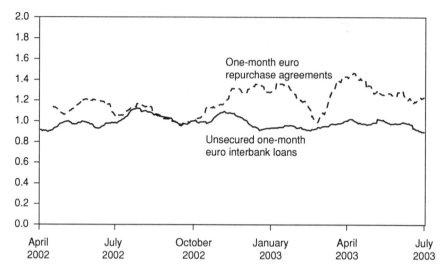

Source: Baele et al. (2004).

ing our interpretation given above, the results suggest that the outcomes in the repo market are systematically different from those that would prevail if the network of relationships were independent of location or nationality. They suggest that the degree of integration in the repo market is lower than in the unsecured interbank market.[6]

Remaining Obstacles to Financial Integration in the Euro Area

Why is the repo market less integrated than the overnight deposit market in the euro area? Interestingly, the answer to this question not only is relevant for the money market but also indicates more generally what are the obstacles to financial integration in the euro area. This means it also identifies obstacles to the further integration of, for example, bond and equity markets.

First of all, repos are relatively complex contracts, because the provision of interbank credit is collateralized with securities. The euro area is characterized by different legal systems in different countries. For example,

---

6. See ECB (2002) for a survey of initiatives aim at increasing repo market integration.

bankruptcy laws and procedures are not fully harmonized. Therefore there coexist a variety of master agreements that can guide repo contracts. And different market participants tend to use different agreements. For example, the importance of the European Masters Agreement—which can be used in multiple jurisdictions according to the respective local law— grows only slowly. So the heterogeneity of repos and their noninterchangeable character is one reason that the law of one price does not hold in the euro repo market with the same degree of precision as in the unsecured euro money market.

A further feature of collateralized lending is that the securities have to be transferred back and forth between the transacting parties. Although this is very easy and cheap within a given country, the same does not apply to cross-border securities transfers. The reason is that each country has its own securities settlement systems and a transfer often involves several of those systems. This handicap is of course very pronounced in Europe, for the euro area is composed of different countries. The fragmentation of securities settlement infrastructures in Europe makes those transfers much more complicated and costly than, for example, in the United States. A recent study by Schmiedel, Malkamäki, and Tarkka (2002) estimates, for example, that the average unit costs of cross-border securities transfers are on the order of $40, whereas within countries they are only about $3. Hence, the large costs of cross-border securities transfers are another reason for the remaining interest rate differentials in the euro repo market.

Legal heterogeneity and fragmented market infrastructures provide obstacles not only for the integration of repo markets. They are similarly important for securities markets in general. For example, the literature has illustrated well the scope for further integration of European bond and stock markets (see, e.g., Baele et al. 2004; Gaspar, Hartmann, and Sleijpen 2003; and Hartmann, Maddaloni, and Manganelli 2003).

Conclusions

In this chapter, we have tried to illustrate the general issues relevant for understanding European financial integration by focusing on the money market. The link between the money market and the framework for implementing the single monetary policy makes it the natural starting point when trying to illustrate the impact of the introduction of the euro on European financial market integration. It is clear that after a short and smooth learning process (of less than three weeks in early 1999), the overnight market for unsecured deposits integrated fully. This is a key development because a common short-term interest rate represents the first step in the transmission mechanism of monetary policy.

More instructive for identifying remaining obstacles to integration are the differences between the unsecured market and the repo market. Cross-border interest rate differentials are only really relevant for the latter. The differentials illustrate that the process of integration is as yet far from complete. To explain the patterns seen, the most relevant factors are likely to be differences in laws, regulations, and practices, and the fragmentation of the market infrastructure, in particular clearing and settlement systems. These factors are also of general relevance for the integration of bond and equity markets.

References

Adam, K., T. Japelli, A. Menichini, M. Padula, and M. Pagano. 2002, Study to Analyse, Compare, and Apply Alternative Indicators and Monitoring Methodologies to Measure the Evolution of Capital Market Integration in the European Union. Paper prepared by the Center for Studies in Economics and Finance for the European Commission, Brussels, January 28.

Baele, L., A. Ferrando, P. Hördahl, E. Krylova, and C. Monnet. 2004. *Measuring Financial Integration in the Euro Area*. ECB Occasional Paper. Frankfurt: European Central Bank.

ECB (European Central Bank). 2002. Main Features of the Repo Market in the Euro Area. *Monthly Bulletin*, October: 55–68.

ECB (European Central Bank). 2003. Financial Integration in Europe. *Monthly Bulletin*, October: 53–66.

ECB (European Central Bank). 2004a. *The Implementation of Monetary Policy in the Euro Area: General Documentation on Eurosystem Monetary Policy Instruments and Procedures*. Frankfurt: ECB.

ECB (European Central Bank). 2004b. *The Monetary Policy of the ECB*. Frankfurt: ECB.

Escrivá, J. L., and G. Fagan. 1996. *Empirical Assessment of Monetary Policy Instruments and Procedures (MPIP) in EU Countries*. EMI Staff Paper 2. Frankfurt: European Monetary Institute of the European Central Bank.

Ewerhart, C., N. Cassola, S. Ejerskov, and N. Valla. 2004. The Euro Market: Stylized Facts and Open Questions. European Central Bank, Frankfurt. Photocopy.

Freixas, X., and C. Holthausen. 2001. *Interbank Market Integration Under Asymmetric Information*. ECB Working Paper 74. Frankfurt: European Central Bank. (Forthcoming in *Review of Financial Studies*.)

Gaspar, V., P. Hartmann, and O. Sleijpen, eds. 2003. *The Transformation of the European Financial System*. Frankfurt: European Central Bank.

Gaspar, V., G. Perez-Quiros, and H. Rodriguez-Mendizabal. 2004. *Interest Rate Behaviour in the Interbank Market*. ECB Working Paper. Frankfurt: European Central Bank.

Gaspar, V., G. Perez-Quiros, and J. Sicilia. 2001. The ECB Monetary Policy Strategy and the Money Market. *International Journal of Finance and Economics* 6, no. 4: 325–42.

Hartmann, P., A. Maddaloni, and S. Manganelli. 2003. The Euro-Area Financial System: Structure, Integration and Policy Initiatives. *Oxford Review of Economic Policy* 19, no. 1: 180–213.

Hartmann, P., M. Manna, and A. Manzanares. 2001. The Microstructure of the Euro Money Market. *Journal of International Money and Finance* 20, no. 6: 895–984.

Santillan, J., M. Bayle, and C. Thygesen. 2000. The Impact of the Euro on Money and Bond Markets. ECB Occasional Paper 1. Frankfurt: European Central Bank.

Schmiedel, H., Malkamäki, and J. Tarkka. 2002. *Economies of Scale and Technological Development in Securities Depository and Settlement Systems*. Bank of Finland Discussion Paper 26. Helsinki: Bank of Finland.

Woodford, Michael. 2003. *Interest and Prices: Foundations of a Theory of Monetary Policy*. Princeton, NJ: Princeton University Press.

Financial Market Integration, the Euro, and the Role of Growth

KRISTIN J. FORBES

> It is significant to see how entirely all the rest of the Geographically Distributed stocks differ in their price movements from the British stock. It is this individuality of movement on the part of each security, included in a well-distributed Investment List, which ensures the first great essential of successful investment, namely Capital Stability.
>
> —Henry Lowenfeld, *Investment: An Exact Science* (1909, 49)

Financial market integration and the comovement of stock prices have been a subject of interest for a century—if not longer. During this period, world equity markets have gone through various phases of integration. Returns in the world's major stock markets were highly correlated in the early 1900s, but then integration declined during the World Wars and in the 1970s (see Goetzmann, Li, and Rouwenhorst 2001). Since the 1980s, however, global financial market integration and the comovement in the world's major stock markets have steadily increased.

This increased comovement in global stock markets is not surprising given the recent surge in capital flows across borders. Between 1992 and 2002, global capital flows increased by an average of about 8 percent a year to nearly $2 trillion (equivalent to about 6 percent of global GDP). As is shown in figure 5.7, if global capital flows continue to grow at this average rate, they could more than double in the next decade to more than $4 trillion.

Almost half of global capital flows in 2002 were in the form of portfolio investment—purchases of stocks, bonds, securities, and notes in one country by citizens of another country. As a result, financial market movements in one country can quickly affect the earnings of investors, corporations, and governments located in other countries. It is not surprising that movements in stock and bond markets in large countries can rapidly spread to financial markets around the globe.

How will this increased financial market integration affect the prospects for the euro? To answer this question, this chapter begins by exam-

Kristin J. Forbes is a member of the White House's Council of Economic Advisers. The author thanks Brent Neiman for assistance in preparing this paper.

Figure 5.7   Actual and extrapolated global capital inflows, 1992–2012

trillions of current dollars

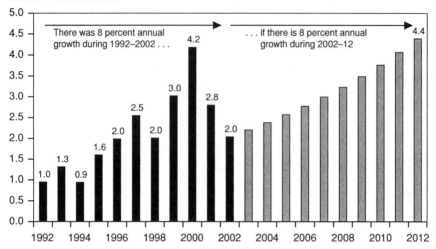

There was 8 percent annual growth during 1992–2002 . . .

. . . if there is 8 percent annual growth during 2002–12

Sources: Capital flow data from 1992 to 2002 calculated using data from the IMF's International Financial Statistics Database and *Global Financial Stability* report.

ining different factors that can drive financial market integration between Europe and the rest of the world—such as increased capital flows and trade flows—and how these factors may evolve in the future. The chapter then takes a different approach to answering this question by examining how stock market integration has already changed since the advent of the euro. No matter which approach is chosen, one recurrent theme is the critical role of economic growth.

If Europe's growth prospects improve, trade and capital flows will increase more rapidly, raising Europe's financial market integration with other countries and increasing the relative demand for the euro and euro-denominated assets. If growth in Europe lags that in other large economies, however, investors will seek higher return opportunities in other regions and companies will seek to expand trade with other countries. Financial market integration between Europe and the rest of the world would proceed more slowly, and although the euro would undoubtedly remain a leading global currency, its role in the global economy may not substantially mature from that of today.

Capital Flows, Financial Integration, and the Euro

As transaction costs fall and investors become more accustomed to holding assets in other countries, cross-border capital flows will continue to increase. This increased willingness to diversify investment portfolios across countries is already apparent in a reduction in home bias in the past decade.[7] This trend not only will cause Europeans to increase their holdings of assets outside of Europe but also will cause non-Europeans to increase their holdings of European assets. The aggregate effect on the demand for European assets, however, is less clear. Will this trend of increased cross-border capital flows lead to net capital flows into or out of Europe? If increased foreign demand for European assets is greater than the increased European demand for foreign assets, this could generate net capital inflows. Conversely, if the increased European demand for foreign assets is greater than the increased foreign demand for European assets, this could generate net capital outflows.

One of the key determinants of whether increased capital mobility will generate net flows into or out of Europe will be European growth prospects. If investors believe that growth in Europe will recover and remain strong, earnings prospects for European companies should improve. Foreigners will seek to increase their investments in European stocks and bonds. Conversely, if growth in Europe lags that in other countries, foreign investors and Europeans will instead seek to increase investments in higher-growth regions.

This situation leads to the next question: What are growth prospects for the eurozone? Blue Chip estimates suggest that growth in the eurozone is expected to improve from 0.9 and 0.6 percent in 2002 and 2003, respectively, to 1.9 and 2.2 percent in 2004 and 2005. (All statistics cited in this paragraph are from the "Blue Chip Economic Indicators," February 2004.) Despite this improvement, figure 5.8 shows that growth in the eurozone is still expected to lag that in many other large economies in the world—such as the United States, which is expected to grow by 4.6 percent in 2004, and even Japan, which is expected to grow by 2.1 percent.

Moreover, the IMF estimates that the potential growth rate for the eurozone is only 2.1 percent. This is substantially below the estimated 3.1 percent for the United States and the 2.6 percent average for the OECD countries (which include the eurozone), although it is higher than the 1.1 percent estimated potential growth rate for Japan. Of course, if European governments embarked on an aggressive agenda of structural reform, removing impediments to growth such as policies limiting labor market flexibility, Europe's long-term potential growth rate could improve. Any such reforms that raised European growth rates should increase demand for European assets, stimulating capital inflows and increasing relative demand for the euro.

---

7. E.g., Greenspan (2003) states that for the countries belonging to the Organization for Economic Cooperation and Development (OECD), the GDP-weighted correlation between domestic saving rates and domestic investment rates (a standard measure of home bias) fell from 0.96 in 1992 to less than 0.8 in 2002.

Figure 5.8 Expected annual GDP growth

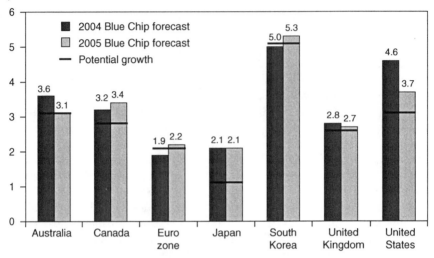

percent

- 2004 Blue Chip forecast
- 2005 Blue Chip forecast
- Potential growth

	Australia	Canada	Euro zone	Japan	South Korea	United Kingdom	United States
2004	3.6	3.2	1.9	2.1	5.0	2.8	4.6
2005	3.1	3.4	2.2	2.1	5.3	2.7	3.7

Source: Blue Chip Economic Indicators, forecasts from February 2004.

In addition to expected growth rates, any other factors that affect the expected return on European assets will influence investors' willingness to hold European assets. One such factor is expected currency movements. If investors believe that the euro will appreciate against other major currencies, this will raise the expected return on European assets relative to assets in other currencies. An extensive literature suggests, however, that predicting currency movements can be extremely difficult and imprecise.

Even though it is difficult to predict future exchange rate movements, increased uncertainty about these movements could also cause investors to increase the diversification of their portfolios. For example, some investors—and especially central banks—tend to have a small proportion of their assets denominated in euros. Figure 5.9 shows that only 19 percent of identified official foreign exchange reserve holdings were held in euros in 2002. In sharp contrast, about 65 percent of these reserve holdings were held in dollar-denominated assets (largely US Treasuries). This large share of dollar holdings is due to factors such as the large size of the United States in the global economy (the United States accounted for about 34 percent of global GDP in 2002, calculated at market exchange rates), the large share of global trade denominated in dollars, the high liquidity and low risk of US assets, and the dollar's historical importance in the global economy.

Despite these compelling reasons to hold a large share of reserves in dollar-denominated assets, standard portfolio theory suggests that some central banks, especially in countries with a large share of trade with

Figure 5.9 Share of identified official foreign exchange holdings
(end of 2002)

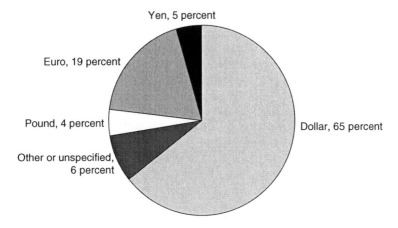

Yen, 5 percent

Euro, 19 percent

Pound, 4 percent

Other or unspecified,
6 percent

Dollar, 65 percent

Source: Data from the revision to the IMF's *Annual Report* (2003).

Europe, might choose to increase their holdings of euro-denominated assets at some point in the future. This will be even more likely if the increasing financial integration of Europe improves the liquidity of euro-denominated assets. There is no reason to expect that any such shift would be rapid, but if foreign central banks did decide to increase their holdings of euro-denominated assets over time, this could cause the euro to slowly appreciate.

Once again, however, a critical determinant of whether foreign central banks would likely increase their holdings of euro-denominated assets in the future is the growth performance of the European economy. Europe accounted for about 30 percent of global GDP in 2002 (calculated at market exchange rates). If the growth rate in Europe does not improve, Europe's share in the global economy will decrease over time (especially given the rapid growth of other large economies, e.g., China and India). In this scenario of slow growth in Europe, foreign central banks would have less incentive to increase their holdings of euro-denominated reserves.

Trade Flows, Financial Integration, and the Euro

Although the effect of trade flows on financial market integration may not be as obvious as the effect of capital flows, the academic literature suggests that trade flows can also be important determinants of financial integration. For example, Forbes (2004) examines why movements in large stock and bond markets affect financial markets around the world. The results show that during the most recent period for which data are available, from 1996 to 2000, bilateral trade flows were large and important determinants of how financial market movements were transmitted to other countries. In fact, the empirical estimates suggest that trade flows may be even more important in explaining financial market integration than cross-country linkages through foreign direct investment and bank lending.

Forbes (2004) also includes estimates of the magnitude of the relationship between trade flows and the integration of stock and bond markets. For example, the study estimates the effect on financial market integration between Chile and the United States if Chile (which just completed a free trade agreement with the United States) increased trade with the United States to a level comparable to that for Mexico (which has had a free trade agreement with the United States since 1994).[8] A 10 percent return in the US stock market is currently correlated with a 2.7 percent return in the Chilean market. If Chile increased its trade integration with the United States to Mexico's levels, however, a 10 percent return in the US market would instead be correlated with a 7.0 to 7.5 percent return in the Chilean market.[9] These calculations are only a rough approximation, but they do suggest that changes in trade flows can have large effects on how financial market movements are transmitted from one country to another.

To predict how trade flows might affect European financial market integration and demand for the euro, it is therefore necessary to discuss expected future trends in European trade flows. Just as global capital flows have increased during the past decade and are expected to continue to grow, trade flows have also increased during past decades and should continue to grow. Granted, increased support for protectionism could slow trade liberalization, but even setbacks such as the disappointing progress in the Doha Development Agenda of trade liberalization are unlikely to stop the steady increase in global trade.

If trade flows between Europe and the rest of the world increase, however, leading to greater financial market integration between Europe and the rest of the world, it is unclear how this will, in turn, affect the value of the euro. Increased demand for European exports would increase demand for the euro and tend to cause it to appreciate (assuming everything else remains constant). But increased imports into Europe would have the opposite effect.

All in all, increased financial integration resulting largely from increased trade flows may not, in and of itself, have any substantial effect on demand for the euro. This is more likely to be true if increased trade is

---

8. More specifically, assume that Chile increased its ratio of imports from the United States to GDP from its average level of 4 percent between 1996 and 2000 to the average ratio of 25 percent for Mexico over the same period.

9. These estimates are based on the version of the model estimated using local currency stock returns and controlling for global and cross-country factors.

Figure 5.10 Japan's trade balance and exchange rate, 2000–03

trade balance/GDP (percent)   yen/dollar

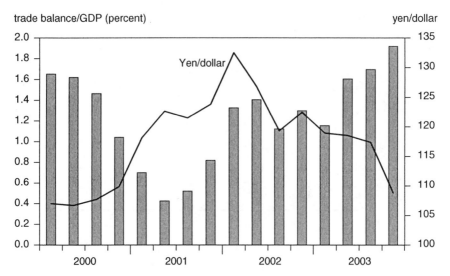

Note: Bars represent quarterly data for each year indicated.

Source: Data from Haver Analytics.

relatively balanced between imports and exports. For the eurozone, trade is currently fairly balanced, with the entire region running a trade surplus in goods and services of about 2 percent of GDP in 2003.

Rather than increased trade flows affecting the value of the euro, more attention has recently been paid to the reverse effect—how recent currency movements affect trade flows. More specifically, as the euro and yen appreciated against the dollar in 2002 and 2003, there has been increasing concern that this will decrease European and Japanese exports. Economic theory and empirical evidence do show that, holding everything else constant, a currency appreciation normally tends to reduce exports, increase imports, and decrease a trade surplus (or increase a trade deficit) after a period of roughly a year.[10] Rarely, however, is "everything else held constant."

Instead, experience suggests that this predicted effect of currency movements on exports and trade balances can be outweighed by differences in growth rates across countries. The recent performance of exchange rates and trade balances in Japan and several European countries reflects this pattern. Figure 5.10 shows that between the first quarter of

10. The immediate effect of an appreciation, however, can be the opposite because prices adjust immediately and trade volumes only adjust with a lag. Due to this "J-curve effect," an appreciation can cause export values to increase, import values to fall, and the trade surplus to increase for several months. Also, in some cases when a country has a large share of debt denominated in foreign currency and/or is highly dependent on imported inputs, the traditional effects of exchange rate movements can be mitigated.

Figure 5.11 Germany's trade balance and exchange rate

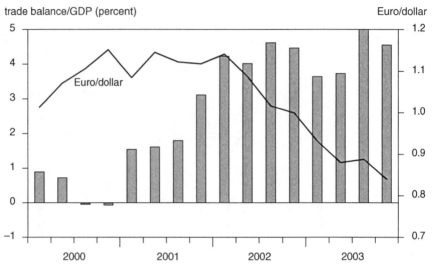

Note: Bars represent quarterly data for each year indicated.

Source: Data from Haver Analytics.

2002 and the fourth quarter of 2003, the yen appreciated by 20 percent against the dollar. During the same period, Japan's trade surplus increased (instead of decreased) from 1.3 to 1.9 percent of GDP. One of the key reasons for the increase in Japan's trade surplus during the period of yen appreciation was faster growth in Japan's major export markets, especially in China and other Asian countries. This trend has recently continued. Japan's trade surplus in goods increased sharply in the first quarter of 2004. This increase was caused by a surge in exports (which increased more than 30 percent in yen during the first quarter of 2003) to high-growth China.

Several countries in the eurozone have also experienced an increase in their trade surpluses (or a decrease in their trade deficits) after the substantial appreciation of the euro (and over a long enough period that any J-curve effect would have disappeared). For example, figure 5.11 shows that when the euro was at its most depreciated level against the dollar in October 2000, Germany's trade in goods and services was basically balanced (with a small deficit of 0.06 percent of GDP). The euro/dollar exchange rate fluctuated for several months, and then the euro steadily appreciated in 2002 and 2003, for a total appreciation of 30 percent between October 2000 and October 2003.

During the same period, however, Germany's trade balance shifted to a large surplus of 4.6 percent of GDP. Despite the appreciation of the euro, slower growth in Germany caused imports to fall by about 9 percent, and faster growth in its major trading partners caused German exports to increase by about 5 percent during the same period. These examples clearly suggest that although exchange rate movements can affect trade balances, these effects can be overwhelmed by the effect of differences in growth rates on trade flows.

The Recent Impact of the Euro on Stock Market Integration

Instead of trying to predict how increased capital flows and trade flows might affect financial market integration and demand for the euro in the future, a different approach is to examine how the recent introduction of the euro has already changed financial integration within Europe and between Europe and other major economies. When the euro was adopted in 1999, it was widely expected that this should increase financial market integration within the region by reducing transaction costs and reducing the uncertainty from exchange rate movements. This increase in financial market integration could have occurred through increased financial flows as well as increased trade flows, all of which would be expected to increase stock market comovements in the region.

As a rough test of whether the introduction of the euro actually did increase stock market comovement, figure 5.12 graphs the weekly correlation in stock market returns between France and each of the eurozone countries, before and after the introduction of the euro (from 1990 to 1999, and then from 1999 to 2003).[11] The figure shows that for most countries in the eurozone, stock market correlations with France did increase substantially after the introduction of the euro. For example, the correlation in stock market returns between France and Italy increased from 54 to 85 percent, and the correlation with Spain increased from 66 to 80 percent. For all 10 countries in the sample, stock market correlations with France increased by an average of 16 percent from the period 1990 to 1999 compared with the period after the introduction of the euro.

As was discussed above, however, financial market integration increased around the world in the 1990s. As a rough test of whether this increase in stock market correlations between France and the eurozone results from the introduction of the euro or is instead part of a broader global trend of increased integration, figure 5.13 performs the same analysis, except that it shows correlations between the eurozone economies and

---

11. I focus on France because it is one of the largest economies in the eurozone. The results from Germany are similar but present a less clear example due to the shock of German unification during this period.

Figure 5.12 Stock market correlations of other EU members with France

percent

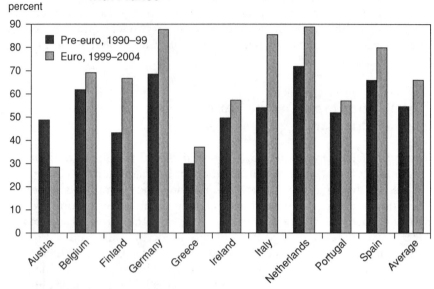

Note: Correlations based on weekly stock market returns for the country's main stock market index.

Source: Author's calculations.

the United States.[12] As would be expected, correlations between most of the eurozone economies and the United States are lower than between the same countries and France. Correlations between almost all the countries and the United States increased, however, after the euro was introduced. For example, the correlation in stock returns between the United States and Italy increased from 36 to 66 percent, and the correlation between the United States and Spain increased from 49 to 63 percent.

In fact, for the 10 countries in the sample (excluding France for consistency), stock market correlations with the United States increased by an average of 25 percent from the period 1990 to 1999 compared with the period after the introduction of the euro—greater than the 16 percent increase between the eurozone countries and France.[13]

---

12. The central results in this section are unchanged (although the point estimates of the correlation coefficients do vary slightly) if stock market correlations are adjusted for changes in volatility across periods, using the correction in Forbes and Rigobon (2002).

13. A similar analysis of stock market correlations between the United Kingdom and the same sample of 10 eurozone countries shows a similar result. The correlations with the United Kingdom increased from the period 1990 to 1999 compared with the period after the adoption of the euro by virtually the same percentage, on average, as correlations with France, despite the United Kingdom's remaining outside the eurozone.

Figure 5.13 Stock market correlations of EU members with the United States

percent

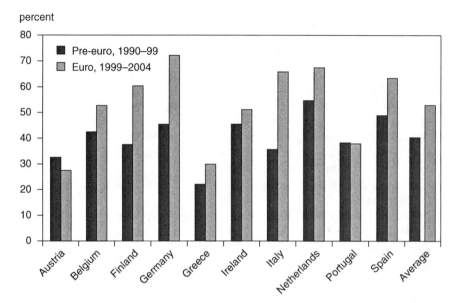

Note: Correlations based on weekly stock market returns for the country's main stock market index.

Source: Author's calculations.

Therefore, although financial market integration within the eurozone has increased since the introduction of the euro, this increase does not appear to have occurred any faster than the increase in financial market integration between the eurozone countries and the United States. One possible explanation for this trend is that faster growth in the United States, which stimulated trade and capital flows between the United States and the eurozone countries, helped stimulate this greater increase in financial market integration. This effect of faster growth on stock market integration may have been even greater than the effect of adopting a single currency. Although this is clearly not a formal empirical analysis, and there are many other factors that determine financial market integration in addition to market comovements, it does support the argument that economic growth can be an important determinant of financial market integration.

Conclusions: The Role of Growth

This chapter has considered various channels by which increased capital flows and trade flows can increase financial market integration, and how all these variables could, in turn, affect demand for the euro. One theme pervading this discussion is the critically important role of growth. Countries that are expected to grow faster will tend to receive greater capital inflows, thereby stimulating greater financial market integration. Central banks are more likely to hold reserves in the currencies of countries with strong growth performance. Increased trade flows are correlated with greater financial market integration, and countries that are more open to trade tend to grow faster. Differences in growth rates across countries can significantly affect trade flows, and even outweigh the standard effects of currency movements. Although stock markets in the eurozone countries became more financially integrated after the adoption of the euro, these stock markets became relatively more integrated with the faster-growing US economy during the same period.

Economic growth is critically important. Its role and effects are so pervasive that it can be difficult "to think about anything else" (Lucas 1988, p. 5). This chapter suggests that Europe's future growth performance will be a decisive factor, and possibly the most decisive factor, in determining the evolution of European capital flows, trade patterns, financial market integration, and demand for the euro. Therefore, it is difficult to discuss the prospects for the euro without simultaneously discussing the even more fundamental question of the prospects for economic growth in Europe.

References

Forbes, Kristin. 2004. A Decomposition of Global Linkages in Financial Markets Over Time. *Review of Economics and Statistics* 86, no. 3: 705–22.
Forbes, Kristin, and Roberto Rigobon. 2002. No Contagion, Only Interdependence: Measuring Stock Market Comovements. *Journal of Finance* 57, no. 5: 2223–61.
Goetzmann, William, Lingfeng Li, and K. Geert Rouwenhorst. 2001. *Long-Term Global Market Correlations*. NBER Working Paper 8612. Cambridge, MA: National Bureau of Economic Research.
Greenspan, Alan. 2003. Remarks at the 21st Annual Monetary Conference, cosponsored by the Cato Institute and the *Economist*. Washington, November 20.
Lowenfeld, Henry. 1909. *Investment: An Exact Science*. London: Financial Review of Reviews.
Lucas, Robert. 1988. On the Mechanics of Economic Development. *Journal of Monetary Economics* 22: 3–42.

The Impact of a Five-Year-Old Euro on Financial Markets

HÉLÈNE REY

In "The Emergence of the Euro as an International Currency," Richard Portes and I argued back in 1998 that the creation of the euro "[would] have substantial implications for the international monetary system; for the currency composition of portfolios; for exchange rates, and hence monetary policies; and for economic efficiency and welfare. The key determinant of the extent and speed of internationalisation of the euro [would] be transaction costs in foreign exchange and securities markets" (Portes and Rey 1998, 307–08). We noted also that the entry (or non-entry) of the United Kingdom into Economic and Monetary Union would play a significant role, because of the size and sophistication of that country's financial markets.

When central banks are equally credible, market size and liquidity become very important factors in determining whether a currency is widely used by market participants around the world or not. We developed the idea that, due to the sheer size of the euro area, a common European currency would have profound effects on international and European financial markets (see also Bergsten 1997). First, it would lead to more disintermediated finance in Europe. It would also increase the liquidity of different financial markets via well-known synergies between the different roles played by a global currency. Efficient capital markets attract more capital inflows, which raises the liquidity of the foreign exchange market. In turn, more liquid foreign exchange markets reduce the costs of portfolio substitution, which raises the turnover on home financial assets and cuts transaction costs even further, and so on.

Having a widely used currency and well-developed financial markets matters for investment and hence for growth. This is a well-established result in recent empirical literature, and it goes beyond the traditional international currency's benefits of seigniorage, lower exchange rate risks for one's exporters and importers, easier current account deficit financing (with issuance of liabilities denominated in one's currency), and political influence.

Hélène Rey is an assistant professor of economics and international affairs at Princeton University.

It is now time, after five years of the euro's existence, to make a preliminary assessment of both its role on the international scene and its contribution to the deep structural changes undergone by European financial markets in recent times. In this chapter, I briefly review the main recent developments in the euro area's government bond, corporate bond, derivative, and equity markets. I argue that the creation of the euro has led to spectacular developments in European financial markets, with the emergence of new markets and in most cases a significant increase in the liquidity and integration of existing markets. I then report on the role of the euro in the international arena and contend that the increase in the use of the euro has been unequally distributed across markets and has been in general quite slow. Finally, I suggest as a possibility that the international use of the euro may be accelerated in the future by a shift of market participants out of dollar assets due to the unprecedented external deficits of the United States.

European Financial Markets and the Euro

Government bond markets, because of their sheer size, are a major component of the financial system. They provide liquid assets for investors to park their funds temporarily.

Government Bond Markets

The spreads of euro area 10-year government bonds versus the German Bund have fallen since the birth of the euro and are now at very low levels. In February 2004, the Austrian bond was trading at 3 basis points above the Bund; the French bond at 2 basis points; the Finnish bond at –2 basis points; the Dutch bond at 0 basis points; and the Italian bond at +14 basis points. Because currency risk is now absent and since there are few reasons to believe that default risks have changed much during the past five years (if anything, they should have increased following the recent breakup of the Stability and Growth Pact!), this suggests that the liquidity risk in those markets has been falling.

There is now as well some evidence that market participants have been coordinating with respect to some key securities, which have become benchmark securities for the government bond market. These are the German Bund at 10 years, the French bond at 5 years, and the Italian bond at 2 years. The existence of such benchmark securities facilitates the process of price discovery and the functioning of markets (see Dunne, Moore, and Portes 2003).

Corporate Bond Markets

Corporate bond markets were almost nonexistent for European nonfinancial institutions in 1998. So were markets for "junk" bonds. These markets emerged as the pool of potential investors increased following the adoption of the euro. But corporate bond markets as a whole underwent a substantial development. Total corporate sector issuances in the euro area amounted to €140 billion in 1999. They increased to €201 billion in 2001, fell back to €118 billion in 2002, and rebounded to €150 billion in 2003.

The Derivatives Market

The euro swap market was at the beginning of 2003 the largest financial market in the world with more than €26 trillion outstanding, just above the dollar swap market.

Equity Markets

European equity markets have traditionally been quite segmented. The advent of the euro seems to have fostered a greater degree of financial integration. The degree of correlation between equity price indices in the major euro area markets has kept on increasing (but it has been doing so ever since the beginning of the 1990s). More strikingly, the share of equities invested in Europe-wide funds has gone up substantially in euro area countries to reach nearly 50 percent. A similar increase has not been observed for the countries that have chosen to remain outside the euro area (Denmark, the United Kingdom, and Switzerland).

Summary

Euro area financial markets have therefore become more liquid, more diverse, and more integrated since the birth of the euro. We now turn to the international side and ask whether the euro has taken on any significant international currency role.

The International Role of the Euro

Foreign exchange trading in euros as a percentage of global trade has not increased compared with the share of European Monetary System (EMS) currencies. In 1998, the dollar was present 87.3 percent of the time at one end of a transaction on the foreign exchange market while the EMS currencies were present 52.5 percent of the time (note that the shares sum to 200 percent because transactions involved pairs of currencies). In 2001, the share of the dollar was 90.4 percent and the share of the euro was a mere 37.6 percent. All the intra-European trades have been netted out with the arrival of the euro, so in fact there has been no dramatic fall in the share of the euro compared with the share of EMS currencies—but there has been no increase either. Similarly, though the share of the euro in reserves has been gradually increasing over time, it amounted to only 18.7 percent of total reserves in 2002 compared with 64.5 percent for the dollar.

The role of the euro for international trade in goods (i.e., the invoicing currency) has also markedly increased but is still below the dollar's level. For example, in 2002, 55.3 percent of French export goods were invoiced in euros. The comparable number was only 48 percent in 2000. Similarly, only 35 percent of French imports were invoiced in euros in 2000. In 2002, 46.8 percent were. As regional integration has been proceeding in Europe, the share of exports and imports invoiced and settled in euros has increased to approximately 60 to 80 percent for countries that acceded to the European Union in May 2004 (Cyprus, the Czech Republic, Hungary, Latvia, Estonia, Lithuania, Malta, Slovakia, Slovenia, and Poland).

But it is in the realm of international debt issuance that the euro has taken on more clearly an international role. The stock of international debt denominated in euros (excluding home-country issuance) rose from below 20 percent at then end of 1998 to just above 30 percent at the beginning of 2003. There are therefore clear signs of the gradual internationalization of the euro on international capital markets.

The First Five Years

The euro has successfully completed its first five years of existence. It has triggered important changes in European financial markets. It has also established itself immediately as the second most important currency in the world and as a potential competitor for the dollar. It has not, however, displaced in any significant way the dollar as the currency of choice for most international transactions and as a reserve currency. The main reason for this is the inherent inertia of the international monetary system (see Krugman 1984, Rey 2001).

Once a currency like the dollar is at the center of the system, it is very difficult for other currencies to compete with the incumbent because no economic agents find it desirable to use a currency different from the one that everyone else is using. It took a long time before the pound lost ground as an international currency and was replaced by the dollar, which had become a credible alternative over the years as the United States grew to become the biggest economy in the world (and the biggest exporter and importer). The dramatic change from the pound to the dollar occurred only after two world wars, after the stability of the pound had been significantly undermined, after the United Kingdom's importance in the world economy diminished, after New York's financial markets developed sufficiently to rival London's, and after the establishment of Bretton Woods.

Scenario for the Future

The euro has become a credible alternative to the dollar, given the size of the euro area economy in the world, and its active trade links with other areas. The European Central Bank has also established the reputation of the euro as a stable currency. But the United States is still the largest economic power in the world (unlike the United Kingdom after World War II). Hence there are reasons to believe that the future of the dollar as the main international currency is not threatened.

There are, however, also some elements pointing toward a potential shift in the relative importance of the euro and the dollar in the world economy. The United States has been running very substantial current account deficits in the past two decades. It has gone from a net creditor to a net debtor position, crossing the zero line around 1986. With US current account deficits now reaching 5 to 6 percent of GDP, a process of adjustment toward external solvency will have to come about. This adjustment will occur in particular through a substantial depreciation of the dollar (see Gourinchas and Rey 2004), which will both stimulate US exports in the long run but also impose sizable capital losses on foreign holders of US assets in the short to medium runs.

This very instability of the dollar, though necessary to restore the long-run external solvency of the US economy, may trigger portfolio shifts out of the dollar into the euro and other currencies, further undermining the stability of the dollar. The key question is therefore whether international investors will still accept taking capital losses on their dollar holdings and keep financing the US current account deficits at a low cost to the United States, as they currently do, or whether they will shift their wealth toward more stable nominal assets. In 2003 and 2004, most of the capital flows financing the deficits have come from Asian central banks accumulating liquid dollar assets as reserves to limit the appreciation of their currency vis-à-vis the dollar. Private flows into the United States have become scarcer. But international investor decisions have proven difficult to foresee, and at this stage it would be quite hazardous to make a definite prediction.

References

(BIS) Bank for International Settlements. 2003. *Quarterly Review,* March.

Bergsten, Fred. 1997. The Impact of the Euro on Exchange Rates and International Policy Cooperation. Paper presented at an IMF Conference, Washington, March 12–18.

Detken, Carsten, and Philip Hartmann. 2002. Features of the Euro's International Role in International Capital Markets. *Economic Policy* 35 (October): 553–70.

Dunne, Peter, Michael Moore, and Richard Portes. 2003. *Defining Benchmark Status: An Application Using Euro-Area Bonds.* CEPR Discussion Paper 3490; NBER Working Paper 9087. London: Centre for Economic Policy Research; Cambridge, MA: National Bureau of Economic Research.

ECB (European Central Bank). 2003. *Review of the International Role of the Euro.* Frankfurt: ECB.

Gourinchas, Pierre-Olivier, and Hélène Rey. 2004. International Financial Adjustment. www.princeton.edu/~hrey (forthcoming NBER Working Paper).

Kenen, Peter. 2003. The Euro and the Dollar: Competitors or Complements. www.princeton. edu/~pbkenen/.

Krugman, Paul. 1984. The International Role of the Dollar: Theory and Prospect, in *Exchange Rate Theory and Practice,* ed. John Bilson and Richard Marston. Chicago: University of Chicago Press.

Portes, Richard, and Hélène Rey. 1998. The Emergence of the Euro as an International Currency. *Economic Policy* 26 (April): 305–43.

Rey, Hélène. 2001. International Trade and Currency Exchange. *Review of Economic Studies* 68, no. 2: 443–64.

Financial Architecture of the Eurozone at Five

GARRY SCHINASI

The role of any currency in international finance reflects the confidence with which it is perceived as a reliably liquid instrument for financial transactions and as a store of value. This confidence must be earned and depends importantly, though not exclusively, on the depth, liquidity, and efficiency of the currency's home or domestic markets and on the array of liquid portfolio investment opportunities in those markets.

The euro area is still developing pan-European markets and is likewise in the process of earning confidence. The dollar already enjoys the confidence of international markets. In this regard, it is unreasonable to assume that the euro and the dollar are competing on equal terms: The dollar has the distinct advantage of having been there first and having gained substantial credibility. It has also demonstrated an ability to sustain this credibility even through some fairly trying times.

Overall, given the head start the dollar has had, I would judge the euro as performing remarkably well in international finance at the young age of five years. It is also fair to say that it has a long way to go before it reaches its full potential, both domestically and internationally.

The euro's role as an international vehicle for finance will grow as Europe develops a full array of deep, liquid, and efficient financial markets, extending well beyond its integrated money markets. So what will it take to further develop the depth and liquidity of Europe's markets?

For four aspects of financial architecture—the plumbing of financial markets—there are still important challenges. The first two, namely, *financial infrastructure* and *regulation*, have more to do with the effective-

Garry Schinasi is an adviser at the International Monetary Fund. The views expressed are his own and not those of the IMF, although much of it is based on material published by the IMF. See Prati and Schinasi (1997, 1999) and IMF (1997, chap. 3).

ness of markets; the second two have more to do with the financial-sector policy apparatus—namely, *prevention* of financial problems and *resolution* of them. Overcoming these challenges in a politically unified Europe would be difficult enough, but European policymakers do not have this convenience.

Financial Infrastructure

With regard to the financial infrastructure, given the observations in the other financially focused chapters in this volume, a simple example will suffice. Before the introduction of the euro, European markets had 31 systems for clearing and settling securities transactions. They also had 25 derivatives exchanges, 20 derivatives clearinghouses, and 15 stock exchanges. Markets were national, each one had a currency, and each nation needed its own system, either run by the government or sanctioned and regulated by it.

Five years after the introduction of the euro, progress has been made in reducing these redundancies, but the euro area still has too many such systems based on national needs rather than European needs. Having to deal with all these systems for clearing and settling securities transactions—mostly involving safe government securities—is very costly, cumbersome, and fraught with differences in accounting, other conventions, and business practices. It also strains liquidity management. There has been progress, but not enough, and this is holding back market integration.

Regulations

Regulations lay out the rules of the game of finance in markets. In the United States, financial regulation is primarily, if not exclusively, the purview of the federal government. There is a uniformity of rules, standards, business practices, and so on for issuing and trading securities, and there is the infrastructure to facilitate this activity that is so vital to the securitized form of finance that takes place in US markets.

The same cannot be said for Europe. Indeed, the opposite is true. There is a lack of uniformity and in fact a largely national orientation to securities regulation. Baron Lamfalussy and his committee have established a process whereby Europe can achieve significant convergence in securities, banking, and even insurance: the Financial Sector Action Plan. The committee was formed to come up with a procedure, and it did, albeit a very complicated and cumbersome one. But it did not have the mandate to examine the scope of each of these important areas requiring regulations. And not all national authorities agree on the procedures.

Crisis Prevention and Resolution

Turning to the prevention and resolution of problems, confidence in a financial system depends in part on perceptions about the ability of the system to withstand problems and resolve them quickly with minimum cost. Europe is still a bank-dominated financial system, so banking supervision is a vital component of crisis prevention.

Prevention

The present approach to banking supervision in Europe reflects three principles inherited from pre-euro Europe: decentralization, segmentation, and cooperation. The first means that the primary responsibility for supervision will remain at the national level, probably for both wholesale and retail institutions. The second means that separate supervisors (or departments within a single authority) are likely to remain for different types of financial institutions such as banks, securities firms, and insurance companies (leaving pension funds aside). The third means that cross-border and cross-sector gaps will have to be handled through closer cooperation between national authorities.

Decentralization, segmentation, and cooperation may work well in Europe, but this still remains to be seen. After all, one can say that the US architecture for financial supervision is even more complicated, multi-institutional, multijurisdictional, and segmented than it is in Europe. And it is at least a defensible statement that the United States has some of the most efficient and effective financial institutions in the world. I would even go further and say that US supervision of financial institutions has been effective overall.

But there are two fundamental differences between Europe's and the United States' architectures for financial supervision and how they work in practice. First, although there is some risk in the US system that a state supervisor would focus on the state's needs rather than the nation's, this is unlikely. If push comes to shove, the disparate parts of the US architecture have tended to focus on the nation's interest if this is what is required, especially because there is a sharing of responsibilities between federal and state regulators.

It is less obvious that national supervision in Europe would tend, as a first priority, to focus on European priorities. After all, there are still different national interests, treasuries, taxpayers, and even laws. And no arrangements for sharing responsibilities and authority for supervision are spelled out in the law or Maastricht Treaty. Cooperation may work smoothly in normal periods of financial activity. But when a large financial institution—with significant cross-border business and exposures—

licensed in one European country is having difficulties, it is difficult to imagine the national supervisor pursuing European interests first and national interests second. In short, there is a strong risk that a propensity to protect national institutions will endure, just as there has tended to be interest in producing national champions before mergers and acquisitions involving foreign institutions.

Second, despite the fragmentation of US supervision, there is a strong and unambiguous supervisor for the banking parts of very large financial holding companies. These holding companies make up the core of the US financial system, in terms of both the payments mechanisms and of providing market-making and liquidity services across the US financial system (and economy and even the global financial system). By payments mechanisms, I include those outside the official payments mechanism Fed Wire, such as CHIPs, and the less formal but perhaps equally important over-the-counter derivatives markets. This supervisor—the US Federal Reserve System—has had its authority over the large institutions solidified if not bolstered by the Gramm-Leach-Bliley Act. There is as yet no such supervisor in the euro zone overseeing the European equivalent of the major European financial institutions.

Resolution

Turning to the last area, the resolution of problems: Crisis management mechanisms are somewhat clearer in Europe today than they were five years ago. But they are still not clear enough to satisfy doubtful international market participants and other outsiders. In particular, it is not clear how a crisis involving a pan-European bank or one occurring across pan-European markets would be handled.

Let me illustrate this ambiguity, which does not appear to be constructive. The European System of Central Banks (ESCB) is entrusted with the "smooth operation of the payments system." In the specific case of a gridlock in the pan-European payments system TARGET, the Maastricht Treaty, which includes the statute establishing the ESCB, implies that the European Central Bank (ECB) has competence to act as lender of last resort.

What does the treaty imply if crisis does not originate in TARGET? It is not clear.

According to at least one legal scholar in Europe, the treaty is silent about whether the ECB has competence to act as lender of last resort (LOLR) (see Lastra 2003). According to Rosa Lastra, some have interpreted this silence as an indication that there is scope to enhance the ECB's authority in this area. Opposing this view, others see silence as an indication that the authority remains where it was before the treaty, namely, with national authorities. Still a third interpretation is that along with other ambiguities in the treaty, the subsidiary principle leaves open the possibility for a European Community competence, which could be exercised directly by the ECB or by the national central banks in their capacity as operational arms of the ESCB. Or perhaps it leaves open the door for some other European institution; it is just not clear.

Some see this ambiguity as constructive, which admittedly is desirable if it is confined to ambiguity about the conditions under which LOLR assistance would be appropriate. But this is not the kind of ambiguity in the treaty. Instead, this ambiguity seems to be about who does what or who has the authority.

There probably are informal, and perhaps even formal, written arrangements about who does what. But unless the markets have confidence that these mechanisms exist and that responsibilities are well defined and can be carried out effectively, they may count for naught in building confidence and establishing credibility in this important policy dimension.

In the case of a general drying up of liquidity related to market developments or an unanticipated shock, the treaty is probably sufficiently silent that the ECB could act through its "market operations approach" and supply liquidity to the markets. But how does it go about distinguishing liquidity from solvency problems when it does not have immediate, independent access to information about the creditworthiness of the major financial institutions, be they of German, Italian, or French nationality?[14]

Looking to the Future

These are some of the remaining but not insurmountable challenges. Overall, there should be little doubt that the euro is a major currency and a major force in international finance, second only to the dollar.

However, it is difficult to see the euro progressing much further without more improvement in each of these areas. First and foremost, this would entail increasing the depth, liquidity, transparency, and integration of European financial markets, which is a necessary condition for further progress internationally. Improving markets would, in my view, also facilitate a more rapid rationalization and consolidation of financial institutions in Europe, which is also needed for capturing the remaining and sizable potential efficiency gains of the European Union.

I do not expect progress to be very rapid. All the challenges outlined here have existed since 1999 when the euro was introduced. Progress has been made in each area. But it has not been rapid, and it has not been sufficient to enable the euro to reach its full potential to either catalyze the

---

14. For two distinct but related discussions of the role of central banks in ensuring financial stability see Schinasi (2003) and Padoa-Schioppa (2003).

creation of deep, liquid, and efficient pan-European markets or serve as an international vehicle for finance.

References

IMF (International Monetary Fund). 1997. *International Capital Markets: Developments, Prospects, and Key Policy Issues*. World Economic and Financial Surveys. Washington: IMF.

Lastra, Rosa. 2003. The Governance Structure for Financial Regulation and Supervision in Europe. *Columbia Journal of European Law* 10: 49–68.

Padoa-Schioppa, Tommaso. 2003. Central Banks and Financial Stability: Exploring the Land in Between. In *The Transformation of the European Financial System*, ed. V. Gaspar, P. Hartmann, and O. Sleijpen. Frankfurt: European Central Bank.

Prati, Alessandro, and Garry J. Schinasi. 1997. *European Monetary Union and International Capital Markets: Structural Implications and Risks*. IMF Working Paper WP/97/62. Washington: International Monetary Fund.

Prati, Alessandro, and Garry J. Schinasi. 1999. *Financial Stability in European Economic and Monetary Union*. Princeton Studies in International Finance 86. Princeton, NJ: Princeton University Press.

Schinasi, Garry. 2003. *Responsibility of Central Banks for Stability in Financial Markets*. IMF Working Paper 03/121. Washington: International Monetary Fund.

6

Can Rubinomics Work in the Eurozone?

ADAM S. POSEN

Most European policymakers view the Stability and Growth Pact (SGP) as vital to the eurozone's survival. Fiscal discipline is necessary to preserve price stability, particularly in a monetary union where countries might have the incentive to issue debt as free riders on other governments' credit ratings. According to this view, the Maastricht Treaty targets for public debt and deficit levels required an enforcement mechanism for members of the eurozone once they entered the currency union. Observers noted from the outset that the SGP constrained the ability of fiscal policy to stabilize the economy at the same time that national monetary policies were being yielded to the European Central Bank (ECB)—though estimates of the empirical relevance of this constraint varied widely.

An influential body of research on "expansionary consolidations" (beginning with Giavazzi and Pagano 1990) contributed to the design of the SGP. Drawing on "tales of two small European countries," the research held that there was actually no meaningful trade-off for policymakers between fiscal discipline and economic stabilization. Not only were the stabilizing benefits of fiscal policy (beyond limited automatic stabilizers such as unemployment benefits) exaggerated, but credible fiscal contractions would actually stimulate growth in the near term by reducing interest rates and increasing efficiency.

Adam S. Posen is a senior fellow at the Institute for International Economics. The author is grateful to his discussants at the conference on which the present volume is based, Jeffrey Frankel and Jürgen Kröger, for helpful comments, and to Daniel Gould for excellent research assistance.

According to this view, once the initial resistance of elected politicians defending pet programs could be surmounted, economies would quickly benefit from a budgetary consolidation. A virtuous circle would emerge of movements toward public surplus, lower interest rates, increased private-sector investment, and economic growth—in turn further improving government balance sheets. By the time the euro was launched on January 1, 1999, the shining example of such a dynamic was to be found across the Atlantic in the United States' expansion tied to a similar policy of "Rubinomics."[1]

If Rubinomics had been easily transferred transatlantically, and similar investment—and productivity-led expansion—had taken place in the eurozone during the first five years of the euro, the SGP would have been hailed as a masterwork of policy design. At present, however, the expansion has not occurred, and the SGP has come in for sharp criticism. The largest countries in the eurozone (France, Germany, and Italy) are currently in violation of the SGP, as are a couple of others, and only one of the smallest eurozone members, Portugal, has been punished for its SGP violations. The European Union's Council of Ministers was even taken to the European Court of Justice by the European Commission for its lax and uneven application of the SGP's sanctions, in a case setting major precedents for the emerging allocation of power between Brussels and the member states. As might have been expected, the European Court of Justice ducked the issue, ruling on a procedural matter, but a proposal to reform the SGP is near the top of the incoming European Commission's agenda. Perhaps contrary to some assumptions about the vulnerability of the euro to fiscal dominance, all of this has taken place without any obvious harmful impact on long-term interest rates, inflation expectations, or the exchange rate of the euro.

Can Rubinomics work in the eurozone? Would a more strict application of the SGP's rules have yielded the hoped-for benefits for European growth and interest rates? Or does the political resistance to the SGP by the eurozone's member states reflect some underlying inapplicability of this logic to their situation?

This chapter addresses these questions in six sections. First, it reviews the intended purposes and perceived problems of the SGP as seen in the first five years. Second, it considers whether the SGP has altered stabilization policy in the eurozone. Third, it assesses whether the channels that made expansionary consolidation possible in the US economy are operative in the eurozone economy. Fourth, it speculates on the likely impact

---

1. A far less salutary example in the other direction both geographically and economically was that of Japan—its tax hikes of 1997, and its fiscal policy in the 1990s more broadly. See Posen (1998b) and Kuttner and Posen (2002). As Fischer (2001) notes, the IMF relied in part on the expansionary consolidation argument to support the 1997 tax increases, and it later recognized that this was a mistaken application to Japan. Below, I list reasons for the policy's inapplicability to the eurozone as well, which are only partly parallel.

of current fiscal policies in the eurozone and the United States on the dollar/euro exchange rate. Fifth, it asks whether fiscal policy rules, like the SGP, can be relied upon as a means to better policy outcomes. Sixth, it concludes that Rubinomics cannot be replicated in the eurozone, because there are neither the responsive investment markets nor the incentives for governments present in Europe necessary to make it work—as is clearly shown by the response of Italy to eurozone membership, even though Italy should have been the greatest beneficiary of expansionary consolidation. As a result, reforms of the SGP that tweak the rules may reduce political friction between Brussels and the national capitals, but they will have little impact upon either member states' fiscal policies or the euro's overall stability.

The SGP's Purposes and Problems

The eurozone supposedly needed the SGP for four reasons: one, to prevent profligate national governments from issuing more public debt in hopes of a bailout from the ECB and/or free riding on more disciplined countries' credit ratings; two, to limit the degree to which member countries would expand their public debt after entering the eurozone, having squeezed to meet the Maastricht criteria; three, to maintain long-run price stability and the autonomy of the ECB by preventing fiscal erosion; and four, to encourage national economies to continue with structural reform during contractions rather than relying on the perceived easy out of expanding government programs. Though all of these were worthwhile goals, their connection to the SGP was based on some dubious assumptions.

First, it was assumed that stabilization policy (in the form of expansion during recessions) tends to increase government deficits in a lasting manner, so the expansion had to be limited. The evidence on this connection is far from clear, however, even drawing on the 1970s (Masson and Mussa 1995), so it is equally unclear that constraining stabilization would lead to fiscal discipline over the longer term. Second, it was assumed that financial markets would not differentiate between countries' public debts, once they were all denominated in euros, so rules were required to prevent free riding. Though interest rates initially did converge among the eurozone member states, there are signs that over time—as the euro itself and the independence of the ECB are taken more for granted—there will be more distinction by markets between different members' debt obligations, just as there is between state governments' debt ratings in the United States. Both of these false assumptions simply overstated the need for the SGP but did little to impinge upon its operation.

Other mistaken assumptions, however, proved more directly dangerous to the SGP's viability. Third, it was assumed that punishments for pact violations would be credible, despite their relying on peer review in

Ecofin (the council of economic and financial ministers). But they were not credible, as was amply demonstrated in the first instances where they might apply. Fourth, underlying the previous assumption, in practice, was the assumption that the major eurozone economies would be largely synchronized with the monetary policy set by the ECB for the zone as a whole, thereby minimizing the need for such fiscal deviations and punishments. In recent years, the opposite unluckily turned out to be the case, with Germany and Italy being most visibly out of sync with ECB policy on the side of excessive tightness.

Fifth, and perhaps most critically, the assumption was made that the loss of countercyclical policy by the national governments would be accepted in any event, both because the room allowed for automatic stabilizers would prove sufficient for most downturns and because the benefits of expansionary consolidations would become evident (and buy off opposition). Neither proved to be the case, with a sharp but not historic recession in 2001–03 justifying greater response than the SGP allowed, and no sign of any investment or productivity boom in those countries whose interest rates dropped upon meeting the Maastricht criteria and entering the eurozone.

Thus, by the time of the euro's fifth anniversary in January 2004, the European Commission had brought suit against the Council of the European Union before the European Court of Justice requesting that the Court (in the convoluted prose of the Court's case law) "annul the Council's failure to adopt decisions to give notice [of sanctions under the SGP's Excessive Deficit Procedure] to France and Germany" for their violations of the SGP.[2] The SGP had been de facto suspended in November 2003, when the Council had given the two major countries passes on sanctions, despite their repeated violations of the 3 percent deficit limit and their lack of credible plans to bring the deficits down in the immediate future (France, in fact, openly stated its unwillingness to constrain its budget policy until it was ready to do so). The major fault pointed to by supporters of the SGP, including the Commission and the ECB, was the failure of the SGP to induce member governments to cut budgets during good times, which in theory would have allowed those governments to expand their deficits more during recessions.

Yet there was more to the SGP's breakdown than the supposed asymmetry of government behavior with respect to budget policy and the business cycle. As noted, a severe recession was centered in Germany and Italy, while eurozone monetary policy was only mildly eased in response

---

2. Press Release 57/04, Judgment of the Court of Justice in Case C-27/04, *Commission of the European Communities v. Council of the European Union*, European Court of Justice, July 13, 2004. Ultimately, the European Court of Justice decided that the EC's desire for giving notice to France and Germany could not be imposed upon the Council, but that the Council could not formally hold the excessive deficit procedure "in abeyance."

to the diminished inflationary pressures continentwide. Moreover, most of the economies in question were undertaking structural reforms, including significant permanent tax cuts and restructuring for efficiency reasons, that made it harder to meet deficit targets. There was also a significant gap between the concerned response of the Commission members, who are the delegated monitors of the SGP, and the tepid responses of the financial markets and the popular opinion, which are the ultimate enforcers of fiscal discipline. Ultimately, the combination of less-than-credible threats and putative benefits of the SGP did not provide sufficient incentive for eurozone member governments to adhere to the SGP under the existing strained, but hardly unlikely, circumstances and the other priorities they had for fiscal policy.

The SGP's Effect on Stabilization Policy

For all the hue and cry about the SGP, has it altered the eurozone economies' fiscal policy behavior, and in particular the response of fiscal policy to the business cycle, from what it had been before the adoption of the euro? The common presumption is that the 12 countries of the eurozone had the worst of both worlds—the SGP had constrained fiscal response to the recent downturn to below desirable levels—but had not constrained policy enough (whether in the upturns or overall) to meet the SGP commitments. This is ultimately an empirical question: Have the eurozone member countries' budget balances responded less to movements in national GDP than they did before Maastricht? The answer to this question gives important information both economically and politically about the SGP: Economically, what is the state of fiscal discipline and its relation to stabilization policy in the eurozone? And politically, were the strictures of the SGP at least partially credible in constraining government behavior?

To make this assessment, I estimate simple fiscal reaction functions of systematic change in public-sector balances in response to variation in economic growth. "Systematic" refers to policies that are undertaken consistently as a result of similar economic conditions, whether or not they would be labeled a priori as formal automatic stabilizers.[3] This builds on earlier work using a similar approach by Bayoumi and Eichengreen (1992) and Posen (1998b). Here, I estimate the relationship between changes in year-over-year GDP growth rates and changes in budget balances for a sample of 18 major economies that belong to the Organization for Economic Cooperation and Development (OECD), including 10 members of

---

3. In the US context, for example, unemployment benefits are regularly extended by Congress during recessions. Even though only the original legislated duration of unemployment benefits could be said formally to be automatic stabilizers, and the extensions require discretionary authorization (a fact honored in the breach during this past recession), this is part of the systematic response of US fiscal policy to recessions.

the eurozone (excluding Greece and Luxembourg) and the three EU members that are outside the eurozone (Denmark, Sweden, and the United Kingdom). The ordinary least squares regression estimate for each country (not a panel), starting with the earliest available annual OECD data, is

$$\Delta Bal/GDP_t = \beta_0 + \beta_1 \Delta \ln GDP_t + \beta_2 Rev/GDP_t + \beta_3 Bal_{t-1}/GDP_{t-1}$$
$$+ \beta_4 (1992\text{--}2003 \text{ dummy})^* \Delta \ln GDP_t + \beta_5 (1969\text{--}79 \text{ dummy})^* \Delta \ln GDP_t \quad (1)$$

The variable *Bal* is the central government balance, including social security funds. The idea is to compare the fiscal response in each country, controlling for prior deficit levels (on the presumption that higher outstanding deficits would lead to diminished willingness or ability to borrow). *Rev* is central government revenues, meant to control loosely for the amount that taxes move with the cycle, ceteris paribus. The coefficient β_1 on GDP growth is the primary measure of the degree of movement in the government's budget position in response to changes in output. A significantly positive β_1 coefficient would indicate a consistently countercyclical fiscal response.

The two period dummies, for 1969–79 and for 1992–2003, are meant to capture cross-national effects. In particular, these are intended to capture shifts in policy norms over time, toward activist fiscal policy in the heyday of the Keynesian response to the oil shocks of the 1970s, and toward fiscal conservatism during the 1990s. If the eurozone's discipline on members' fiscal policy were to have an effect, it would show up in a significantly negative coefficient β_4 for members only, or rather a significantly larger coefficient for members than for the non–eurozone members (if all countries moved toward discipline during this period). The period of the 1992–2003 dummy variable of course extends beyond the period of the SGP itself (which runs 1999 to present), which had to be done for statistical reasons. That said, because it covers the period from the Maastricht Treaty onwards, it includes the period of putative fiscal consolidation to meet the public debt and deficit targets for entry to the eurozone and so, if anything, should bias towards finding in the results evidence of a shift away from countercyclical fiscal policy and towards discipline. The SGP was always meant to enforce maintenance of these targets once they were attained in the run-up to EMU.

Because the SGP is an adjunct to the Maastricht Treaty, drafted and signed at the same time, it is fair to suggest that the prospect of the SGP's implementation should have been affecting fiscal policy formulation in prospective eurozone members from the time of the treaty's adoption. If anything, this should bias the results toward finding a significant negative β_4 coefficient (i.e., a constraining effect of the SGP on stabilization policy), because it includes the pre-euro years where countries undertook one-time efforts to bring down debt and deficits to qualify for euro membership.

The estimated results are presented in table 6.1. The results are broadly sensible, with most coefficients on revenue/GDP positive (consistent with

Table 6.1 Countercyclical response of fiscal stance; dependent variable: Change in the general government budget balance (percent of GDP)

Country	Change in ln GDP	Revenue/GDP	Lagged government balance	1992–2003 dummy	1969–79 dummy	Adjusted R^2	Years covered
Australia	0.115	-0.003	-0.149	0.237	-0.181	0.1285	1962–2003
Austria	0.189	-0.051	-0.326*	0.064	0.067	0.1886	1964–2003
Belgium	0.272	0.202	-0.144	0.407	0.025	0.0897	1970–2003
Canada	0.460**	0.079	-0.098	0.242	n.a.	0.4992	1981–2003
Denmark	0.739**	0.284**	-0.053	-0.456*	0.023	0.5649	1971–2003
Finland	0.383**	0.016	-0.063	0.261	-0.059	0.3675	1960–2003
France	0.502**	0.040	-0.315**	-0.032	0.058	0.5292	1963–2003
Germany	0.348**	-0.093	-0.570**	0.454*	0.127	0.2049	1962–2003
Ireland	0.240	0.418*	-0.004	-0.039	-0.429	0.3308	1977–2003
Italy	0.460**	0.0875*	-0.109*	0.320	0.039	0.3658	1960–2003
Japan	0.434**	0.000	-0.159*	-0.227	-0.286*	0.3958	1970–2003
Netherlands	0.094	-0.049	-0.396**	0.370	0.226	0.2960	1969–2003
Norway	0.297	0.809**	-0.639**	0.718**	-0.161	0.7631	1975–2003
Portugal	0.136	0.0828*	-0.362**	0.134	0.247	0.3594	1969–2003
Spain	0.259**	0.010	-0.134	0.246*	0.001	0.3186	1964–2003
Sweden	0.756**	0.076	-0.118	0.005	-0.207	0.2803	1963–2003
United Kingdom	0.283	0.331	-0.245	0.558	-0.148	0.3237	1970–2003
United States	0.414**	0.298**	-0.240**	0.307**	0.023	0.6484	1960–2003

*, ** indicates significance at the 5 and 1 percent levels.

Note: A positive coefficient on change in GDP indicates a countercyclical response of the overall fiscal stance. OLS regression estimated: $\Delta(Bal_t/GDP_t) = \beta_0 + \beta_1 {}^*\Delta lnGDP_t + \beta_2 {}^*Rev_t/GDP_t + \beta_3 {}^*Bal_{t-1}/GDP_{t-1} + \beta_4 {}^*(1992–2003 \text{ dummy} {}^* \Delta ln[GDP_t]) + \beta_5 {}^*(1969–79 \text{ dummy} {}^* \Delta ln[GDP_t]) + error$. A dummy was added for 1991 in Germany to take into account the one-time fiscal and data effects of reunification (it was significant at the 1 percent level).

Source: Organization for Economic Cooperation and Development, Economic Outlook 74.

a procyclical variation in tax receipts) and all on lagged government balance negative (consistent with a tendency for recent deficits to constrain current spending). Most important for our present purposes, not a single eurozone member has a significant negative coefficient on the 1992–2003 dummy, which is consistent with no reduction in the countercyclicality of budget deficits post-Maastricht.[4] In fact, the bulk of estimates of β_4, and a majority of the significant coefficients on the 1992–2003 dummy, are positive irrespective of eurozone or even EU membership. Even the United States during the Bill Clinton administration if anything increased its responsiveness to the business cycle while paying down its debt during the boom years (and going into debt during the 2001–03 downturn under President George W. Bush).

Because this includes the mid-1990s, as well as the post-euro-adoption period, this result indicates that even during the run-up to euro membership covering a time of expansion for most EU economies, budget positions did not improve more than would be accounted for by the usual procyclical factors. Figures 6.1, 6.2, and 6.3 bear this out, plotting the fitted versus actual year-over-year change in government balance for the three major eurozone countries. Germany was indeed more countercyclical than forecast for the period 1992–2003, but was symmetrically so on both the up and down cycles. France as well appears to have become more countercyclical than expected based on past behavior since the adoption of the euro in 1999, but again in both directions not simply toward ease. Italy's fiscal behavior after Maastricht is fit well by the estimated reaction function for the entire post-1960 period, only deviating toward surplus in 1997, as one might expect with one-off privatization measures to show motion toward the Maastricht targets. Figure 6.4 plots the debt/GDP ratios of these three economies; relatively steady increasing trends are evident for France and Germany, while Italy has fluctuated around an already high level. In short, the picture that emerges is one in which the Maastricht Treaty and the SGP have had no significant impact on eurozone fiscal policy.[5]

---

4. In fact, two eurozone member countries, Germany and Spain, have significant positive coefficients on the 1992–2003 dummy, and Italy's is positive and nearly significant. This holds even when knocking out the observation for 1991 in Germany due to the effects of reunification (significant at the 1 percent level). The next section offers a partial explanation for this result.

5. Gali and Perotti (2003), using a different statistical approach, come to a similar broad conclusion: that fiscal policy did not change with monetary integration in Europe, and if anything became more countercyclical. Buti and van den Noord (2003) also conclude that the SGP did not constrain stabilization policy. McNamara (2003) usefully points out that the standard deviation of eurozone member states' deficits has been increasing slightly over time, a fact inconsistent with what was supposed to be a move toward keeping deficits within a common limited range and a more synchronized eurozone business cycle.

Figure 6.1 German fiscal response, 1990–2003: A bit more countercyclical, but symmetrically

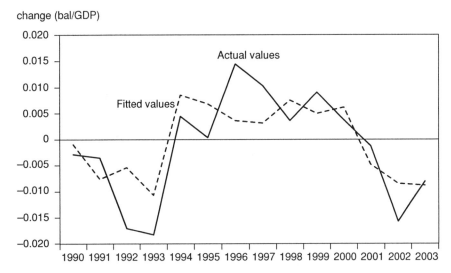

change (bal/GDP)

Note: Estimated: $\Delta(Bal_t/GDP_t) = 0.021 + 0.348^*\Delta lnGDP_t - 0.093^*Rev_t/GDP_t - 0.57^* Bal_{t-1}/GDP_{t-1} + 0.454^*(1992–2003 \text{ dummy}^*\Delta ln[GDP_t]) + 0.127^*(1969–79 \text{ dummy}^*\Delta ln[GDP_t])$. A 1991 dummy variable was added to the specification. It was significant at the 1 percent level. Fitted values were calculated for the entire 1960–2003 period, but only the 1990–2003 results are shown here.

Source: Organization for Economic Cooperation and Development, *Economic Outlook 74.*

Blocked Channels for Expansionary Consolidations

Some supporters of the SGP insist that if only the member governments had carried through on their budgetary commitments, there would have been growth benefits aplenty. As was noted above, the work of Giavazzi and Pagano (1990) gave birth to an influential literature promising such a virtuous circle.[6] Working from the examples of apparent expansionary consolidations in Denmark (1983–84) and Ireland (1987–88)—as well as the infamous converse example of France's contractionary expansion (under François Mitterrand's first term of "Socialism in One Country") and later emerging-market examples championed by IMF researchers—the European Commission drew inspiration for an eventually self-enforcing

---

6. The European Commission (2003, 99–123) gives a very thorough summary of the empirical and theoretical literature.

Figure 6.2 French fiscal response, 1990–2003: Also did more in both directions

change (bal/GDP)

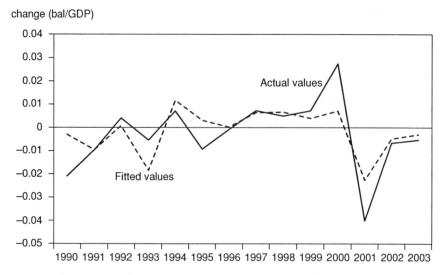

Note: Estimated: $\Delta(Bal_t/GDP_t) = 0.039 + 0.502^*\Delta lnGDP_t + 0.040^*Rev_t/GDP_t - 0.315^*Bal_{t-1}/GDP_{t-1} - 0.032^*(1992\text{--}2003\ \text{dummy}^*\Delta ln[GDP_t]) + 0.058^*(1969\text{--}79\ \text{dummy}^*\Delta ln[GDP_t])$. Fitted values were calculated for the entire 1960–2003 period, but only the 1990–2003 results are shown here.

Source: Organization for Economic Cooperation and Development, *Economic Outlook 74.*

SGP and reform cycle.[7] The greatest exponent and example of such a policy dynamic, however, was Rubinomics in the United States during the Clinton administration:

> The restoration of fiscal discipline reduced or eliminated the possibility that continued fiscal morass would eventually lead either to an effort to inflate our way out of debt problems or to higher taxes to pay debt service. And that increase in confidence affected business decisions about investment, expansion, and hiring, as well as consumer decisions, and produced a greater flow of foreign capital into our savings-deficient nation to finance investment here, lowering our cost of capital . . . a virtuous cycle of debt reduction promoting growth which further reduced the deficit, which then in turn further increased growth, and so on back and forth. (former US Treasury secretary Robert Rubin, in Frankel and Orszag 2002, 132)

Would a similar virtuous cycle have taken hold in the eurozone if only the member governments had abided by the letter and the spirit of the

---

7. It needs to be noted that even the Danish case has come under scrutiny by experts on that economy as to whether it truly was an example of an expansionary consolidation. See Bergmar and Hutchison (1999).

Figure 6.3 Italian fiscal response, 1990–2003: Only deviated a lot in 1997—toward *surplus*

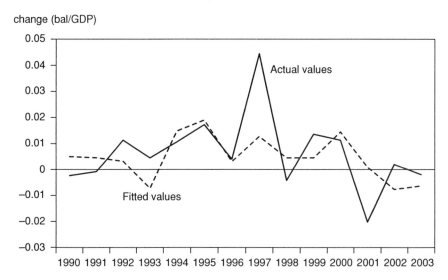

change (bal/GDP)

Note: Estimated: $\Delta(\text{Bal}_t/\text{GDP}_t) = 0.054 + 0.46^*\Delta\ln\text{GDP}_t + 0.088^*\text{Rev}_t/\text{GDP}_t - 0.108^*\text{Bal}_{t-1}/\text{GDP}_{t-1} + 0.32^*(1992\text{–}2003 \text{ dummy}^*\Delta\ln[\text{GDP}_t]) + 0.039^*(1969\text{–}79 \text{ dummy}^*\Delta\ln[\text{GDP}_t])$. Fitted values were calculated for the entire 1960–2003 period, but only the 1990–2003 results are shown here.

Source: Organization for Economic Cooperation and Development, *Economic Outlook 74.*

SGP? Leaving aside the echoes of those monetarists in decades past who insisted that inflation would have been controlled if only the central banks had adhered to those targets, this hypothesis has to be assessed empirically. Unfortunately, because the governments in question did not follow the SGP even partially, let alone follow more ambitious fiscal consolidation agendas, the eurozone offers few data with which to examine this question empirically. So instead, let us break down logically what is required for an expansionary consolidation cycle to occur:

- Interest rates must respond strongly to fiscal consolidation. This usually requires beginning in a state of low confidence and/or a high debt/GDP ratio. The share of debt owed to foreigners usually must be large enough that consolidation reduces the interest rate paid (i.e., an exchange rate premium).

- Business investment must respond strongly to interest rate reduction. This usually requires forward-looking financial markets and flexible corporations. There should be a shortage of capital funds available rel-

Figure 6.4   Gross government debt/GDP ratios, 1990–2003

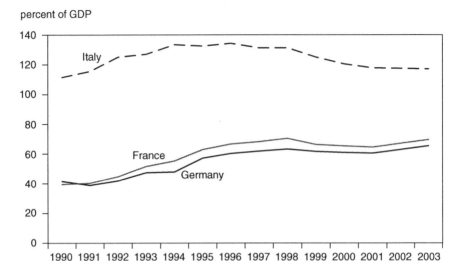

percent of GDP

Source: Data from Organization for Economic Cooperation and Development, *Economic Outlook 75.*

ative to the number of possible productive investment projects outstanding. It helps if consumers have access to credit and are not dependent upon fixed-rate income if their expenditure response is to feed the dynamic.

- Growth in productivity and in employment must respond strongly to the increases in investment and consumption.

- And, to complete the cycle, government revenue must respond strongly to the increase in growth (e.g., through capital gains taxes on rising equities).

These attributes were all present in the United States, giving rise to the virtuous cycle of the 1990s. But these are not the attributes of the large eurozone economies. They are instead the attributes of the smaller eurozone economies and of the euro "outs" (Denmark, Sweden, and the United Kingdom) to varying degrees.

Only one of the large eurozone member economies (Italy) entered the eurozone in 1999 with high indebtedness and low confidence that its debt would be fully repaid, and thus was a candidate for immediate benefits from fiscal consolidation. France and Germany had the lowest interest rates on their sovereign debt among EU members in the years running up to EMU, and both still have public debt to GDP ratios well under 70 percent even after recent years' SGP-violating deficits. Italy itself still has too little debt held abroad to see much of an interest rate response on its borrowing, and Germany and France have hardly any foreign-held debt. Domestic saving in all three countries is very high, much higher than in the United States, and in Germany and Italy savers are far more risk averse. The willingness of savers to reallocate their funds in response to interest rate movements is rather low in these countries. All these factors limit the interest rate response to public consolidation.

The transmission channels from interest rate declines to growth are even more dubious for the major eurozone economies. Due to the government-protected overbanking and public-sector financial institutions in these economies, the return to capital is too low and the intermediaries do not tend to invest in risky projects either (Posen 2003). The result is an excess of loanable funds rather than a shortage, as the United States had, and a shortage of productive investment projects because "long-term" banking relationships lock funds up and distort incentives, also the opposite of the US situation.

Various other regulatory barriers to best practices and competition limit the productivity or employment response in Europe to even productive investment, as compared with the United States (Baily and Kirkegaard 2004). Thus, what worked for the United States and for (say) Ireland in terms of an expansionary consolidation would probably not work for Germany, France, or Italy. And even if they did begin to work, the effect on government revenues would be lower than in the United States, given the structure of taxation in these countries (including higher dependence on taxation of labor and consumption than of capital compared with the United States) and of the social safety net (including long-term unemployment, which is less responsive to the business cycle than in the United States).

In this light, one begins to see the major eurozone economies' unwillingness to adhere to the SGP or to undertake major fiscal consolidation as more of a rational, if not optimal, response to economic realities than a case of pusillanimous policymakers.[8] On the one hand, these countries are unlikely to reap much in the way of benefits from fiscal consolidation in the near term, unless they are facing crowding-out constraints, which they are not, given their low returns on capital and extensive household savings. These economies are not candidates for Rubinesque virtuous cycles, given their structural problems as well as simply their structures.

On the other hand, being the largest and least open eurozone economies, these three countries give up the most by passing up fiscal stabilization policy after Maastricht. In general, the larger and less open the economic zone

---

8. This does not refer to the need for all aging societies—especially Italy and Germany, but also including the United States—to take on the long-term fiscal dangers from rising old-age and health entitlements. The reluctance of politicians in almost all countries to confront such distant but real threats is well established. It is also of little relevance to the discussion here, because any fiscal consolidation that might result from adherence to the SGP would be only a partial first step toward balancing the generational accounts. See Peterson (1999).

Figure 6.5 Size and countercyclical response, 1980–2003

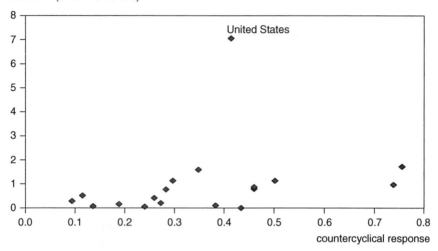

real GDP (trillions of dollars)

Note: Spearman correlation = 0.69.

Source: GDP data from Organization for Economic Cooperation and Development, Economic Outlook 74.

over which fiscal policy acts, the larger the impact of stabilization measures on the economy. This is borne out in the countercyclicality of policies estimated in table 6.1. If one plots the estimated degree of budget response to the cycle versus economic size, as is done in figure 6.5, one finds a clear positive association—the Spearman rank-order correlation (thereby giving equal weight to observations rather than overweighting by size) between the two is 0.69. Similarly, if one plots the estimated countercyclical fiscal response versus openness (defined as imports + exports/GDP), as is done in figure 6.6, there is an obvious negative association; the Spearman correlation is –0.58. Because the relative share of eurozone member countries' exports priced in their own currency has gone up as a result of eurozone entry, the effective openness of their economies is even lower than this ratio, and one would expect the utility of countercyclical policy to increase accordingly.

And given the well-recognized fact that a eurozone-wide monetary policy is inherently less targeted toward Germany's business cycle than the Bundesbank's policy was (when it set monetary policy for the Exchange Rate Mechanism countries), the relative worth to Germany of utilizing countercyclical fiscal policy has increased. To the degree that France and Italy were more synchronized with the German cycle than with the output gaps implied by the ECB's eurozone-wide inflation and monetary targets (which recent years' price and output trends in Italy at least seem to indicate), the same increase in the relative importance of fiscal stabilization

Figure 6.6 Openness and countercyclical response, 1980–2003

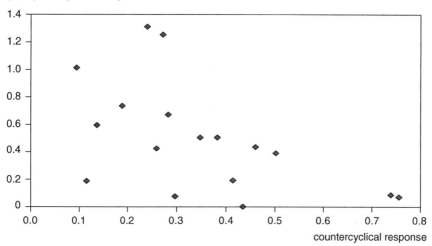

(X+M)/GDP (real values)

Note: Spearman correlation = –0.58.

Source: GDP data from Organization for Economic Cooperation and Development, *Economic Outlook 74.*

holds. If France and Italy were able in the pre-euro times to reset their currencies' parities to the deutsche mark more often than vulnerable small economies—as the historical record seems to reveal by comparison with, for example, Austria's and Belgium's strict adherence to pre–Economic and Monetary Union deutsche mark pegs—that adds to the loss of stabilization from coming under the eurozone's one monetary policy to fit all.[9]

Thus, on all economic counts—their low likelihoods of attaining a Rubinesque virtuous circle, their size and decreasing openness, and their loss of a meaningful degree of monetary stabilization—it is rational for policymakers in the major eurozone economies to ignore the SGP and to increasingly utilize fiscal stabilization policy. And that is in line with the results of our investigation of the direction fiscal behavior has taken in Europe since 1992. It needs to be noted as well that this argument is made without

9. In its excellent meta-study of empirical work on expansionary consolidations in Europe, the European Commission (2003) notes that more than half of expansionary consolidations identified were accompanied by monetary easing. Taking into account the inherent lags of fiscal policy as well—meaning that consolidations often take place when the business cycle has already turned up, so the subsequent expansions are not fully attributable to the budgetary consolidations—the number of "pure" expansionary consolidations is few. This only strengthens the argument that the big three eurozone economies are rational to forswear consolidation or limits on their countercyclical policies in the absence of accommodation by or coordination with the ECB.

reference to political pressures, elections, or politicians' high discount rates, which there is no reason to think would be systematically different in France, Italy, or Germany than in other eurozone member countries.

Fiscal Gaps, Euro Strength, and Dollar Weakness

Does the fiscal behavior of the eurozone economies, and the big three's disregard of the SGP in particular, really matter for the euro and for monetary policy? Most European policymakers—whether at the ECB, at the European Commission, or outside the current governments in question—believe it does matter very much.[10] Some market observers claim to agree, though long-term interest rates for the eurozone have not risen noticeably in response to SGP violations more than cyclical and oil-price factors alone would require. As the IMF's 2004 Article IV Consultation Discussion with the Euro-Area Countries points out in its Concluding Statement, there has been little slippage in the euro area's overall debt position (even though more progress on the long-term sustainability issues would be desirable). Figure 6.7 shows the overall debt/GDP and deficit/GDP ratios of the eurozone. Even with French and German fiscal expansion in recent years, the deficit ratio has remained below its 3 percent target, while the overall debt ratio has been essentially stable at below 80 percent and, thus, below the level when the euro was launched.

Certainly, by comparison with the erosion of the US fiscal position during the 2000–03 period, a shift from nearly 2 percent of GDP surplus to 5 percent deficit annually, the eurozone economies have little to bemoan—and that fiscal erosion occurred while the Federal Reserve was aggressively easing monetary policy and the dollar was depreciating, both of which should have lessened the need for stabilization policy.[11] The mounting public debt and record deficits of the Japanese government also made the eurozone look good by comparison.[12] If inflation differentials drive ex-

---

10. See, inter alia, Issing (2003), Tanzi (2003), and of course the European Commission's court case.

11. Of course, countercyclical stabilization was not the primary motivation for the Bush administration's tax cuts or Congress' spending increases, as acknowledged by both the administration's critics and advocates. It merely served as a useful additional excuse for pursuing a policy previously desired. See the discussions by Hubbard (2004) and Frankel (comment in this volume). Muehleisen and Towe (2004) provide an extremely useful and objective analysis of the shift in US fiscal policies.

12. Broda and Weinstein (2004) point out, however, that a fairer and more careful comparison of the Japanese and other OECD members' public accounts puts the level of net Japanese public debt much lower than is commonly recognized. Though I strongly agree with their assessment, there is no question that the decline in Japanese public balances over the post-1992 period was sharp, and the eurozone saw nothing comparable.

Figure 6.7 Eurozone total debt and deficit, 1990–2003

government debt/GDP
(percent of GDP)

government balance/GDP
(percent of GDP)

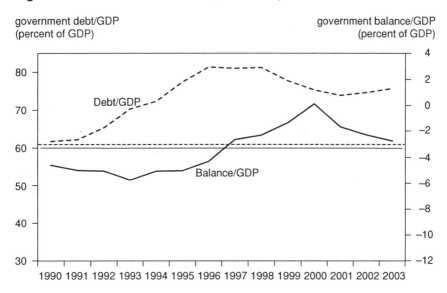

Notes: "Deficit to GDP" limit imposed by Maastricht Treaty (right scale = 3 percent of GDP).
"Debt to GDP" limit imposed by Maastricht Treaty (left scale = 60 percent of GDP).

Source: Organization for Economic Cooperation and Development, Economic Outlook 74.

change rate trends toward purchasing power parity, and fiscal overhang drives long-run inflation expectations (assuming central banks equally committed to price stability), Europe's relative fiscal probity should be a recipe for relative euro appreciation over time.[13] Though this may not be of consolation to central bankers concerned about increasing global liquidity and the eventual effect on the world price levels (if such things exist), it should be reassuring to the ECB and European citizens about the relative purchasing power of the euro, even in the long run.

Macroeconomists, however, actually are split in their analysis of the likely impact of fiscal consolidation (or expansion) upon exchange rates in the short to medium run. This is best illustrated by the debate between Laurence Ball and N. Gregory Mankiw on one side, and Alan Greenspan on the other, at the Federal Reserve's annual Jackson Hole meeting in 1995 on "Budget Deficits and Debt." Ball and Mankiw (1995) suggested that a fiscal consolidation would reduce interest rates by reducing crowding out, thereby narrowing interest rate differentials in favor of the home currency

---

13. Chinn (1997) and Cheung, Chinn, and Pascual (2002) discuss the relevance of such fundamentals to long-term movements (and their irrelevance to short-term movements) in exchange rates.

and leading to a depreciation. Greenspan (1995) agreed that a fiscal consolidation would reduce interest rates, but (foreshadowing Rubinomics) he argued that an increase in confidence and productivity would result, leading to an appreciation. Realistically, both effects are in play for all governments at all times; the question is which one predominates.[14]

In Europe, the more traditional crowding effect cited by Ball and Mankiw should dominate, because the Rubinesque effect is weak for all the reasons offered above. In addition, because financial markets are relatively illiquid in the eurozone, the crowding-out effect should be larger than in the United States.[15] Thus, fiscal laxity in the form of ignoring the SGP should at the margin push up both interest rates and the euro. In the United States, where the economy is much more dependent upon forward-looking asset markets and flows of foreign capital, the confidence effect is likely to dominate. Accordingly, fiscal laxity in the United States should lead to a currency weakening, as expressed by Greenspan.

In addition, the fiscal laxity in the eurozone is being treated by the ECB as a reason to avoid premature loosening, thus emulating for the euro the Paul Volcker–Ronald Reagan monetary-fiscal policy conflict that pumped up the dollar in the early 1980s. By contrast, despite some rhetoric about the need for attention to the long-term growth of entitlements, the current Federal Reserve is accommodating the George W. Bush administration's fiscal expansion, and in particular its tax cuts. This will tend to push the dollar down as well.

These fiscal factors should not be oversold as determinants of exchange rates in the near to medium term. Chinn and Frankel (2003) establish that US interest rates still have a significant effect on eurozone interest rates, without evidence of a complementary influence in the other direction; the US current account deficits require some amount of dollar depreciation to be brought back to sustainability (see Bergsten and Williamson 2003), whatever happens on the fiscal front from here; a lack of savings resulting from fiscal excess is a far greater problem in the United States than in the eurozone. Accordingly, all the fiscal policy factors, even taken solely on their own terms, seem to point over the next few years to a stronger euro versus the dollar, despite the major eurozone economies ignoring the SGP.

---

14. There is clear evidence of a meaningful but not huge crowding-out effect of budget deficits in the United States, despite the forward-looking markets present. See the recent convergence of empirical results in Engen and Hubbard (2004), Gale and Orszag (2004), and Laubach (2003).

15. However, that has improved significantly since the adoption of the euro, as is documented in the contributions to this volume by the members of the panel on financial markets and by Bernanke.

Are Fiscal Policy Rules Ever-Binding?

The Stability and Growth Pact is widely and properly seen as a use of rules-based fiscal policy.[16] Although macroeconomic policy rules were once primarily the province of monetary policy, such measures as the SGP, the balanced-budget rules in the United States, and the adoption of PAYGO by Congress in the 1990s have brought attention to the use of such rules in fiscal policy as well. This is part of the more general European thrust since the Single European Act toward treating economic problems in the European Union as matters of institutional design, with an emphasis on the creation of "binding commitments" on governments to adopt "time-consistent" policies (see Posen 1998a). Essentially, the idea is that while elected politicians have short time horizons and high discount rates, given their electoral incentives, the economy as a whole is better off if the politicians can be constrained from acting on those short-term incentives. Budgetary rules like the SGP are meant to keep politicians from spending too much or taxing too little in the hopes of immediate gains.

Ultimately, for such fiscal rules to work, there either must be a benefit from adherence to the rules that shows up sufficiently strongly and credibly for some groups in society to insist on enforcing the rules, or the rules must themselves be enforced by threats and if necessary punishments from an outside authority. The declared existence of a rule itself does not become self-enforcing, whatever the claims about reputational effects, if the incentives are not present. Bond markets alone cannot be the enforcement mechanism of the rules, for if those markets' sanctions, such as increases in interest rates in response to budgetary laxity, were sufficiently scary to the governments, there would be no need for the rule in the first place.

As we have seen, the SGP fails on both counts to be a viable fiscal rule: The unlikely benefits of expansionary consolidation in the eurozone context are not credible; whereas the very real benefits for large, less open eurozone members to use countercyclical policy to offset the loss of monetary autonomy are credible. The European Commission (EC) does not have sufficient authority to impose punishments on eurozone member states, and the member states have no interest in punishing themselves. This would explain why, as shown above, the SGP ultimately made no significant difference to the fiscal behavior of the eurozone's major member economies.

This outcome is not peculiar to the SGP, however, or an indication that careful tweaking of the SGP's rules and design would change that outcome. In general, fiscal rules that seem to work are more often indicators that a will to pursue fiscal consolidation exists in a powerful political coalition than that are causal factors of consolidation in and of themselves.

---

16. See the treatments of the SGP in Brueck and Zwiener (2004), Daban Sanchez et al. (2003), and Sapir et al. (2003) in this explicit framework of "rules-based fiscal policy."

Take the example of PAYGO rules, discussed in Frankel and Orszag (2002). This constituted a useful rhetorical device and means of coordination between the president and Congress over budget issues, once the president and a working majority in Congress agreed that they wanted deficit reduction—but PAYGO was also tossed aside when changing circumstances (and a changed president and Congress) led to less desire for deficit reduction. Though the rule did not leave the books immediately, when the desire for fiscal rectitude waned, tactics to get around PAYGO emerged, such as the "tax expenditures" noted disapprovingly in Rubin (2002), and then PAYGO itself receded.

Two senior veterans of the US budget process, Rudolph Penner and Eugene Steuerle (2004), persuasively make the case for this interpretation of budget rules as an aid when the will is there, but not as an independent causal factor. Looking at the longer view of US budgetary history, Dixit (1996, 121) argues in a similar spirit:

> But the transaction-cost view of the political process points to a need to look deeper and to identify the true underlying political problems, of which the [fiscal] procedures are merely symptoms. Why were the [budget deficit] problems allowed to occur, and why did they last so long? The answer must be that the currently dominant forces in the political process wanted just those outcomes and quite deliberately installed or persevered with those procedures.

Dixit associates the rise in US government spending in the 1870s, 1930s, and 1970s, and the enabling institutional changes in budgeting procedures, with political demands for the expansion of government, and the reversions back to centralized appropriations procedures (more conducive to budgetary constraint) as reflecting periods when the political consensus emphasized fiscal restraint. From a practitioner's viewpoint, Penner and Steuerle (2004) make much the same interpretation of the rise and fall of budget rules and of surpluses, with the desire for the latter in the United States from the mid-1980s to present. Putting it graphically, one may reach for a blanket in bed when one wants to be warmer, and the blanket does help one stay warm, but it will be thrown off whenever one gets too hot—the blanket cannot force the sleeper into staying at the temperature the blanket allows.[17] To extend the metaphor into the current eurozone context, the SGP may be the ECB's and EC's security blanket for fiscal developments, but as with Linus's blanket in *Peanuts*, its only service may be as a psychological comfort, not as a source of security itself.

---

17. Analogous cases can be drawn from monetary policy. Central bank independence can be seen as evidence of a desire by a powerful political coalition to keep inflation down, and as an instrument in that pursuit, rather than as a cause of low inflation itself (Posen 1993, 1995). As McCallum (1997) and Blinder (1998) point out, central banks appear to have chosen just not to play the time-inconsistent inflationary game, given the ease with which the "inflation bias" disappeared. See Posen (1998a) for a general discussion of whether institutions make better policy and of this approach to political economy.

Without Rubinesque Effects, What Should We Expect from the Euro?

The Stability and Growth Pact apparently has a lot of difficulties, with its design, with its enforcement, and with its credibility, particularly in light of its repeated violation by France and Germany, and the inability of the EC to enforce it over the objections of the member states. As was assessed above, the SGP had no impact on the countercyclical fiscal behavior, or on the long-term term trend of deficits and debt, of the eurozone members—with the exception of little Portugal, the one member state to be sanctioned under the SGP for violating budgetary guidelines. It is important, however, that this appears not to be the result of the SGP's design or implementation. Rather, as was discussed above, the violations of the SGP by the larger eurozone economies are a rational if not optimal response by European policymakers to two factors: first, the absence of direct benefits in the form of expansionary consolidations, given the structure of the eurozone economies; and second, the evidence of direct benefits for larger, less open eurozone economies from using countercyclical fiscal policies to offset the asymmetries of eurozone-wide monetary policy.

This should not erode the relative worth of the euro on international markets, as argued above, in part because the relative predominance of crowding-out versus Rubinesque effects should mean that fiscal expansion in the eurozone should drive up interest rates and the euro exchange rate. It also must be noted that the failure to live up to the SGP does not represent fiscal indiscipline on the scale of that practiced by the United States in the 2000s. Nor should the failure of the eurozone governments and their leading politicians to adhere to the strictures of the SGP be viewed as a unique shortfall of the eurozone membership. It was pointed out above that even in the United States, fiscal rules have largely been endogenous responses to the changing political coalitions for and against budgetary restraint, and there is a good general reason to be suspicious of the independent efficacy of fiscal policy rules in any context. So perhaps the SGP not only fails but also largely fails to matter, as long as the visible credibility gap between the SGP's strictures and the member states' policies is closed.[18]

Yet there remains at least one major policy concern, not so much with the SGP itself, but emerging from one of the reasons why the SGP did not bind. If Rubinomics has not worked and will not work in the eurozone, then one of the major and often-cited motivations for eurozone member-

---

18. Blanchard and Giavazzi (2004); Fatas et al. (2003); Gros, Mayer, and Ubide (2003); Hallerberg, Ubide, and Walton (2004); and Sapir et al. (2003)—among others—make sensible proposals for technocratic fixes of the SGP to allow for more countercyclical policy, i.e., getting the SGP to better conform to the underlying economic incentives and actual behavior, as well as shifting its focus to longer-term sustainability (with more dubious prospects).

Figure 6.8 Economic performance before and after the Maastricht Treaty for five eurozone members, 1984–93 compared with 1994–2003

percentage point difference between
1984–93 and 1994–2003 averages

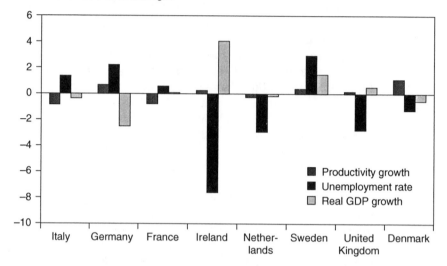

Source: Computed from Organization for Economic Cooperation and Development, *Economic Outlook* data.

ship goes away.[19] Numerous eurozone member countries, Belgium and Italy prominent among them, joined the zone in part because of the "binding oneself" logic of Giavazzi and Pagano (1990) and the Italian Political Economy school that followed—if the commitment to the zone forced fiscal discipline upon these countries, they should have experienced a decline in interest rates, a boom in investment, a surge in productivity growth, and ultimately an improvement in GDP growth and reduction in unemployment. Any growth forgone in the process of consolidating budgets to meet the Maastricht Treaty's criteria during the run-up to eurozone membership would be more than compensated for by the credible ongoing improvement in fiscal position, and the resulting Rubinesque virtuous cycle, according to this theory.

Unfortunately, things have not worked out this way. Figure 6.8 compares the economic performance before and after Maastricht for five eurozone members and the three non-member EU nations. The bars compare

---

19. Of course, there were and are many other motivations for eurozone membership beyond this one, such as France's desire to have more say over European monetary policy than leaving it to Bundesbank control, and Germany's desire to advance European unification and the acceptance of enlargement to the east.

the change in average annual productivity growth, unemployment, and GDP growth rates between the periods 1984–93 and 1994–2003.[20] In 1994, the Maastricht Treaty was signed, including the budget deficit and public debt targets that gave birth to the SGP. This two-period comparison should then give some idea of whether economic performance improved markedly once expectations kicked in for the eurozone, and also for the credible commitment to fiscal consolidation.[21] Such an exercise can be no more than indicative, given the number of factors that feed into overall macroeconomic performance, but it does give some measurement of the positive impact, if any, of fiscal consolidation and eurozone membership.

The record is not reassuring. Italy, which should have had the greatest benefits from getting on a path to fiscal rectitude, saw its productivity growth and real GDP growth decline slightly, and unemployment rise, after Maastricht. The other four eurozone members had mixed records, with Germany suffering on all three criteria, and only Ireland—which completed its expansionary consolidation itself in the late 1980s, well in advance of even discussing the Maastricht Treaty—benefiting on all three counts. Meanwhile, the three non–eurozone EU members (Denmark, Sweden, and the United Kingdom) all improved on at least two of the three measures during the same period versus pre-Maastricht days.

The Italian case merits greater scrutiny, because it should have been the poster child for the benefits of fiscal consolidation through eurozone membership. If ever there was an exogenous interest rate decline on public debt that was likely to be sustained, it was the one Italy enjoyed upon admission to the eurozone. Whether because entry raised the prospect of free riding by Italy on Germany's credit rating, or of greater discipline on Italian fiscal policymakers by tying their hands (the idea that motivated Italian elites' advocacy of the euro from the start), Italy was suddenly able to issue debt at a much lower interest rate. Of course, its very high initial debt/GDP level also made it a candidate for a Rubinesque virtuous cycle, not least because debt-service payments were a nontrivial part of GDP and the government budget, and part of that debt was foreign denominated.

Yet Italy's experience since getting serious about meeting the Maastricht Treaty's fiscal criteria in 1997 and joining the eurozone in 1999 very well illustrates the channels blocking any consolidation from becoming expansionary, at least in the medium term. Figure 6.9 presents the course of interest rates and private fixed investment in Italy during the decade since Maastricht. In accord with what one would expect, Italian govern-

---

20. The 10-year averages should smooth out the effects of business cycles, though obviously there were one-time shocks, such as German reunification and the exit of Italy from the Exchange Rate Mechanism.

21. One could also split the time sample at the start of 1999, with the launch of the euro. That would, however, not only ignore any beneficial expectation effects for consolidating countries, it would also shorten the sample to just five years, including a global recession.

Figure 6.9 Italian interest rates and investment, 1994–2003

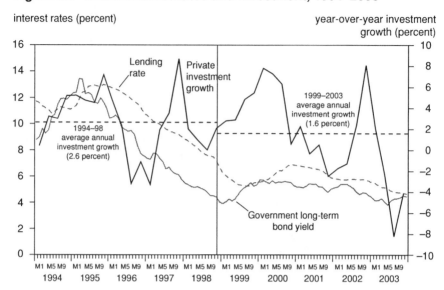

Sources: IMF, *International Financial Statistics*, September 2004, and Organization for Economic Cooperation and Development, *Economic Outlook 75*.

ment bond yields and the average private-sector lending rate declined from the time of the Maastricht Treaty, and they have remained low since the entry of Italy into the eurozone at the time of the euro's launch in January 1999. This came both through the importing of monetary credibility (i.e., the removal of exchange rate and inflation risks) and the deepening integration of eurozone capital markets. No boom in investment, growth, or productivity has ensued, however.

In fact, in accord with the general discussion above, private-sector investment does not seem to have responded to the drop in interest rates, which grew by an annual average of 2.6 percent in the period 1994–98 versus 1.6 percent in 1999–2003. The channels of expansionary consolidation—in terms of translating any interest rate and investment moves into productivity and employment gains—also appear to have been blocked in Italy, consistent with the view stated above (and the spirit of Baily and Kirkegaard 2004). Figure 6.10 shows the limited decline and then plateauing of the Italian unemployment rate, and the slight downward trend of both GDP and productivity growth in Italy during the past 20 years, irrespective of Maastricht and eurozone membership. As shown in figure 6.4 above, the ratio of Italy's gross debt to GDP only fell from a high of 134 to 117 percent, and has since plateaued, despite the marked decline in interest rates reducing outlays for debt service, a lot of one-time asset sales and privatizations (see the 1997 spike of positive change in government balance shown in figure 6.3), and the existence of the SGP. Real GDP growth declined on average in the 1990s after

Figure 6.10 Italian macroeconomic performance, 1984–2003

percent

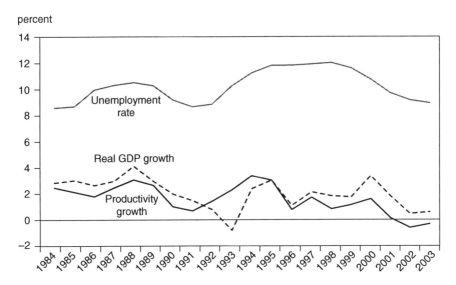

Source: Organization for Economic Cooperation and Development, *Economic Outlook 74.*

the short-term boost from adjusting the Exchange Rate Mechanism peg in 1992–93, again despite the fact that Italy had more to gain from the credibility bonus of eurozone membership than perhaps any other economy.

This is not to say that Italy or any other EU member economy would have been better off staying out of the eurozone. The point is the positive empirical assessment of whether the Banca d'Italia's and other Italian economic elites' strategy of using euro entry and membership as a means to fiscal reform and improved performance worked. Unless controlling more carefully for the business cycle would radically change these longer-term averages, all indications are that the binding-the-hands policy approach did not work.[22] It was arguably a sensible strategy ex ante, as was the theory of expansionary consolidation in Europe, but upon more practical examination and with the benefit of subsequent data, it is clear that it did not work out ex post.

Thus, we are left with even less hope than before that the creation of the euro, though a major political and monetary accomplishment, will in and of itself lead to improved growth and employment prospects in Europe.[23]

---

22. Such a controlled assessment of performance would also have to take into account the fact that Italy entered the eurozone with an undervalued currency, particularly against the deutsche mark, given Italy's exit from the Exchange Rate Mechanism and depreciated reentry in the mid-1990s, which should have led to faster growth and lower unemployment, at least for some initial years.

23. This disappointing outcome was predicted in Posen (1999).

The hard work of structural reform beyond bond markets remains independent of the euro's existence—and the relative value of using counter-cyclical fiscal policy in the eurozone versus pursuing fiscal consolidation in hard times has if anything increased for eurozone members. The worth of the SGP itself and its importance to the euro project, however, come further into question.

References

Baily, Martin, and Jakob Kirkegaard. 2004. *Transforming the European Economy*. Washington: Institute for International Economics.
Ball, Laurence, and N. Gregory Mankiw. 1995. What Do Budget Deficits Do? In *Budget Deficits and Debt: Issues and Options*. Volume on August 13–September 2 Symposium. Kansas City: Federal Reserve Bank of Kansas City.
Bayoumi, Tamim, and Barry Eichengreen. 1992. Restraining Yourself: The Implications of Fiscal Rules for Economic Stabilization. *IMF Staff Papers* 42, no. 1 (March): 32–48.
Bergmar, U. Michael, and Michael Hutchison. 1999. Economic Expansions and Fiscal Contractions: International Evidence and the 1982 Danish Stabilization. In *Macroeconomic Perspectives on the Danish Economy*, ed. Torben Andersen, Sven Hougaard Jensen, and Ole Risager. New York: Macmillan.
Bergsten, C. Fred, and John Williamson. 2003. *Dollar Overvaluation and the World Economy*. IIE Special Report 16. Washington: Institute for International Economics.
Blanchard, Olivier J., and Francesco Giavazzi. 2004. Improving the SGP Through a Proper Accounting of Public Investment. CEPR Discussion Paper 4220 (February). London: Centre for Economic Policy Research.
Blinder, Alan. 1998. *Central Banking in Theory and Practice*. Cambridge, MA: MIT Press.
Broda, Christian, and David Weinstein. 2004. Happy News from the Dismal Science: Reassessing Japanese Fiscal Policy and Sustainability. Columbia University, New York. Photocopy (August).
Brueck, Tilman, and Rudolf Zwiener. 2004. Fiscal Policy Rules for Stabilization and Growth: A Simulation Analysis of Deficit and Expenditure Targets in a Monetary Union. Deutsches Institut für Wirtschaftsforschung, Berlin. Photocopy (March).
Buti, Marco, and Paul van den Noord. 2003. Fiscal Policy in EMU: Rules, Discretion and Political Incentives. Paper presented at a conference on rethinking economic and social policies, Madrid (November).
Cheung, Yin-Wang, Menzie Chinn, and Antonio Garcia Pascual. 2002. *Empirical Exchange Rate Models of the Nineties: Are Any Fit to Survive?* NBER Working Paper 9393. Cambridge, MA: National Bureau of Economic Research.
Chinn, Menzie. 1997. *Sectoral Productivity, Government Spending, and Real Exchange Rates: Empirical Evidence for OECD Countries*. NBER Working Paper 6017. Cambridge, MA: National Bureau of Economic Research.
Chinn, Menzie, and Jeffrey Frankel. 2003. The Euro Area and World Interest Rates. Paper presented at a conference on the euro area as an economic entity sponsored by the Centre for Economic Policy Research, Frankfurt (September).
Daban Sanchez, Maria T., Enrica Detragiache, Gabriel Di Bella, Gian M. Milesi-Ferretti, and Steven A. Symansky. 2003. *Rules-Based Fiscal Policy in France, Germany, Italy, and Spain*. IMF Occasional Paper 225. Washington: International Monetary Fund.
Dixit, Avinash. 1996. *The Making of Economic Policy: A Transaction-Cost Politics Perspective*. Cambridge, MA: MIT Press.

Engen, Eric, and R. Glenn Hubbard. 2004. *Federal Government Debts and Interest Rates.* NBER Working Paper 10681. Cambridge, MA: National Bureau of Economic Research.

European Commission. 2003. Can Fiscal Consolidations in EMU Be Expansionary? In *Public Finances in EMU 2004: Part IV, European Economy 2004,* no. 3, ed. Directorate General for Economic and Financial Affairs. Brussels: European Commission.

Fatas, Antonio, Andrew Hughes Hallett, Anne Siebert, Rolf Strauch, and Juergen von Hagen. 2003. Stability and Growth in Europe: Towards a Better Pact. *Monitoring European Integration 13.* London: Centre for Economic Policy Research.

Fischer, Stanley. 2001. Comments on "The Great Recession." In *Brookings Papers on Economic Activity.* Washington: Brookings Institution Press.

Frankel, Jeffrey, and Peter Orszag, eds. 2002. *American Economic Policy in the 1990s.* Cambridge, MA: MIT Press.

Gale, William, and Peter Orszag. 2004. Budget Deficits, National Saving, and Interest Rates. Brookings Institution, Washington. Photocopy (September).

Gali, Jordi, and Roberto Perotti. 2003. *Fiscal Policy and Monetary Integration in Europe.* NBER Working Paper 9773. Cambridge, MA: National Bureau of Economic Research.

Giavazzi, Francesco, and Marco Pagano. 1990. Can Severe Fiscal Contractions Be Expansionary? Tales of Two Small European Countries. In *NBER Macroeconomics Annual 1990,* ed. Olivier Blanchard and Stanley Fischer. Cambridge, MA: MIT Press.

Greenspan, Alan. 1995. General Discussion: What Do Budget Deficits Do? In *Budget Deficits and Debt: Issues and Options.* Volume on August 13–September 2 Symposium. Kansas City Federal Reserve Bank of Kansas City.

Gros, Daniel, Thomas Mayer, and Angel Ubide. 2003. *The Nine Lives of the Stability Pact: Rapid Reaction Report of the CEPS Macroeconomic Policy Group.* Brussels: Centre for European Policy Studies.

Hallerberg, Mark, Angel Ubide, and David Walton. 2004. How Should the Stability and Growth Pact be Reformed? *Finance & Development,* June, 26–28.

Hubbard, R. Glenn. 2004. Remarks on the Panel on Policy Coordination. In *Stabilizing the Economy: Why and How,* ed. Adam Posen and Benn Steil. Oxford: Blackwell.

Issing, Otmar. 2003. Standpunkte/Stabiles Geld und solide öffentliche Finanzen gehören zusammen/Durch die gröbliche Verletzung des Stabilitätspaktes steht die Glaubwürdigkeit der europäischen Institutionen insgesamt auf dem Spiel. *Frankfurter Allegemeine Zeitung,* December 6, 12.

Kuttner, Kenneth, and Adam Posen. 2002. Fiscal Policy Effectiveness in Japan. *Journal of the Japanese and International Economies* 16: 536–58.

Laubach, Thomas. 2003. New Evidence on the Interest Rate Effects of Budget Deficits and Debt. Board of Governors of the Federal Reserve System, Washington. Photocopy (May).

Masson, Paul, and Michael Mussa. 1995. Long-Term Tendencies in Budget Deficits and Debt. In *Budget Deficits and Debt: Issues and Options.* Volume on August 13–September 2 Symposium. Kansas City Federal Reserve Bank of Kansas City.

McCallum, Bennett. 1997. Critical Issues Concerning Central Bank Independence. *Journal of Monetary Economics* 39, no. 1: 99–112.

McNamara, Kathleen. 2003. Globalization, Insights, and Convergence: Fiscal Adjustment in Europe. In *Governance in a Global Economy: Political Authority in Transition,* ed. Miles Kahler and David Lake. Princeton, NJ: Princeton University Press.

Muehleisen, Martin, and Christopher Towe, eds. 2004. *U.S. Fiscal Policies and Priorities for Long-Run Sustainability.* IMF Occasional Paper 227. Washington: International Monetary Fund.

Penner, Rudolph, and Eugene Steuerle. 2004. Budget Rules. Urban Institute, Washington. Photocopy (May).

Peterson, Peter. 1999. *Gray Dawn: How the Coming Age Wage Will Transform America and the World.* New York: Random House.

Posen, Adam. 1993. Why Central Bank Independence Does Not Cause Low Inflation: There Is No Institutional Fix for Politics. In *Finance and the International Economy* 7, ed. Richard O'Brien. Oxford: Oxford University Press.

Posen, Adam. 1995. Declarations Are Not Enough: Financial Sector Sources of Central Bank Independence. In *NBER Macroeconomics Annual 1995*, ed. Ben Bernanke and Julio Rotemberg. Cambridge, MA: MIT Press.

Posen, Adam. 1998a. Do Better Institutions Make Better Policy? *International Finance* 1, no. 1: 173–205.

Posen, Adam. 1998b. *Restoring Japan's Economic Growth*. Washington: Institute for International Economics.

Posen, Adam. 1999. Why EMU Is Irrelevant for the German Economy. Public lecture, Frankfurter Volkswirtschaftliches Kolloquium, Frankfurt (May).

Posen, Adam. 2003. *Is Germany Turning Japanese?* IIE Working Paper 03-2. Washington: Institute for International Economics.

Rubin, Robert. 2002. Comments on Elmendorf et al. In *American Economic Policy in the 1990s*, ed. Jeffrey Frankel and Peter Orszag. Cambridge, MA: MIT Press.

Sapir, Andre, Philippe Aghion, Giuseppe Bertola, Martin Hellwig, Jean Pisani-Ferry, Dariusz Rosati, Jose Vinals, and Helen Wallace, eds. 2003. *An Agenda for a Growing Europe: Making the EU Economic System Deliver*. Oxford: Oxford University Press.

Tanzi, Vito. 2003. Role and Future of the Stability and Growth Pact. Cato Institute, Washington. Photocopy (November).

Comment

JÜRGEN KRÖGER

I share Adam Posen's view that the mere observation that in many cases fiscal consolidation has coincided with high economic growth does not imply causality. He refers to monetary policy, which can support this desirable combination. A broader perspective would also include exchange rate movements, which if appropriately managed may support fiscal adjustment, as witnessed for example by the Italian fiscal consolidation path after 1995. And in many cases, fiscal consolidation was supported by a market-driven monetary stimulus in the run-up to Economic and Monetary Union (EMU).

But a comparison of US and European fiscal policy effectiveness is difficult, for at least two reasons. First, because the public-sector share in GDP is much larger in Europe than in the United States, the automatic stabilizers smooth the cyclical volatility to a greater extent than in the United States. Second, given the greater rigidities in most EU countries, the output costs of reducing inflation are higher. In Europe, each cycle has tended to raise the nonaccelerating inflation rate of unemployment. Therefore, given the lags involved, discretionary fiscal policy may have longer-term adverse effects on growth and employment.

It is useful, however, to try to assess the fiscal policy framework of EMU. Where do we stand after five years? I offer 10 observations. First, my old undergraduate textbooks on fiscal policy distinguished three functions:

Jürgen Kröger has been the director for economic studies and research at the European Commission in Brussels since 2002.

- allocation of resources toward public spending;

- stabilization of output in the presence of demand shocks; and

- redistribution of income (or wealth), according to social (national) preferences.

Membership in the EMU potentially has a profound influence on all three functions, depending among other things on the institutional arrangements.

Privatization and liberalization, the development of the single internal market, and the integration of the EU economies into a global market economy have had an impact on the optimal size of the state and the optimal degree of redistribution. There is a general recognition in the European Union that from an economic point of view both of these probably lie below the present level, and that there are potential gains to be made by all the EU states moving together in that direction.

However, it is also the case that national preferences differ, and that coordination takes the form of broad orientations and learning from best practices, and is therefore not very binding.

I concentrate my remarks here on the stabilization aspect of fiscal policy, because this is where the existing rules-based framework has inspired discussion.

Second, the experience of EU members has shown that the policy of countercyclical activism has often resulted in an increase in the size of the state, persistently higher deficits, and an accumulation of public debt. In some cases, this has resulted in a threat to fiscal sustainability. The consolidation of public budgets, including the gradual reduction of debt levels, has become a policy priority in Europe. In the run-up to monetary union, the Maastricht criteria clearly helped to make fiscal discipline politically more acceptable and substantially accelerated the process of budgetary consolidation before the introduction of the euro. The question was, however, would fiscal discipline prevail once entry into the EMU was accomplished?

Third, it is difficult to say a priori whether a country's incentives to run excessive deficits would increase or decrease after joining a monetary union such as the EMU. The risk premium on interest rates over some benchmark rates that a member state has to face for its debt is likely to be significantly lower in the EMU than before it.

This is inviting moral hazard. The currency risk disappears—by definition—completely. The default risk is also likely to decrease, because of intra-EU solidarity. In other words, the "non-bail-out clause" is not (fully) credible. At least, this seems to be the perception of markets. Financial markets have up to now only partly distinguished between fiscally good and bad performers. However, the interest spreads vis-à-vis Germany have been reduced markedly and even become negative in some cases (e.g., Finland).

On the optimistic side, it has been argued that the loss of the option to finance public deficits by printing money would impose a hardened budget constraint on countries. The experience of five years of EMU suggests that the discipline imposed by financial markets has been reduced while the "hardening of the budget constraint"—the inability to finance deficits by printing money—plays only a minor role, as long as deficits remain sustainable.

Fourth, why is it in the European Community's interest to have binding deficit rules? The most important argument in favor of common deficit rules is based on the risk to the sound functioning of EMU, which would emerge if public debt in some (even small) member states became too high for their public finances to remain sustainable. Unsustainable public finances would likely impose hard choices on the European Central Bank's monetary policy, possibly threatening its prime objective of price stability.

Obviously, debt sustainability is a long-term concept, and it is easier to reduce the debt/GDP ratio for a country with high average potential growth like Finland (4 percent) than for a low-growth country like Germany (1.8 percent). Therefore, an evaluation of debt sustainability cannot be made on the basis of today's debt ratio alone. The dependence of fiscal debt sustainability on trend growth is one criticism that some observers put forward as an argument against a simple deficit benchmark.

In addition, the risk premium required by financial markets on euro areawide interest rates may depend on credible fiscal rules. From the Community's viewpoint, binding deficit rules appear justified because of the risk of free riding and the potentially adverse effects on real interest rates. Free riding—a moral hazard problem—is typically more tempting to smaller countries, because their fiscal expansion will likely have only a minor effect on areawide interest rates (including the European Central Bank's policy rate). The adverse effect on areawide interest rates—a negative externality—will, conversely, be stronger after a fiscal expansion in larger countries, or in a group of countries.

Fifth, another question discussed at the time the fiscal rules for EMU were negotiated was: How binding, or how flexible, should such rules be? (Or how can strict rules be applied flexibly?) We are currently witnessing a renewed debate on this issue. Strictly binding rules clearly have enforcement problems; there are strong incentives to circumvent them by moving items off budget, using the flexibility of accounting rules, one-off measures, and the like.

The empirical evidence taken from existing monetary unions (e.g., the United States and its constituent states) was not very encouraging. And in the run-up to EMU, the European Union has gained some experience of its own. The European Commission has made progress in limiting these kinds of problems through surveillance, clarifying and tightening of accounting rules, and other means. Unfortunately, the Community rules are currently facing enforcement problems, which are in many ways more fundamental and more difficult to tackle.

Sixth, the four main shortcomings and weaknesses of the Stability and Growth Pact (SGP), as they appear to us, can be summarized as follows. The first is that the SGP appears static. In particular, the definition of medium-term balance should take account of country-specific characteristics. A country with a high rate of growth can sustain a somewhat higher deficit than one with a low rate of potential growth. Also, the initial debt level has an impact on the desired medium-term deficit. Furthermore, countries differ in terms of the size of the automatic stabilizers. Countries in which the automatic stabilizers are large (e.g., the Scandinavian countries) should seek to have a medium-sized surplus so as not to breach the 3 percent ceiling during an economic downturn. Finally, medium-term sustainability also depends on factors like population aging, which should be taken into consideration in defining the fiscal policy strategy.

The second shortcoming is that the SGP has worked asymmetrically over the cycle. In periods of high economic growth, fiscal discipline has been insufficient to preserve the room for maneuver to let the automatic stabilizers work during the downturn. Therefore, one condition for improving the SGP's workability must be stronger enforcement during times of high economic growth.

The third shortcoming is that the quality of public finances is an important factor in assessing a country's medium-term growth performance. The Broad Economic Policy Guidelines should put greater emphasis on growth-enhancing structures in public finance. And the fourth shortcoming is that the enforcement of commonly agreed-on rules has become more uncertain, which may have undermined the credibility and predictability of the European Union's policy framework.

Seventh, what is the way forward? It would seem that, given the current political climate, any decision about changes to the European Union's fiscal rules will have to wait until more legal certainty is established by the forthcoming European Court of Justice ruling on the SGP's implementation procedures. However, the court's ruling is primarily about interinstitutional responsibilities and procedures rather than about the economic rationale for the SGP.

In any case, changes to either the SGP or its interpretation would try to improve on the weaknesses described above. However, any change of the Maastricht Treaty in this area should be avoided. Let us consider several options for appropriate changes.

One option could be to introduce more flexibility into the definition of medium-term balance, taking into account the level of debt, growth performance, and special characteristics like population aging.

Another option, when applying the Maastricht Treaty procedures, should be envisioning compliance with both the reference values of 60 and 3 percent of GDP for the debt and the deficit, respectively, rather than focusing unduly on deficit targets alone. A stronger focus on debt developments should reduce the current short-term bias shown by member states, thus increasing the incentive to lower high debt levels.

A third option that should be pursued is ambitious action in good times and prudent and symmetric-over-the-cycle behavior. The enforcement mechanisms (including early warnings) should be used promptly, with a view to preventing the 3 percent reference value from being breached.

In addition, the European Commission should be able to use its capacity for intensified surveillance. Past experience has shown that member states are unwilling to apply the rules of the SGP against each other. The authority of the institutions involved needs to be strengthened to permit a more flexible and nuanced interpretation of the rules. The Commission should therefore have greater independence in launching excessive deficit procedures.

Eighth, however, more flexible rules are difficult to implement. In particular, the principle of equal treatment of member states—a political necessity in Europe—makes it very hard in practice to take account of the subtle differences in the specific economic situation of each country. Differences in economic circumstances, such as the fiscal cost of German unification or the direct-deficit-reducing effects of interest rate convergence in the run-up to the euro in some other member states, represent a very variable environment in which fiscal consolidation has to take place. The principle of equal treatment, as it is implemented in practice, leaves very little room for discretion.

In addition, experience has shown that it is very hard to get agreement among all the member states on methodological issues. For example, it took years for the Community to agree on a common method for the measurement of output gaps. In the end, a fairly crude formula was found: the same form of the production function (Cobb-Douglas), the same inputs (aggregate capital stock, employment) filtered with the same method and parameters (Hodrik-Prescott). This necessarily excludes any additional information that is available for individual countries over and above the agreed-on data inputs. Therefore, no element of reasoned judgment is allowed, something for which the method is often criticized.

Ninth, conversely, a strong case can be made for the Commission to gain a more independent role in the enforcement process. The present arrangement has its weaknesses, as we have seen. The Commission is well placed to take a Community position, and it is independent of the political realities in individual member states. It is therefore in a unique position to advance good economics, even in a difficult political environment.

Tenth and finally, as we have learned from the optimum currency area literature, a monetary union should have either fully flexible markets, with complete price and wage flexibility, or a very high degree of factor—in particular labor—mobility. In the absence of a very high degree of flexibility, which is certainly the case in EMU, some degree of fiscal transfers to compensate for the impact of asymmetric demand shocks might in principle be required, although the asymmetry of demand shocks may be greater within countries than between them.

However, the European Community's budget is certainly too small to serve this purpose, and it is not very well designed to do so. Other forms of automatic income transfer have been discussed, including a common areawide unemployment insurance scheme. However, there is little hope, in today's political climate, that rapid progress toward a bigger fiscal union will be made any time soon.

Comment

JEFFREY FRANKEL

American economists' skeptical predictions regarding the Economic and Monetary Union (EMU) were in some respects too pessimistic, in light of experience so far. But two predictions have turned out to be accurate. First, *a permanent 3 percent ceiling on deficits, without flexibility (e.g., for recessions) would not be fully enforceable.* The provision for monetary penalties against countries that violate the limits does not increase the credibility of enforcement; it may reduce it. At the same time, the continuing contradiction between word and deed undermines the credibility of other agreed-on aspects of the European unification project—for example, vis-à-vis the accession of the 10 new EU members.

Second, members of Euroland would suffer from occasional asymmetric shocks. In that light, *discretionary fiscal policy would become more, not less, necessary now that monetary independence has been lost.*

Adam Posen's chapter contains a number of very interesting findings. Perhaps his primary conclusion is that the Stability and Growth Pact (SGP) has not in fact limited countercyclical responses of fiscal policy among EMU members since 1999. That is in part due to the willingness to violate the limits of the SGP, especially on the part of the larger countries. He concludes that the countries that are smaller and have high ratios of trade to GDP have found the SGP less onerous, for several reasons. First, fiscal policy has less of an effect on the domestic economy

---

Jeffrey Frankel is a professor at Harvard University.

in a country where much spending leaks out: some of the increased spending, that would otherwise have shown up as purchases of domestic goods, instead goes into imports or other purchases of internationally tradable goods. Thus, these countries are giving up less when they give up some flexibility of fiscal policy.

Second, the larger countries—Germany, France, and Italy (and perhaps Spain should be added)—felt the loss of monetary autonomy more keenly, and they felt the need to compensate with active fiscal policy, whereas most of the smaller countries had already given up monetary autonomy to Frankfurt years ago and had come to terms with this change. Actually, Posen finds that even the smaller countries did not have a statistically significant decrease in countercyclicality in fiscal policy during the period 1999–2003, despite the SGP. But with so few observations, we may have to settle for point estimates rather than statistical significance. He finds that three of the larger countries—Germany, Spain, and Italy—actually show an *increase* in countercyclicality under EMU. This is consistent with the idea that they have relied more on the fiscal policy tool now that the monetary policy tool is gone.

Third, the larger countries can get away politically with breaking the rules in a way that the less powerful countries cannot. These are all important points, some of which are not widely recognized.

Is Europe Less Well Suited to Expansionary Consolidation than the United States?

The United States is even larger than the large European countries, and it has a correspondingly lower ratio of trade to GDP. If Posen's generalizations are correct, why, then, did the United States pursue and achieve fiscal discipline during the 1990s? That question can be broken down into two questions, one concerned with politics and the other with economics. The political question is: Why were tough fiscal measures—raising tax revenue and cutting the rate of growth of spending—taken in the United States? The economic question is: Why did the new fiscal policy apparently succeed in helping to raise the growth rate—the "expansionary consolidation" of Giavazzi and Pagano (1990)?

These two questions are more closely linked than is at first apparent. If fiscal policy is defined in terms of tax revenue or the budget balance, then of course an important component of the improvement was the result of rapid growth; in other words, causality goes in both directions. But assume that we limit our definition of fiscal discipline to specific policy measures. An important reason why President Bill Clinton and Treasury Secretary Robert Rubin took the measures they did was that they believed it would help the economy. Given that this turned out to be right, one does not need to say a lot more about the politics.[24] So the main question concerns economics: Why did Rubinomics work in the United States and not in Europe? Here, my view diverges a bit from Posen's. And so it is to this question that I will devote most of my comments.

Posen's answer to the question posed in the title of his chapter is, essentially, "No, Rubinomics cannot work in Europe." He argues that the main channel of Rubinomics runs from fiscal consolidation to lower interest rates and thereby to higher investment, and that this channel is less operational in continental Europe. One reason he gives is that the United States, unlike Europe, is a large net debtor internationally, so there can be a large default premium built into the interest rate, which fiscal consolidation then works to reduce.

I see two problems with this argument. First, high domestic debt (and unfunded future pension liabilities), which the Europeans have, can in theory drive up the default premium as easily as high foreign debt. Second, the United States—despite its debts, both domestic and foreign—has never (as yet) had to pay a perceptible default premium on its debt. Even when its fiscal policies have been at their most irresponsible, the dollar has retained its status as premier reserve currency, and the US Treasury bill market has retained its extra attractiveness to international investors.

Perhaps a better argument for why the interest rate channel does not work in continental Europe is that the money markets and securities markets are less well developed and less flexible there. Interest rates are traditionally considered to be less responsive to a given reduction in national saving, and investment is not as adversely responsive to a given increase in interest rates.[25] In other words, the *LM* curve is flatter and/or the *IS* curve is steeper in Europe, so crowding out is less of an issue. But this argument will not necessarily get you there either. The national saving identity must hold one way or another. There are other channels of crowding out besides the interest rate channel that has long been emphasized by the macroeconomics textbooks, including stock markets and the exchange rate. In the case of continental Europe, there may be channels that work through the quantity of credit extended to firms—without showing up in interest rates or other price measures. For instance, if banks are lending to Airbus, then they are not lending to private start-up companies.

---

24. No less interesting is the story of how, after the 1992 election, the Rubin view came to win out over the priorities of other Clinton advisers—Clinton (2004), Rubin (2002, 131), and Woodward (1994). The most effective argument was that the bond market would react negatively, if investors heard that all the spending programs contemplated during the campaign were to be carried out in full.

25. Posen's example of Italy is particularly interesting here. As he points out, some combination of EMU and fiscal discipline did succeed in sharply reducing real interest rates in Italy, and yet there was no investment boom.

Table 6.2 Determinants of long-term interest rates, United States and Europe, 1988–2002

Determinant	United States	Germany	France	Italy	Spain	United Kingdom
Constant	−0.001	−0.122***	−0.022	−0.081	−0.043*	−0.034
	(0.008)	(0.038)	(0.027)	(0.041)	(0.023)	(0.030)
Inflation	1.00	1.00	1.00	1.00	1.00	1.00
Debt ratio	0.060**	0.182***	0.027	0.109	0.031	0.067
	(0.019)	(0.047)	(0.040)	(0.062)	(0.051)	(0.044)
Expected change in debt ratio	0.144**	0.112***	0.177**	0.324**	0.289***	0.066
	(0.061)	(0.032)	(0.073)	(0.106)	(0.048)	(0.110)
Output gap	0.388**	0.608**	0.252	0.297	0.218	−0.316
	(0.174)	(0.219)	(0.202)	(0.484)	(0.223)	(0.324)
Foreign interest rate	0.096	1.529***	0.923***	0.390	1.204***	0.815**
	(0.122)	(0.327)	(0.241)	(0.446)	(0.145)	(0.348)
Number of observations	15	15	15	15	15	15
Adjusted R^2	0.32	0.51	0.82	0.77	0.82	0.55
DW	2.24	2.50	2.47	1.70	2.47	1.44

*, **, *** = indicates significance at the 10, 5, and 1 percent level.

Note: Ordinary least squares regression using annual data, in levels (Newey-West robust standard errors in parentheses). Percentage variables are defined in decimal form. DW is Durbin-Watson statistic.

Source: Chinn and Frankel (2003).

Furthermore, the generalization that the interest rate channel is not fully operational in continental Europe may no longer be true. Table 6.2, from Chinn and Frankel (2003), reports estimates of an equation for the determination of the long-term real interest rate in the United States and five European countries. The estimated effect of contemporaneous debt is stronger in Germany than in the United States, though weaker in the other four European countries. The more striking result is that the estimated effect of the *expected future* change in debt is statistically significant in all four large countries of the euro zone, and the effect is actually stronger than in the United States—in magnitude, significance, or both. This is important, because the possibility of expansionary consolidation lies in expected future deficits, not in contemporaneous deficits. Though in standard textbook theory contemporaneous deficits drive up short-term interest rates and lead to the crowding out of investment and other sectors, this effect can only partially offset the expansion in government spending and consumption. The net contemporaneous effect is expansionary. Only future deficits can be contractionary. (We look more at the two effects below.)

Three Regimes That Have Been Proposed to Achieve Fiscal Discipline

In any case, I do not accept the premise that expansionary fiscal consolidation is rendered possible by some structural feature in the United States that is absent in Europe. The most powerful pieces of evidence are the fiscal records of the 1980s and the 2000s. The fiscal consolidation of the 1990s was the exception, not the rule. By this I mean not just that the George W. Bush administration in 2001 launched an irresponsible fiscal expansion, which in many respects was modeled on that of the Ronald Reagan administration's first term in 1981. I mean also that there has not been an economic price paid in higher interest rates and slower growth, at least not yet.

In other words, as with the achievement of fiscal discipline in the 1990s, there is both an interesting political question (How have they been able to do this, politically?) and an interesting economic question (Why have financial markets not yet responded?). Although expansionary consolidation seemed to work, both politically and economically, in the United States in the 1990s, the converse approach, the return during the period 2001–04 of a "cut taxes and spend" philosophy, failed to have both the political and economic consequences that one would have predicted. This suggests that there was something different about US policy in the 1990s, more than that there is something permanently different about the United States.

I suggest that the key lies in the political economy regime that is adopted to achieve fiscal discipline. Everyone at least pays lip service to fiscal discipline, even when seeking to justify large deficits. The question is how it is achieved, in a world where there are always interest groups clamoring to receive benefits in the form of specific tax cuts and spending.

I see three categories of regimes that have been proposed as mechanisms for achieving fiscal discipline. The first is "Starve the Beast," the rationale that the Republicans gave to the regime that I call "cut taxes and spend," in the first Reagan term and the George W. Bush administration. (More precisely, in both cases, it is the rationale they began to give in the second or third year of these terms, after the clear failure of events to bear out their initial rationale—that reductions in tax rates would lead to so much economic growth that the budget would get better rather than worse.) Starve the Beast is the argument that large tax cuts, though they will create temporary deficits, will soon force cuts in spending because "Congress cannot spend money it does not have."

The second category of proposed mechanisms is "rigid rules." Two prominent examples are the balanced-budget amendment that was rejected in the United States (the proposal was part of the Contract with America in the Newt Gingrich revolution of 1994) and the SGP that was adopted in Europe.

The third regime is the one that was actually in place in the United States in the 1990s, which I will call the "regime of Shared Sacrifice." This category of mechanisms includes laws and guidelines to facilitate fiscal discipline by spreading the pain relatively broadly. Three of the important mechanisms used in the 1990s were (1) caps on the rate of growth of discretionary spending (which were adopted in the Budget Enforcement Act of 1990 and extended by the Clinton administration in 1993); (2) "PAYGO" (the "Pay as you go" rule, also legislated in 1990 and 1993, which said that any member of Congress proposing a tax cut or entitlement spending increase had to show how to pay for it); and (3) the principle of preserving the new on-budget surplus, under the slogan "Save Social Security First" (proposed by Clinton in his State of the Union message in 1998, and accepted by both parties until George W. Bush assumed office in January 2001). My claim is that what was different about the 1990s in the United States is that the regime in effect, Shared Sacrifice, is one that works, whereas the others do not.

Let us begin with the rigid rules, and why they do not work. As everyone knows, any gain in credibility that is achieved through a rigid rule carries a loss in flexibility. With rigid monetary rules such as a currency board, for example, the government loses the ability to respond to recessions or overheating by mitigating moves in monetary policy. With rigid fiscal rules, such as a balanced-budget amendment, the government loses the ability to respond to such disturbances by mitigating moves in fiscal policy.

Less often appreciated is that commitments to ever more stringent rules eventually run into negative returns, even when the payoff is measured solely by credibility. This is especially true when the commitment is made by an elite that may not have democratically sought or received a sign-off from the people. Which is more credible: a statement by a central banker that he will resign if he misses a particular monetary target, or a statement that he will shoot himself? The latter commitment is less credible, precisely because it is a stronger statement than the first, and is too strong to be believable. The same is true of a balanced-budget amendment and the SGP. A severe and inflexible commitment not to step over a particular line with respect to the budget deficit carries such high costs that it is not credible in the first place. This is the underlying explanation for Posen's important finding that the SGP has in fact not reduced the fiscal activism in Euroland by even a little.

Let us consider, next, why Starve the Beast does not work. It is not literally true that a government cannot spend money it does not have. Governments do it all the time, and on a very large scale. (Only under a rigid balanced-budget rule would it be true, and that we have just considered.) The claim is that cutting taxes and creating budget deficits puts strong political pressure on the government to cut spending, because people do not like the deficits. But "strong pressure to cut spending" compared with

Figure 6.11 US federal budget deficit and spending, 1977–2003
(percent of GDP)

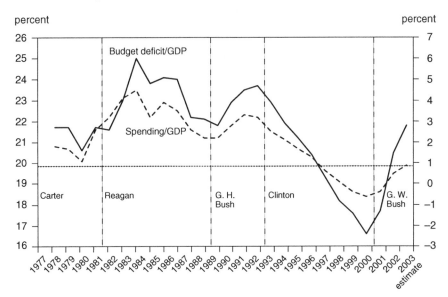

Source: US Office of Management and Budget data.

what? For the claim to be meaningful, it should be stronger pressure than under the alternative of the 1990s regime, the one I have called Shared Sacrifice.

In support of my claim that Starve the Beast is a sham, I offer four exhibits: figure 6.11, econometric citations, an a priori argument, and a fascinating fact. Figure 6.11 illustrates the US budget during the terms of the past five presidents. The first striking lesson is: When a Republican president comes in, the budget deficit takes off. It may sound surprising, but there it is. Ronald Reagan becomes president in 1981—and the budget deficit shoots up. George H.W. Bush takes office in 1989—and the same thing happens. George W. Bush arrives in 2001—the same. In between, during the Clinton administration, the budget deficit is eliminated and is replaced with a record surplus.

Now, you might think this pattern was entirely because of Republican tax cuts and Democratic tax increases. That is, you might think that if you fell for the line that the Republican Party is the party of small government. But the striking pattern in the budget is not entirely, or even primarily, due to taxes. Figure 6.11 also shows federal spending, by presidential term. When a Republican becomes president, spending increases sharply. It was true when Reagan became president, when George H. W. Bush became president, and when George W. Bush became president—in 1981, 1989, and 2001. The deficit-spending correlation casts doubt on the claim that their tax cuts were part of a plan to reduce the rate of growth of spending.

Niskanen (2002) and Gale and Kelly (2004) have conducted more formal econometric tests, and they reject the Starve the Beast proposition statistically. It appears that, rather than a positive correlation between tax revenue and spending, there is a negative correlation. The reason is that the historical data exhibit two regimes, one in which budget discipline is achieved through tax increases and spending cuts simultaneously (Shared Sacrifice), and another in which budget profligacy is achieved through the reverse policies. The hypothesized combination of tax cuts followed closely by spending cuts just does not describe American history. Only after presidents have reversed their low-tax campaign platforms (Clinton also originally had one in the 1992 campaign) has progress been made at cutting both government spending and the deficit.

Consider now the a priori case. What is the mechanism through which, in theory, the Starve the Beast approach is supposed to restrain spending? The mechanism is that if you create huge deficits, citizens will worry so much about the national debt that they will come complaining to their representative in Congress: "I'm worried about raising taxes on my grandchildren." The representative will then be less likely to vote higher spending. Maybe people do worry about the national debt, about taxes on their grandchildren. But surely they do not worry about such uncertain prospective future taxes (as hypothesized in the Starve the Beast paradigm) *more* than they worry about *certain taxes today* (as they must, in the Shared Sacrifice paradigm). Unpopular taxes today must surely put more pressure on representatives in Congress. Thus, as a political economy argument, Starve the Beast just does not make sense, if the alternative is the regime of the 1990s.

Starve the Beast is an ex post rationalization that some Republicans have found convenient to use in some circles and not in others, but it does not describe the motives of those who passed George W. Bush's tax cuts. How can such an assertion be supported? One final piece of evidence (also from Gale and Kelly 2004) is that almost half the members of Congress, together with President Bush, have signed a "no new taxes pledge"—which, based on the Starve the Beast rationale, would make the new tax cuts permanent and prevent most tax increases. But an examination of the voting records of the congressional pledge signers shows that they have been *more prone to vote for spending increases* than have the nonsigners. It is thus hard to believe that their motives are genuinely to force their colleagues to cut spending.

The Shared Sacrifice mechanisms of the 1990s—spending caps, PAYGO, and Save Social Security First—have in common budget neutrality as a criterion for future changes relative to the baseline. The strategy comes from the logic that to achieve budget balance, the country must recognize the need for sacrifice and agree to share the burden. It is the idea that "I will agree to forgo my tax cuts, if you agree to forgo your spending increases." The only way the country will ever get budget discipline, in the long run, is through a common spirit along the lines "I would like to get my pork-barrel project funded for my constituents, but I will hold back if everybody else is holding back."

The 1990s showed that the principle of Shared Sacrifice works. Notice the difference from the principle of Starve the Beast. The first is "I will give up the tax cut I want if you give up the spending you want." The second is "I will take the tax cut I want, and in return you give up the spending you want." Which sounds like a more politically plausible route to a deal in Congress?

The problem is that the caps and PAYGO expired in 2001 and that there has been no effort to restore them, at least not from the White House.

How Has Bush Achieved Such Large Deficits? Pointers for European Politicians

I have discussed how Clinton achieved a surplus by the end of the 1990s. How has George W. Bush been able to achieve such big deficits in the 2000s? The 2001 recession helped. And it is always easier to give away money than it is to collect money—an important principle of political economy. But there is a third factor: The government made forecasts of future budgets that were overly optimistic, and predictably so. This enabled the White House to say that the country could afford these huge tax cuts. The forecasts were part of the mechanism that allowed the fiscal mess to come about. Officials release their budget forecasts twice a year and, to date, every time they have been forced to admit that last time they were wrong. And then, every time, they have done it again—"they" being both the Congressional Budget Office (CBO) and the Office of Management and Budget (OMB). (A qualification: CBO has little choice but to base its projections on current legislation, even when administration policy and informed prediction both call for costly future changes in legislation, such as new tax cuts.)

When the new administration came to power in January 2001, it boosted the revenue estimates, helping it to claim that we were going to have record surpluses rising as far as the eye could see. The first set of three bars in figure 6.12 illustrates this. In May 2001, the administration admitted that the surpluses were not going to be quite as big as it had said four months earlier, but it still saw substantial surpluses, and still ones that rose in the future. In January 2002, the same thing happened: It was admitted that the surplus was small now but still positive and still supposedly rising in the future. (This forecast came after the recession and September 11, 2001.) Then, in August—whoops!—we were in deficit after

Figure 6.12 Three years of budget forecasts that soon proved overly optimistic, 2002–04

billions of dollars

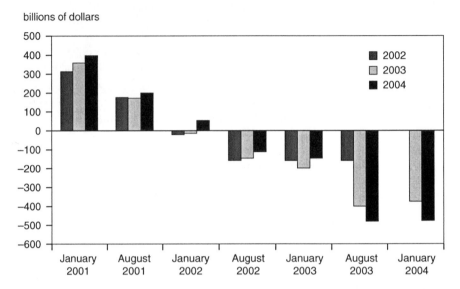

Source: US Office of Management and Budget data.

all, but it was going to go away gradually in the future. Each time, the administration was forced to revise its estimates.

CBO is still forecasting deficits for the next few years but a path to a surplus by 2013. (OMB has decided to stop forecasting at the 10-year horizon.) That is still overly optimistic, for many reasons.[26] It is surprising that the press goes on reporting these forecasts, largely at face value. But the misleading forecasts might help explain why voters and market participants alike do not yet seem to have fully understood the magnitude of the coming deficits.

To justify their large deficits, in violation of the SGP, European leaders might increasingly want to rely on the George W. Bush defense: Yes, we are running high deficits at the moment, but our projections indicate that the fiscal situation will improve in the future. It may be helpful for them to consider some elaboration on the tricks that the American authorities have found useful:

■ Make unrealistically optimistic economic assumptions. If forecasting record real growth is too obvious—this trick has been used so often in the past that even the American press will sometimes report it—instead

---

26. Frankel (2003, 37–45) lists 10 reasons, and also discusses the coining of the word "Rubinomics" by Glenn Hubbard.

play with other, more obscure, parameters that affect tax revenues. For example, in January 2001 OMB raised the predicted share of income going to wages and salaries, a subtle way to achieve this effect.

■ Assert that you will cut spending in the future—even in absolute terms, even if it has been rising sharply as a share of GDP during the past four years, and even if you are proposing expensive new programs. When spending turns out to be higher than your budget forecast, you can always pretend it is a surprise and ask for a "supplemental appropriation." If you pretend it is part of the national defense or homeland security, the public is unlikely to question it.

■ Keep pension funds in the budget while they are running a surplus. (When the baby boomers start to retire during the next decade, move these funds back off the budget.)

■ Whenever you reduce a tax, always give the legislation a phony sunset a few years in the future. If politically important constituents complain that they want a permanent tax cut, reassure them that this is entirely your intention. That does not mean that you have to put it into the budget forecast.

■ Switch among 1-year forecasts, 5-year windows, and 10-year windows, depending on which, at a particular moment, allows you to claim that the trend is in the right direction.

Rubinomics, and Expansion Versus Contraction

Rubinomics is supposedly the claim that fiscal consolidation has a positive effect on growth. To answer the question of whether fiscal contraction can be expansionary, we must consider two offsetting effects: the contemporaneous effect and the confidence effect. They are the same two effects that Posen identifies with Larry Ball and Greg Mankiw, on the one hand, and Alan Greenspan, on the other.

In the short run, fiscal expansion is expansionary. But at the same time, market expectations that the economy is on a future path of a rising debt/GDP ratio can put a lot of upward pressure on long-term interest rates today, and that in itself is contractionary. The two effects go in opposite directions—the contemporaneous Keynesian expansionary effect and the contractionary effect via long-term interest rates. In practice, it is hard to separate the two. This is because actual moves toward fiscal discipline, rather than rhetoric alone, are usually required to influence expectations and achieve credibility.

Table 6.3 is a stylized account of recent fiscal history in this light. It covers four presidential terms, two for Clinton, and two for George W. Bush. (The years 2005–08 would have been heavily influenced by the Bush legacy

Table 6.3 Stylization of the two channels of fiscal policy, by presidential term

Effects on growth	Clinton administration		Bush administration	
	1st term, 1993–96	2nd term, 1997–2000 and beyond	1st term, 2001–04	2nd term, 2005–08 and beyond
As, over time, the numbers show the promises of fiscal responsibility . . .		To be increasingly credible		To be less and less credible
(1) Effect of contemporaneous fiscal stance, via demand ("Keynesian effect")	Mild contraction	Mild contraction	Positive stimulus	Approximately neutral
+ (2) Effect of expected future fiscal path, via long-term interest rates ("confidence effect")	Mild expansion	Strong positive effect	Mild contraction	Strong negative effect
= Overall impact of fiscal policy on growth	Approximately neutral	Positive	Weakly positive	Strongly negative

of debt whether he was the president again or not.) The effects of contemporaneous fiscal stimulus appear in the first Clinton column and the first Bush column. Clinton's mildly contractionary fiscal policy had a mildly contractionary effect contemporaneously, and Bush's expansionary fiscal policy had a modestly positive stimulus contemporaneously.

Now, however, let us look at expectations—the effects on the economy of expected future fiscal paths—which come through long-term interest rates. They are illustrated in the second and fourth columns of table 6.3. Both Clinton and Bush claimed to be on a good long-term path. Initially, it was not entirely credible on either part. But Clinton even in his first term got some credibility benefit. In his second term, when the markets saw that these promises were coming true, interest rates declined, the stock market rose, investment boomed, and the economy achieved a record expansion.

Clinton set numerical goals to cut the deficit by the end of his first term and then again in his second one. These claims of fiscal responsibility became increasingly credible over time, so long-term interest rates fell (with the help of accommodation from the Federal Reserve). I think that in Bush's second-term presidency, we will once again see the emergence of deficit numbers far larger than are currently officially forecast, and that this has not yet been properly absorbed by the public and the markets. Meanwhile, the Fed is beginning to withdraw its extraordinary monetary stimulus of 2001–04. Interest rates will go up, which will start to have a negative effect on the economy.

How Might Europe Salvage the SGP?

But let us return to the fiscal problems of Europe, the topic of this volume. What is to be done, if neither Starve the Beast nor a rigid rule works? How can Shared Sacrifice be formalized and institutionalized?

Some proposals for a balanced-budget amendment or SGP do introduce much-needed flexibility, allowing cyclical adjustment of the targets while maintaining an average balance of zero. But if you allow more flexibility in the form of cyclical adjustment, then you will lose even more credibility; governments will always claim that their budget shortfalls are due to temporary bad luck in the economy (bad weather, terrorist attacks, the dog ate my homework). They will always be tempted to use the tricks that US policymakers have used so effectively in recent years.

I do like, more than Posen, a proposal that is a formalized version of an institution in Chile. The rule is a cyclically adjusted budget balance of, say, zero. But to enforce this rule, you appoint an independent fiscal authority or commission of experts—analogous to the Federal Reserve and other independent central banks—which has the responsibility to say what constitutes deviations from potential output, to compute the cyclically adjusted budget, to make forecasts, and to announce whether this year's budget satisfies the rule. The rest of the government still has the responsibility to allocate spending and taxes within the total, as it should in a democracy. I see this proposal as offering the flexibility that the regimes of the balanced-budget amendment and SGP lack, while preventing the abuse that the regime of Starve the Beast has so abundantly experienced.

References

Chinn, Menzie, and Jeffrey Frankel. 2003. *The Euro Area and World Interest Rates*. Paper 03-17. Santa Cruz, CA: Santa Cruz Center for International Economics.

Clinton, Bill. 2004. *My Life*. New York: Alfred A. Knopf.

Frankel, Jeffrey. 2003. What an Economic Adviser Can Do When He Disagrees with the President. *Challenge*, May–June, 29–52.

Gale, William, and Brian Kelly. 2004. *The No New Taxes Pledge*. Washington: Brookings Institution and Tax Policy Center.

Giavazzi, Francesco, and Marco Pagano. 1990. Can Severe Fiscal Contractions Be Expansionary? Tales of Two Small European Countries. In *NBER Macroeconomics Annual 1990*, ed. Olivier Blanchard and Stanley Fischer. Cambridge, MA: MIT Press.

Niskanen, William. 2002. Comments on Tax Policy. In *American Economic Policy in the 1990s*, ed. Jeffrey Frankel and Peter Orszag. Cambridge, MA: MIT Press.

Rubin, Robert. 2002. Comments on Fiscal Policy. In *American Economic Policy in the 1990s*, ed. Jeffrey Frankel and Peter Orszag. Cambridge, MA: MIT Press.

Woodward, Bob. 1994. *The Agenda*. New York: Simon & Schuster.

7

Building on the Euro's Success

TOMMASO PADOA-SCHIOPPA

The title of this chapter was suggested by the organizers of the conference of which this book is the record. With this title, I could be tempted to indulge in describing such important achievements as the smooth introduction of the new currency, the maintenance of price stability, and the growing international role of the euro. Important as they are, however, we should not forget that such achievements are means to an end. The end is to enhance economic prosperity in a stable and safe environment, and to do so both in Europe and worldwide. Indeed, in an increasingly globalized world, we cannot take a domestic perspective only. Spillovers between countries and regions are so powerful and frequent that prosperity and stability can be achieved and preserved domestically only if they are at the same time safeguarded globally.

In this chapter, I describe the euro's success from this broader perspective, and discuss how Europe can help meet the challenges faced by the global economy today. Let me state clearly up front what I see as the euro's three main elements of success from this perspective. First, the European Monetary Union—or, in short, the euro—has brought monetary stability to an economic area that constitutes the world's largest trading partnership and had been for very long an area of instability. Second, it has helped anchor policies in its region, and most particularly in central and eastern Europe, thereby contributing to guiding one of the most profound processes of economic transformation the world has experienced in many decades. And third, the euro is contributing to global adjustment

Tommaso Padoa-Schioppa is a member of the Executive Board of the European Central Bank.

patterns with an active and constructive commitment to the principles of the post–Bretton Woods global, multilateral arrangements.

The Domestic Dimension

To start with the domestic dimension, European Monetary Union has put an end to Europe as an area of monetary tensions, exchange rate crises, and macroeconomic imbalances. The euro has turned it into an area of stability. Not only has it eliminated exchange rate disruptions among the participating countries, but it has also established an environment of low long-term interest rates throughout the euro area. Long-term rates have declined by about 5 percentage points from 1994 to the start of the single monetary policy in January 1999. At the same time, interest rate dispersion has virtually disappeared. Given the weight of the euro area in the world economy, this has contributed to global stability in a significant way.

Success was not guaranteed from the outset. Rather, it was dependent on the degree of confidence the euro would inspire among the more than 300 million euro area citizens when they use it as a means of payment, a store of value, and a unit of account. Five years ago, the Eurosystem had still to prove its capability to build and maintain such confidence.

At that time, some skeptical observers predicted that inflation expectations and outcomes in the euro area would rise again once the beneficial effects of the convergence process ebbed. Others argued that the quality of the new currency would correspond only to some average of all legacy currencies, rather than to the benchmark set by the strongest ones. We can say now that both views turned out to be wrong. The Eurosystem has been successful in keeping inflation and inflation expectations stable and anchored to its very demanding definition of price stability.

The euro has also been a central element of the integration process among EU members. For example, it has enhanced competition across borders and acted as a catalyst for structural change.

All these are very important achievements. Yet when discussing economic success, I am acutely aware that Europe is far from meeting one key requirement of that success, namely, combining price stability with healthy rates of growth. This is indeed a crucial issue, to which I shall return when examining the global dimension.

The Regional Dimension

Let us now turn to the second element of success: the anchoring role for policies in central and eastern Europe. The prospect of joining the European Union and eventually the euro area has been crucial in guiding the fundamental economic change implied in the transition from a command to a market economy. This prospect has also fostered macroeconomic stability in the region.

In May 2004, 75 million people joined the European Union, and the euro will ultimately become their currency. The path toward the full monetary integration of the new entrants is clearly laid out and will be implemented as they progress in convergence. Many of the benefits are already visible now. Trade integration has already fully occurred, and many of the prospective new member states are trading as much with the current EU members as those members are doing among themselves. Financial integration is also highly advanced, through the ownership links between EU commercial banks and the banking systems in central and eastern Europe.

As for nominal convergence, inflation rates five years ago were still at 10 percent in the region and had declined to 2 percent by last year, without economic growth suffering. As a matter of fact, several of the new entrants are closer to meeting the numerical Maastricht criteria today than the current euro area members were five years before the euro. This means that the prospect of euro adoption has already helped anchor policies in this part of the global economy and is entrenching progress in transition, integration, and nominal convergence.

Of course, the impressive progress in *nominal* convergence should not hide the enormous task of *real* convergence. The purchasing power per head in the prospective member states is only about half that in the current European Union. The major challenge is indeed catching up in terms of prosperity. But the conditions are in place for these countries to grow by more than 5 percent a year for many years. This would be in line with the experience of regions and countries such as the south of Germany, the northeast of Italy, and Ireland. The main challenge for new member states will thus be to preserve and strengthen nominal convergence while succeeding in the real catching up.

The anchoring effect of the euro in the region neighboring the euro area goes, however, well beyond the scope of prospective new member states. The European Union has significantly tightened its economic, financial, and institutional links with many countries surrounding it. The European Union's enlargement is the best-known example, but there are also the Stabilization and Association Process with the countries of the western Balkans; the Barcelona Process with Mediterranean countries; and the Partnership and Cooperation Agreements with countries of the Commonwealth of Independent States, notably Russia. Indeed, from an institutional point of view, current developments in Europe represent an expansion of the cooperative framework that has characterized the European integration process since the early 1950s.

The euro is, of course, only part of this whole process, but not a minor one. In terms of *official* use, most of the roughly 50 countries for which the euro is—in various degrees of intensity—an anchor or a reference currency are located in the immediate geographical neighborhood of the euro area—in particular, the countries of central and eastern Europe, the Mediterranean, and the Balkans. In terms of *private* use, the euro is an important financing currency for borrowers and a major vehicle currency in foreign exchange markets in countries close to the euro area. In addition, a significant use of the euro as a parallel currency can be observed in the European Union's neighboring regions.

The Global Dimension

Turning now to the global dimension, the euro has well established itself as the second international currency. In some areas, in particular in international financial markets, its importance has grown during the past five years. Financial institutions and nonfinancial corporations, in particular those from the United Kingdom, the United States, and Canada, have taken advantage of the greater size and liquidity provided by the increasingly integrated euro bond market. As a result, the share of the euro in the stock of international debt securities rose from about 20 percent in 1999 to more than 30 percent in 2003. In other areas, the international role of the euro has remained relatively stable. An example is the foreign exchange market, where the share of the euro in foreign exchange transactions today is not significantly bigger than that of the deutsche mark in the past, accounting for about one-quarter.

Beyond this rather specific role, however, what matters most is the contribution the euro provides to global monetary and financial stability. This contribution consists in the euro area's constructive participation in the post–Bretton Woods arrangements, and in its active commitment to multilateral cooperation. It is useful to elaborate on this point, because in this area we are now confronted with a most pressing issue, namely, how to achieve the adjustment of the large global imbalances as smoothly as possible, avoiding—or at least minimizing—negative effects on global economic growth.

What should the euro and the euro area do to meet this challenge? To answer this question, I refer to four key features of the post–Bretton Woods regime. First, no single currency performs the anchoring role for the other major currencies. Second, exchange rates are determined by market forces and ought to be in line with economic fundamentals; as such, their movements are expected to contribute to the adjustment of external imbalances. Third, because exchange rate markets may be very volatile and may produce disorderly movements among the major currencies, occasional public action through verbal or, in some special circumstances, market intervention might be undertaken. Fourth, the appropriate framework for international cooperation is a multilateral one, mainly through the Group of Seven and the IMF.

Let me say that the euro area's policy is fully consistent with these four key features. Exchange rate developments enter into the European Central Bank's (ECB's) monetary policy strategy, together with all pertinent economic variables, to the extent that they have a bearing on its primary objective of price stability. The ECB respects the fact that the exchange rate of the euro is essentially market determined. At the same time, the ECB has—on a very few occasions during the past five years—made its view clear about specific developments in the exchange rate of the euro. For instance, it has recently observed that the current magnitudes of exchange rate swings could create momentum and excessive volatility in financial markets that might be unwarranted on the basis of economic fundamentals.

It is by accepting the logic of the post–Bretton Woods regime that Europe has fully supported the adjustment process during the past two years. It has done so in spite of the fact that Europe is not contributing—in either direction—to the gravity of present global imbalances. As part of this adjustment process, the euro has appreciated against the dollar by about 46 percent since March 2002, with more than one-third of this (17 percent) concentrated between September 2003 and February 2004. Perhaps even more striking, the euro has appreciated by virtually the same percentages on average vis-à-vis the currencies of China, Japan, South Korea, and the other main Asian economies. This is due to the link these currencies have maintained with the dollar. Such an appreciation is striking if one considers how strong competitors these economies already were before depreciating and how large their external surpluses are.

From experience, we know that to bring large external imbalances back on a sustainable path, changes are required both in prices and quantities. The exchange rate alone is not sufficient; growth differentials must also adjust. And here is where lies the main challenge for Europe today: to increase its potential and actual growth. For the world economy not to slow down, it will be necessary, in the years to come, to step up European growth.

During the past decade, real GDP in the euro area grew at the disappointingly low rate of 2 percent a year, whereas in the United States it exceeded 3 percent. I am always struck with admiration when I think that the United States' actual growth exceeded its potential growth for six of the last seven years of the 1990s. Even if one considers that part of the EU-US growth differential is attributable to a difference in demographic trends, the extraordinary performance of the US economy remains.

Not only is *potential* growth relatively low in Europe; the *actual* growth performance is also persistently falling short of that potential. At this moment, prospects for recovery seem to lie ahead, given the establishment of macroeconomic stability and very low interest rates (indeed, the lowest in 50 years). Moreover, important structural rigidities have been dismantled in Europe in recent years, and the integration of 10 new catching-up economies is an implicit promise for growth. However, there is no room for complacency: Europe still falls short of its aim to become a fully competitive and dynamic economy. Only by significantly stepping up its own growth performance will Europe complete its contribution to overcoming the challenges facing the world economy.

But I think that there is yet another, no less relevant European contribution to the functioning of the global economy. This is to strengthen the multilateral character of international cooperation. To this end, Europe can build on its success in applying multilateralism to its regional integration. A close look at the origins of the current imbalances suggests that they have emerged—at least partly—from a policy environment characterized by a degree of unilateralism.

As we know, the reserve buildup in Asia has become the main source of financing of the US current account deficit. This unprecedented buildup has been motivated to a significant extent by the desire of Asian governments to protect their economy against external shocks and by the pursuit of a growth strategy that was largely export led. The pursuit of such a strategy is understandable, because it combines domestic development with international integration. After all, Europe followed a similar path in the 1950s and 1960s. However, a policy in which the countries peg, or tightly manage, their currencies vis-à-vis the dollar implies that the latter becomes the informal common monetary standard both in the region and in relation to the outside. Actually, although formal efforts at regional economic integration have recently increased in Asia, monetary issues have not yet become a significant part of this process.

For some years, a policy of unilateral dollar pegs in Asia has benefited all parties involved. The United States has been able to finance fiscal and current account deficits in an environment of low interest rates despite a falling dollar. Asian countries have received strong growth impulses, and some have even welcomed the buildup in reserves as a further measure to fight deflationary tendencies. However, one may wonder how long this mutually beneficial outcome will last. Indeed, since mid-2003 there have been increasing calls, particularly from US authorities, for more flexibility in Asia's exchange rate management. This has been advocated with a view of leading to some orderly and progressive appreciation of the currencies of emerging Asia. The Group of Seven statement at Boca Raton in February 2004 points in the same direction.

The adjustment of global imbalances is a delicate process, which has a global and multilateral character even when such imbalances are not evenly distributed across the world. At the same time, we should be aware of the fragility and incompleteness of the system of open trade we have constructed over the years. I know of no country where the constituency of protectionism takes long vacations. Recently, there have been suggestions in some quarters, both in the European Union and the United

States, in favor of protectionist measures to tackle increasing competition by Asian countries.

I mention this to stress that in an increasingly globalized economy, the preservation and strengthening of a satisfactory multilateral framework is crucially important. As a European, I am aware that the move toward exchange rates more in line with underlying fundamentals can be difficult. This is all the more true when exchange rate policies not only bear on trade and financial relations with the anchor country but also on those with important trading partners in the region. But at the same time, and against the background of the European experience, I venture to say that it will be difficult to secure progress in economic and financial integration—both within Asia as well as between Asia and the rest of the world—without addressing at some point the monetary dimension of such cooperation.

Conclusions

In discussing the euro's success, I have said relatively little about the achievements of introducing a single currency for 12 sovereign nations, the maintenance of price stability in the euro area, and the euro's gradually increasing international role. I have said relatively little about these issues because I regard them as necessary foundations for the euro's success but not as its essence. In my view, the essence lies deeper—in having brought stability to Europe, both in the euro area and its neighboring regions, in contributing to global adjustment through a commitment to exchange rate arrangements fully consistent with the post–Bretton Woods setting, and in reinforcing principles of multilateral cooperation that are applicable at the regional as well as global levels.

It is in these areas that the euro contributes to a more efficient and stable international monetary system, and it is also here that we must continue to work to further improve the functioning of this system—domestically, in fostering sustainable growth in the euro area, and globally, in working toward a framework that accompanies globalization in the real economic sphere with an appropriate framework in the monetary sphere. The positive experience of the euro reminds us that a multilateral framework is the best choice to make.

8

The Euro at Five: An Assessment

BEN S. BERNANKE

> What is the appropriate domain of a currency area? It might seem at first that the question is purely academic since it hardly appears within the realm of political feasibility that national currencies would ever be abandoned in favor of any other arrangement.
>
> —Robert A. Mundell (1961, 657)

The successful introduction five years ago of an entirely new currency over a wide range of polities and economies was, at a minimum, a remarkable technical achievement. As a card-carrying member of the club of monetary economists, I like to think that our collective expertise was helpful in making that achievement possible. As both a policymaker and an economist, I welcome this opportunity to look back on the first five years of the euro to see what can be learned from the experience and to consider what this grand experiment implies for the future.

The economic analysis of optimal currency areas began, of course, with Robert Mundell's seminal 1961 paper, quoted above.[1] As you know, Mundell argued that, ideally, economic similarity, not political boundaries, should define the geographic area spanned by a common currency. He was the first to state the classic trade-off implied by the decision to adopt a common currency. According to Mundell, the principal advantage of a

Ben S. Bernanke is a member of the Board of Governors of the Federal Reserve System. This is the text of a keynote address to the Euro at Five conference, held February 26, 2004, at the Institute for International Economics. Karen Johnson and members of the board's International Finance Division provided helpful assistance and comments. These remarks reflect the author's views and not necessarily those of his colleagues in the Federal Reserve System.

1. McKinnon (1963) extended Mundell's analysis.

common currency is the reduction in transaction costs implied by the use of a common medium of exchange across a broad area. The disadvantage of a common currency is the loss of the shock-absorber properties of flexible exchange rates and independent monetary policies. Flexible exchange rates and independent monetary policies will be useful shock absorbers to the extent that macroeconomic shocks are imperfectly correlated across regions, wages and prices are sticky, and other macroeconomic adjustment mechanisms—such as factor mobility or fiscal transfers among regions—are weak or absent. Thus, from the Mundellian perspective, the case for a common currency within a broad area is stronger the greater the actual or potential economic and financial integration within the area, the greater the correlation of macroeconomic shocks among regions within the area, and the more effective the nonmonetary shock absorbers, such as factor mobility.

Whether the nations that compose the European Monetary Union (EMU) form an optimal currency area in Mundell's sense has been widely debated by researchers. For example, Barry Eichengreen (1992) argued early on that Europe was perhaps not well suited for a common currency on economic grounds (though he found the political motivations more compelling). According to Eichengreen, the factors reducing the desirability of a monetary union in Europe included the historical variability of real exchange rates among European nations, the low degree of labor mobility between countries, and a lower correlation of underlying shocks among European countries than among regions of the United States.[2] Other critics of monetary unification, such as Martin Feldstein, have stressed the limited extent of fiscal transfers within the European Union. Differences across countries in the nature and strength of the monetary policy transmission mechanism are another factor that may reduce the attractiveness of a monetary union.[3] However, some more recent assessments, which have emphasized factors such as the high propensity of European countries to trade with each other and the increased coherence of national business cycles within Europe, have generally been more favorable (Alesina, Barro, and Tenreyro 2002; Agresti and Mojon 2001). Of course, analyses that look only at historical conditions ignore the important possibility that monetary union itself may induce endogenous changes in trade propensities, the pattern of macroeconomic shocks, and other components of the Mundellian analysis, a point that Eichengreen and many other authors have made.

Rather than pursuing the question of whether Europe is in fact an optimal currency area in Mundell's sense, I think it is useful simply to recognize that the European experiment in economic and monetary union has

---

2. See also Bayoumi and Eichengreen (1992).

3. The volume edited by Angeloni, Kashyap, and Mojon (2003) documents these differences in detail.

not been motivated primarily by Mundellian factors. (Mundell himself did not expect that such considerations would be sufficient to lead to monetary unions, as the quote with which I began suggests.) Political factors rather than economic ones have played the dominant role. The nations of Europe share a remarkable cultural heritage in philosophy, politics, science, religion, and the arts, and advanced thinkers have long recognized that this common heritage might serve as a basis for the formation of a cohesive European political entity. Such an entity presumably could influence world events and provide for a common defense more effectively than could a collection of nation-states.

Indeed, political and economic integration within regions of Europe has occurred on a number of occasions—for example, in Germany and Italy. Another important motivation for political integration has been the desire to reduce the risk of intra-European conflict. From Napoleon to Bismarck to the Kaiser to Hitler, Franco-Prussian and then Franco-German conflicts were flash points for continentwide and worldwide wars. European Economic and Monetary Union (EMU) holds the promise of binding so closely the economic interests of these two powers, as well as those of other European nations, as to make future intra-European conflict unthinkable. Such arguments have been part of the debate over European integration at least since the 1957 Treaty of Rome. Indeed, the hope of policymakers is to create a virtuous circle, in which closer economic integration promotes greater political cooperation, which enhances opportunities for economic integration, and so on.[4]

The largely political origin of the union has several implications for the economic analysis of the common currency. First, from a purely economic point of view, the creation of the EMU is at least partly an exogenous event. Thus, something of a natural experiment exists from which to learn about the effects of such institutional innovations. Second, an assessment of the success of the euro, indeed of the entire experiment in European integration, rests not only on economic criteria but also on the success of Europe as a political entity.

If one thinks of the introduction of the euro as representing to some degree a natural experiment in monetary economics, what can be said about the costs and benefits, at least thus far, of this sweeping institutional change? One can look in a number of areas for effects of monetary unification, including the patterns of trade, developments in the financial sector, changes in macroeconomic stability, and the international role of the new currency. Many of these areas have already been examined elsewhere in this volume in much greater detail than I can do here. Rather than trying to be exhaustive, I will instead assert and briefly defend a hypothesis.

---

4. The importance of political factors in the European economic union has also been illustrated by the importance of noneconomic considerations in the debates about joining the union in nations such as Sweden and the United Kingdom.

The hypothesis is that the most significant effects of monetary unification have been felt, and will continue to be felt, in the development of European financial markets and that the greatest economic benefits to Europe in the long run will accrue through the improved functioning of these markets.

Effect on Trade

To defend this hypothesis, I need first to consider briefly the effects of monetary unification in some other key areas. Let us begin with trade. The debate about monetary unification was influenced to some extent by a tradition of empirical research that provided some basis for optimism about the effects of a common currency on trade. For example, the extensive literature on so-called border effects concluded that nations trade with each other far less than would be expected based on the extent of trade between regions within a country, opening up the possibility that differing national currencies are among the factors that inhibit trade.

In a recent study, Reuven Glick and Andrew Rose (2001) provided some support for the idea that currency unions promote trade. Glick and Rose analyzed a panel data set of 217 countries for 1948–97. They found that entering or leaving a currency union had large effects on trade flows. Indeed, they estimated that a pair of countries that begins to use a common currency should see a doubling in bilateral trade. However, as Glick and Rose themselves note, many of the countries entering or leaving currency unions during their sample period were small and poor, not rich and (in some cases) large like the nations of western Europe. Moreover, their analysis does not rule out either reverse causality (that is, that increasing trade may promote the adoption of a currency union, rather than vice versa) or the possibility that a third, unmeasured factor (such as political relationships) may have influenced both trade and currency policies.

In contrast to the findings of Glick and Rose, evidence drawn directly from the recent European experience does *not* generally support the view that adoption of a common currency has a major effect on the magnitude or direction of trade.[5] True, euro-area exports did surge after the adoption of the euro in January 1999. However, cyclical conditions and the early weakness of the new currency no doubt played a critical role in that increase, an inference confirmed by the substantial slowing in European export growth since the beginning of 2001. Also striking is the fact that the share of total euro-area exports destined for other members of the eurozone did not increase with the introduction of the currency, as would be likely if the common currency promoted trade. Indeed, at about 50 per-

---

5. Micco, Stein, and Ordonez (2003), using bilateral trade data from the early years of the monetary union, find modest trade-enhancing effects.

cent of total exports, the intra-euro-area export share today remains noticeably below the recent peak of about 57 percent reached in the early 1990s.

The most decisive evidence on the trade question can be found by looking at microdata. In an important study, John Rogers (2003) of the board staff analyzed annual data on the prices of 139 items, collected by the Economist Intelligence Unit for 25 European and 13 US cities. For his main results, Rogers divided the items into traded and nontraded categories, though he considered many other ways of slicing the data as well. He then analyzed the cross-city dispersion of prices in each year. Of course, the reduction of barriers to trade, the harmonization of tax policies, and the increased efficiency of cross-national markets should lead to reduced dispersion in the prices of goods, especially actively traded goods, as competition and arbitrage reduce local monopoly power and differences in prices.

Rogers found a substantial decline in the dispersion of traded goods prices across European cities over 1990–2001. Indeed, by the end of the period, the variability of traded goods prices across cities within EMU countries had declined by more than half, and it was not substantially different from the variability found among cities in the United States. This convergence of prices suggests a powerful, ongoing process of increased economic integration and elimination of barriers to trade among the members of the EMU. Crucially, however, Rogers found that the bulk of this convergence occurred between 1990 and 1994, the period of the "single market" initiative. Only a small part of the convergence in traded goods prices occurred after 1998, the period during which the euro was introduced and national currencies were withdrawn from circulation. Rogers's evidence therefore suggests that the increased integration of product markets in Europe has been an ongoing process, which may have been assisted by the adoption of the euro but for which a common currency has hardly proved essential.

Effect on Stability

A second question of interest is the degree to which adoption of the euro has affected macroeconomic stability in the eurozone. In Mundell's taxonomy, adoption of a common currency is a strictly negative factor for stability because it eliminates the shock-absorbing features of flexible exchange rates and independent monetary policies. In fact, however, the effects of the common currency on macroeconomic stability in Europe have been positive as well as negative. Notably, the structure and mandate of the European Central Bank (ECB), as well as the perception of continuity with the policies of the pre-euro Bundesbank, have enhanced the ECB's credibility and contributed to low and stable inflation in the eurozone.

Although Germany and several other countries in the union enjoyed low inflation before the adoption of the common currency, with some partial exceptions to be discussed below, the ECB has been able to "export" that benefit to other members of the monetary union. The common currency has also eliminated periodic exchange rate crises, which had plagued European monetary arrangements and generated real and financial disturbances at least since the days of the gold standard.

On the other hand, the ECB has faced the challenge of making policy for Europe as a whole despite differing macroeconomic conditions in member countries, a dilemma that Mundell would have predicted. For example, since 1999 a few countries, such as Ireland, have had inflation rates consistently above the eurozone average. Irish inflation peaked at 7 percent on a 12-month basis in November 2000 and has since been in the 4 to 5 percent range. At the same time, other countries, such as Germany, have experienced low—perhaps uncomfortably low—rates of inflation.[6]

Patrick Honohan and Philip Lane (2003) investigated the sources of relatively high inflation in Ireland after the adoption of the euro. These authors found that the loss of exchange rate flexibility and monetary autonomy played important roles in the Irish inflation. For example, a relatively large share of Ireland's trade is with non-European partners, so that the early weakness of the euro stimulated Irish exports and economic activity disproportionately. Ireland was also unable to resort to monetary restraint to cool down an economy that, for a variety of reasons, was experiencing faster demand growth than most of the rest of Europe.[7] Ireland's relatively high inflation rate may in turn have had destabilizing effects, because, in combination with low pan-European nominal interest rates, it implied that the Irish economy faced a negative real rate of interest. One possible consequence of the low real rate is the boom in Irish property prices, which has fed back into higher domestic spending.

Of course, at the other end of the spectrum, Germany has experienced weak growth and very low inflation in the past few years (Sinn 2003). Without the ability to use stabilizing monetary policy, Germany has eased fiscal policy and thus has come into conflict with its obligations under the Stability and Growth Pact.

In short, with respect to macroeconomic stability, the common currency appears to have had both positive and negative effects. More time will be needed before we can assess whether the common currency will ultimately be a stabilizing or a destabilizing influence at the macroeconomic level.

---

6. Some cross-country differences in inflation might simply reflect convergence in price levels, resulting from the Balassa-Samuelson effect or from initial conversion factors from national currencies to the euro not precisely consistent with the law of one price for tradables. Rogers (2003) finds some evidence for the latter effect but not the former.

7. Of course, fiscal policy remained available, though most economists agree that fiscal policy is less effective than monetary policy as a short-run stabilization tool.

International Role

Yet a third area in which potential benefits of the euro have often been cited is in respect to the common currency's potential international role. The phrase "international role of the euro" covers a number of disparate possible functions of the currency. These functions include the use of euro-denominated assets as official reserves, the use of the euro as a vehicle currency in foreign exchange transactions, the denomination in euros of financing instruments issued by borrowers not resident in the eurozone, the acceptance of euro-denominated or euro-linked assets in international investment portfolios, and the invoicing in euros of internationally traded goods and services. Of course, during the post–World War II period the dollar has been the dominant international currency with respect to each of these functions. It seems plausible that the euro, a low-inflation currency used by an economy comparable to that of the United States in size and sophistication, will over time increase its "market share" in each of these areas. However, the euro's potential international role, and, more importantly, the benefits to eurozone countries of an increased role for the euro differ significantly by function.

A summary evaluation of the euro's international position is that the common currency's role has been increasing but that so far the euro has posed less of a challenge to the dollar as an international medium of exchange than some analysts expected. For example, in foreign exchange markets the US dollar accounts for nearly 50 percent of transaction "sides" compared with about 25 percent for the euro, implying that the overwhelming majority of foreign exchange transactions involve the dollar (European Central Bank 2003, 26; data are from Continuous Linked Settlement). Hence, the dollar appears to remain the international "vehicle currency," serving as a temporary abode of value for foreign exchange transactions involving third currencies, whereas the euro's role in foreign exchange markets is similar to that played in earlier times by the deutsche mark (Solans 2003).

The dollar also remains the dominant invoicing currency for internationally traded raw materials, such as oil. The dollar is even dominant in US-European trade, with more than 90 percent of US exports to Europe and somewhat more than 80 percent of European exports to the United States being invoiced in dollars as of September 2003 (European Central Bank 2003, 33). With regard to the currency composition of official reserves, dollar-denominated assets accounted for 64.5 percent of world reserves at the end of 2002, down from 67.5 percent at the end of 2000. During the same period, the euro's share of international reserves rose from 15.9 percent to 18.7 percent (European Central Bank 2003, 45).

Although economists and financial market participants will observe the developing role of the euro in international transactions with interest, the direct benefits to eurozone economies of having the euro play an international medium-of-exchange role are relatively modest. Arguably, the more significant aspects of the euro's international role arise from the strengthening and expansion of euro-denominated financial markets as these markets take on a greater international character. Internationalization of European financial markets increases investment opportunities, opportunities for diversification, and sources of funding, and it improves liquidity and market efficiency.

Effect on European Financial Markets

As suggested above, the most important benefit of the currency union has been and will likely continue to be its strengthening of European financial markets. Traditionally, the efficiency and scope of these markets has been hampered by the costs and risks associated with the use of multiple currencies as well as by the fragmentation arising from international differences in legal structure, accounting rules, and other institutions. Given the rapidity and frequency of trade in financial markets, even small transaction costs can hamper the efficiency and liquidity of those markets. The common currency, with ongoing efforts to harmonize financial regulations and institutions, has significantly reduced those transaction costs. Together with lower country-specific macro risks arising from the adoption of the common currency, this reduction in transaction costs has greatly improved the breadth and efficiency of European financial markets.

Importantly, the benefit of more efficient financial markets goes well beyond the benefits to financial investors and the financial industry itself. A growing academic literature suggests that financial development is a critical precursor to broader economic development (King and Levine 1993). In this vein, a study for the European Commission estimated that financial development that brought the European financial system close to US norms might add almost a percentage point to the growth of value added in manufacturing in the European Union (Giannetti et al. 2002). Whether one accepts this optimistic assessment or not, there are evidently significant potential benefits to financial deepening that go beyond the financial sector itself.

How has the common currency improved financial efficiency? Perhaps the most dramatic effects of the monetary union in the financial sphere have been in fixed-income markets, both government and private. Government debt markets, because of their size, safety, and benchmark status, are central to a vibrant fixed-income market, and they have been particularly strengthened by the adoption of the euro. Notably, since the run-up to the monetary union began, sovereign debt yields have converged to a remarkable extent. For example, between 1990 and 1996, spreads on Italian and Spanish government bonds, relative to German bonds of comparable maturity, averaged about 430 and 350 basis points, respectively. Today the spreads paid by these governments are quite small, in the vicinity of 15 basis points over the German equivalent for Italy and essentially zero for Spain.[8] Clearly, these governments have benefited substantially by the reduction in inflation risk and exchange rate risk provided by the common currency.[9] The addition of some sovereign default risk (now relevant because individual countries are no longer able to inflate away their debts) has evidently not offset these benefits, perhaps because of the effects of the Stability and Growth Pact.

Beyond improving the fundamentals of government finances, the common currency has also increased the depth and breadth of government bond markets. In particular, the development of a large market in euro-denominated government debt and the resulting expansion in cross-border holdings of debt has improved market liquidity and opportunities for risk sharing. For example, in their excellent survey of developments in European financial markets since the introduction of the euro, Gabriele Galati and Kostas Tsatsaronis (2003, 174) note that nonresident holdings of French government bonds rose from about 15 percent at the end of 1997 to about 35 percent by 2002. Moreover, as of 2002, foreigners held three-quarters of Belgian government long-term bonds and 63 percent of Irish government debt. A broader investor clientele implies more potential bidders in primary markets and more transactions in secondary markets, improving liquidity. This broadening is the sense in which an international role for the euro, by which here I mean more internationalized European financial markets, seems to promise the greatest potential benefits.

The European government bond market has been substantially strengthened by the adoption of the common currency, but it has not attained the liquidity of the US Treasury market (and may never do so). Although aggregate issuance of eurozone government debt is of the same order of magnitude as US Treasury issues, there remains the fundamental difference that eurozone debt is the debt of 12 sovereign entities rather than one, as in the United States. Naturally, the European Union accepts no collective responsibility for the debts of individual governments, the Stability and Growth Pact notwithstanding. Moreover, so far the coordination of issuance schedules, the structure of issues, and other technical details has been limited. However, opportunities for further strengthening of the eurozone government bond market appear to remain. For example, if the technical details can be worked out, one can imagine the issuance of securities backed by the obligations of multiple European gov-

---

8. So-called convergence plays proved very profitable for financial investors who bet on the success of the EMU and its implication that government debt spreads would largely disappear.

9. It is interesting, however, that even nonmembers such as Sweden and the United Kingdom have seen their bond yields converge to the German benchmark since about 1997 or 1998.

ernments. These securities could be made uniform by fixing the country shares of the underlying debt, or by stripping off country-specific default risks through such instruments as credit default swaps. Such securities would provide a benchmark yield curve, among other advantages.

The benefits of the euro for government bond markets have carried over to corporate bond markets as well. Issuance of euro-denominated bonds by corporations took off soon after the introduction of the new currency. Although much of the boom no doubt reflected general macroeconomic conditions and other factors, potential access to a much larger base of investors willing to hold bonds in the common currency and resulting improvements in pricing and liquidity also played a role. Underwriting costs have also fallen, the result of both greater competition and the reduced costs of bringing issues to market (Santos and Tsatsaronis 2003). The rapid development of Europe's corporate bond market, including a nascent high-yield market, should prove highly beneficial to European economic development.

The benefits of the common currency for other types of securities markets have been more mixed thus far, but the potential is there. The European interbank market was strengthened substantially in tandem with the creation of the eurosystem of central banks. In contrast, markets for securities lending (repo markets) remain somewhat fragmented, and commercial paper markets are underdeveloped. European stock markets, which in any case account for a smaller share of financing activity than in the United States, have not been successfully harmonized thus far, and cross-border equity investments may still involve high transaction costs (McAndrews and Stefanadis 2002). However, it is widely observed that the perspectives and strategies of European equity analysts have changed toward a deemphasis on country-specific factors and greater attention to industry and company factors in the valuation of stocks (Adjaouté and Danthine 2002). This change indicates that financial market participants see increased financial and economic integration in Europe as an irreversible trend. Efforts to adhere to the Lamfalussy process, which aims to streamline the harmonization process for financial market legislation and regulation, should hasten the integration of European securities markets.

European finance has traditionally been bank centered. What will happen to banks in the new regime? Banks may lose some loan customers to the growing securities markets, but they will also benefit from increased access to finance, both in the interbank market and in the corporate bond market. Indeed, the banks were large players in the early boom in the issuance of euro-denominated corporate bonds, accounting for more than half the new issues thus far (Galati and Tsatsaronis 2003, 181). On the lending side, banks' local knowledge and specialized services should allow them to retain an important market share.

In a study that illustrated the importance of banks' knowledge of local conditions, Allen Berger and David Smith (2003) found that European affiliates of multinational corporations strongly prefer working with a bank in the country of their operation rather than a bank from the country of the multinational's corporate headquarters. Moreover, having chosen a bank in the country of operations, the affiliates were more likely to select a bank with local or regional operations than a bank with global reach. These results are consistent with the view that bankers' competitive advantage relative to security markets is their knowledge of local firms, markets, and economic conditions and their ability to establish long-term relationships with local customers. Perhaps the European banking situation will begin to look more like that of the United States, where borrowing through securities issuance and banking coexist, providing different services and meeting the needs of different clienteles. Moreover, the composition of banks may settle into the pattern of the United States, where very large banks with a global reach and the capacity to engineer highly complex transactions and community banks that specialize in lending to the local area have both found room to flourish. However banking may evolve in Europe, increased financial integration that makes local banking markets more "contestable" will likely improve the efficiency with which local banking services are delivered.

I have only scratched the surface of a large topic, but it seems safe to conclude that the common currency has had and will continue to have large benefits for European finance. At a minimum, the single currency eliminates exchange rate risks that exist when securities are denominated in different currencies. The single unit of account seems also likely to reduce transaction costs and eliminate a portion of the fixed costs involved in issuing similar securities in multiple currencies. These factors are already serving to moderate home bias in borrowing and lending, leading to larger, more liquid, and more diversified financial markets.

Clearly, a great deal more work needs to be done, both by the government and by the private sector, to realize the full benefits of the common currency for European finance. Beyond the markets that I have mentioned as needing special attention, like equity markets, further harmonization is also required to coordinate national systems for payments, clearing, and settlement. A larger, more integrated financial system may carry greater systemic risks and raise new challenges for the system of financial oversight and supervision. Further challenges will arise as new countries, including those currently at a relatively low level of financial development, join the European monetary system. Their accession will greatly complicate the harmonization process, but given what is known about the role of finance in economic development, the benefits for both the new members and the current ones could be very large.

References

Adjaouté, Kpate, and Jean-Pierre Danthine. 2002. European Financial Integration and Equity Returns: A Theory-Based Assessment. Paper prepared for the Second ECB Central Banking Conference on The Transformation of the European Financial System, October 24–25, Frankfurt-am-Main.

Agresti, Anna-Maria, and Benoit Mojon. 2001. *Some Stylized Facts on the Euro Area Business Cycle.* European Central Bank Working Paper 95 (December). Frankfurt: European Central Bank.

Alesina, Alberto, Robert Barro, and Silvana Tenreyro. 2002. *Optimal Currency Areas.* National Bureau of Economic Research Working Paper 9072 (July). Cambridge, MA: National Bureau of Economic Research.

Angeloni, Ignazio, Anil Kashyap, and Benoit Mojon, eds. 2003. *Monetary Policy Transmission in the Euro Area.* Cambridge, UK: Cambridge University Press.

Bayoumi, Tamim, and Barry Eichengreen. 1992. *Shocking Aspects of European Monetary Unification.* National Bureau of Economic Research Working Paper 3949 (January). Cambridge, MA: National Bureau of Economic Research.

Berger, Allen, and David Smith. 2003. Global Integration in the Banking Industry. *Federal Reserve Bulletin* 89 (November): 451–60.

Eichengreen, Barry. 1992. Is Europe an Optimum Currency Area? In Silvio Borner and Herbert Grubel, eds., *The European Community after 1992.* London: Macmillan.

European Central Bank. 2003. *Review of the International Role of the Euro.* Frankfurt-am-Main (December).

Galati, Gabriele, and Kostas Tsatsaronis. 2003. The Impact of the Euro on Europe's Financial Markets. *Financial Markets, Institutions, and Instruments* 12 (August): 165–221.

Giannetti, Mariassunta, Luigi Guiso, Tullio Jappelli, Mario Padula, and Marco Pagano. 2002. *Financial Market Integration, Corporate Financing and Economic Growth.* European Commission, Directorate-General for Economic and Financial Affairs, Economic Paper 179 (November). Brussels: European Commission.

Glick, Reuven, and Andrew Rose. 2001. *Does a Currency Union Affect Trade? The Time Series Evidence.* National Bureau of Economic Research Working Paper 8396 (July). Cambridge, MA: National Bureau of Economic Research.

Honohan, Patrick, and Philip Lane. 2003. *Divergent Inflation Rates in EMU.* Working Paper, World Bank and Trinity College (October).

King, Robert, and Ross Levine. 1993. Finance and Growth: Schumpeter Might Be Right. *Quarterly Journal of Economics* 108: 717–37.

McAndrews, James, and Chris Stefanadis. 2002. The Consolidation of European Stock Exchanges. *Current Issues in Economics and Finance* 8 (June). Federal Reserve Bank of New York (June).

McKinnon, Ronald. 1963. Optimum Currency Areas. *American Economic Review* 53 (September): 717–25.

Micco, Alejandro, Ernesto Stein, and Guillermo Ordonez. 2003. The Currency Union Effect on Trade: Early Evidence from EMU. *Economic Policy* (October): 315–56.

Mundell, Robert. 1961. A Theory of Optimum Currency Areas. *American Economic Review* 51 (September): 657–65.

Rogers, John H. 2003. *Monetary Union, Price Level Convergence, and Inflation: How Close Is Europe to the United States?* Working Paper. Washington: International Finance Division, Board of Governors of the Federal Reserve System.

Santos, João, and Kostas Tsatsaronis. 2003. *The Cost of Barriers to Entry: Evidence from the Market for Corporate Bond Underwriting.* Federal Reserve Bank of New York and Bank for International Settlements Working Paper.

Solans, Eugenio. 2003. The International Role of the Euro in a Globalised Economy. Speech delivered at the Pareto Securities Economic Conference, Oslo, March 27.

Sinn, Hans-Werner. 2003. The Laggard of Europe. *CESifo Forum* 4, Special Issue (Spring).

About the Contributors

C. Fred Bergsten has been director of the Institute for International Economics since its creation in 1981. He is also chairman of the "Shadow G-8," which advises the G-8 countries on their annual summit meetings. He was chairman of the Competitiveness Policy Council, which was created by Congress, throughout its existence from 1991 to 1995 and chairman of the APEC Eminent Persons Group throughout its existence from 1993 to 1995. He was assistant secretary for international affairs of the US Treasury (1977–81); assistant for international economic affairs to Dr. Henry Kissinger at the National Security Council (1969–71); and a senior fellow at the Brookings Institution (1972–76), the Carnegie Endowment for International Peace (1981), and the Council on Foreign Relations (1967–68). He is the author, coauthor, coeditor, or editor of 34 books on a wide range of international economic issues, including *The United States and the World Economy* (2004), *Dollar Adjustment: How Far? Against What?* (2004), *Dollar Overvaluation and the World Economy* (2003), *No More Bashing: Building a New Japan–United States Economic Relationship* (2001), *Global Economic Leadership and the Group of Seven* (1996), and *The Dilemmas of the Dollar* (2d ed., 1996).

Ben Bernanke is member, Board of Governors of the Federal Reserve System. He was the Howard Harrison and Gabrielle Snyder Beck Professor of Economics and Public Affairs and chair of the economics department at Princeton University (1996–2002). He had served as a professor of economics and public affairs at Princeton University since 1985. He held a Guggenheim Fellowship and a Sloan Fellowship and is a fellow of the Econometric Society and of the American Academy of Arts and Sciences. In July 2001, he was appointed editor of the *American Economic Review*. He was a visiting scholar at the Federal Reserve Banks of Philadelphia (1987–89), Boston (1989–90), and New York (1990–91, 1994–96) and served on the Academic Advisory Panel at the Federal Reserve Bank of New York (1990–2002). His publications include *Essays on the Great Depression* (Princeton University Press, 2000) and *Inflation Targeting: Lessons from the International Experience* (Princeton University Press, 1999).

Günter Burghardt is the ambassador for the European Union to the United States. Before his present posting, he was at the Commission's headquarters in Brussels, most recently as the director general for external relations under Commissioners Chris Patten (1999–2000) and Hans van den Broek (1993–99). From 1985 to 1993 he was a close aide to Commission President Jacques Delors, holding the posts of deputy chief of staff and the Commission's political director. From 1970 to 1985 his assignments included deputy chief of staff to the commissioner for internal market, environmental protection, nuclear safety, and innovation (1981–84); assistant to the Commission's then–director general for external relations, Sir Roy Denman, who during the 1980s also served as the Commission's ambassador in Washington; and desk officer for relations with the United States, Canada, and Australia (1972–80). He entered the Commission as a member of the legal service in 1970.

Hervé Carré is the minister for economic, financial, and development affairs at the Delegation of the European Commission in Washington. He joined the European Commission in Brussels in 1973, specializing in the monetary area. He has since led divisions dealing with national and European Community monetary policies, the EMS, ECU and exchange markets, and international monetary and financial matters. In 1991 he was seconded to the US Federal Reserve Board in Washington, and in 1992 to the Government of Portugal as adviser to the minister of finance. He returned to the European Commission in 1994 as director for monetary matters and in 1999 became the director for the economy of the eurozone and the European Union. As a member of the Economic and Financial Committee (formerly the Monetary Committee) he was involved in all negotiations concerning the creation of the euro.

Richard Clarida is professor of economics and international affairs at Columbia University and has been the chair of the economics department since 1997. He was senior staff economist, President Reagan's Council of Economic Advisers (1986–87), and a consultant to President Reagan's Council of Economic Advisers (1987–89), Federal Reserve Bank of New York (1991–92, 1995–97), and the Group of 30, Project on Exchange Rate Regimes (1999). He was a member of the Cowles Foundation for Research in Economics (1983–88) and codirector of the Columbia Center for Economic and Political Analysis (2000). He is a research associate at the National Bureau of Economic Research. He was a visiting scholar at the International Monetary Fund, Federal Reserve Board, Bank of England, Bank of Italy, Reserve Bank of Austria, Bank of Canada, Deutsche Bundesbank, and the European Central Bank.

Richard N. Cooper is the Maurits C. Boas Professor of Economics at Harvard University and chairman of the Advisory Committee of the Institute for International Economics. He was the chairman of the National Intelligence Council (1995–97), chairman of the Federal Reserve Bank of Boston (1990–92), undersecretary of state for economic affairs (1977–81), deputy assistant secretary of state for international monetary affairs (1965–66), senior staff economist at the Council of Economic Advisers (1961–63), and professor of economics (1963–77) and provost (1972–74) at Yale University. He is the author, editor, coeditor, or coauthor of *What the Future Holds: Insights from Social Science* (MIT Press, 2002), *Environment and Resource Policies for the World Economy* (Brookings Institution, 1994); *Macroeconomic Policy and Adjustment in Korea, 1970–1990* (Harvard University Press, 1994); *Boom, Crisis, and Adjustment: The Macroeconomic Adjustment in Developing Countries* (World Bank, 1993); *Economic Stabilization and Debt in Developing Countries* (MIT Press, 1992); and *Can Nations Agree? Issues in International Economic Cooperation* (Brookings Institution, 1989).

Kristin Forbes is a member of the President's Council of Economic Advisers. She is on leave from the Massachusetts Institute of Technology's Sloan School of Management, where she is the Mitsubishi Career Development Chair and associate professor of international management. During 2001–02 Forbes worked in the US Treasury Department as the deputy assistant secretary of quantitative policy analysis, Latin American and Caribbean nations. She has written extensively on stock market contagion and coedited *International Financial Contagion* (2001). She is a faculty research fellow at the National Bureau of Economic Research. She was a visiting scholar at the Federal Reserve Board, Indian Council of Research on International Economic Relations, and International Monetary Fund. Before joining MIT, she worked in the investment banking division at Morgan Stanley, in the policy research department at the World Bank, and in the economics group at Fleet Financial Institutions.

Jeffrey Frankel is James W. Harpel Professor of Capital Formation and Growth at the Kennedy School of Government, Harvard University. He directs the National Bureau of Economic Research program in International Finance and Macroeconomics and is a member of the NBER Business Cycle Dating Committee, which in 2001 officially declared the US recession. He came to Harvard in 1999 from the Council of Economic Advisers, to which he was appointed by President Clinton in 1996 and subsequently confirmed by the Senate. His responsibilities as a member included international economics, macroeconomics, and the environment. He was a professor of economics at the University of California, Berkeley. Past appointments include the Brookings Institution, Federal Reserve Board, Institute for International Economics, International Monetary Fund, University of Michigan, and Yale University. Recent books include *American Economic Policy in the 1990s* (coeditor, MIT Press, 2002).

Vítor Gaspar has been the director general, DG Research, at the European Central Bank since 1998. Before this appointment he served as director of research at the Banco de Portugal. He was director of economic studies at the Portuguese Ministry of Finance and the personal representative of the finance minister in the Intergovernmental Conference that eventually led to the Maastricht Treaty. He held a teaching position in the economics department of the Universidade Nova de Lisboa. He is the author of numerous research papers and coeditor of *The Transformation of the European Financial System* (European Central Bank, 2003).

Philipp Hartmann is principal, DG Research, European Central Bank. He is an affiliate at the Centre for Economic Policy Research. He was a research fellow in financial regulation, London School of Economics. He is the author of *Currency Competition and Foreign Exchange Markets: The Dollar, the Yen, and the Euro* (Cambridge University Press, 1998), coeditor of *The Transformation of the European Financial System* (European Central Bank, 2003), and coauthor of *Financial Regulation* (Routledge, 1998).

Jürgen Kröger has been the director for economic studies and research at the European Commission in Brussels since 2002. He joined the commission in 1983 and has since held several positions, including head of division, monetary affairs of the euro area and other members states (1996–2002); counsellor in the Cabinet of Yves-Thibault de Silguy (commissioner responsible for monetary, financial, and economic affairs); and head of unit, directorate for national economies, Germany, France, and Denmark (1990–94). He also served at the commission's monetary directorate (1987–90) and the directorate of macroeconomic analysis (1983–87). He was assistant professor at the University of Hamburg (1977–83).

Tommaso Padoa-Schioppa is a member of the Executive Board of the European Central Bank. He was deputy director general of the Bank of Italy (1984–97) and director general for economic and financial affairs at the Commission of the European Communities, Brussels (1979). He is the president of the International Center for Monetary and Banking Studies, member of the G-7 Deputies and G-20 Deputies, member of the advisory committee of the Institute for International Economics, observer at the Financial Stability Forum, and chairman of the G-10 Committee on Payments and Settlement Systems. He was the chairman of the Basel Committee on Banking Supervision (1993–97), chairman of the Banking Advisory Committee of the Commission of the European Communities (1988–91), and chairman of the Working Group on Payment Systems of the Central Banks of the European Community (1991–95).

Adam S. Posen, senior fellow, was an economist in international research at the Federal Reserve Bank of New York (1994–97). He was Okun Memorial Fellow in Economic Studies at the Brookings Institution. In 1992–93, he was resident in Germany as a Bosch Foundation Fellow and worked for the Bundesbank in Frankfurt and for Deutsche Bank in Berlin. He is a consultant to the IMF and to several US government agencies, and a visiting scholar at central banks worldwide. He is a term member of the Council on Foreign Relations and serves on its Working Group on Transatlantic Relations and on its Independent Task Force on US-Japan Economic Relations. He is the founding US editor of the refereed journal *International Finance*. He is the author of *Restoring Japan's Economic Growth* (1998; Japanese translation, Toyo Keizai, 1999), coauthor of *Inflation Targeting: Lessons from the International Experience* (Princeton University Press, 1999), editor and coauthor of *The Future of Monetary Policy* (Blackwell, forthcoming), and coeditor and coauthor of *Japan's Financial Crisis and its Parallels to US Experience* (2000; Japanese translation, Toyo Keizai, 2001) and *Stabilizing the Economy* (Blackwell, forthcoming).

Randal Quarles is the assistant secretary for international affairs, US Treasury. From August 2001 through March 2002, he served as the United States executive director at the International Monetary Fund. The current appointment as assistant secretary is his second stint at the Treasury Department. He served as special assistant to the secretary for banking legislation from 1991 to 1992 and as deputy assistant secretary of the Treasury for financial institutions policy from 1992 to 1993. In the private sector, he is co-head of Davis Polk & Wardwell's Financial Institutions Group. He has advised both domestic and international banks and bank holding companies on a broad variety of matters, including mergers and acquisitions and venture capital operations, as well as the full range of bank securities activities and capital markets transactions. He has published on a variety of issues in international finance. He is a member of the American Bar Association and the Bar Association of the City of New York.

Hélène Rey is an assistant professor of economics and international affairs, Princeton University. She was a lecturer at the London School of Economics and Political Science (1997–2000). She was a visiting professor at CERAS and Ecole des Ponts, Paris; resident scholar at the International Monetary Fund's research department; and visiting scholar at NBER/ Harvard, Institute for International Economic Studies, Stockholm, Princeton University, and CentER, the business and economic research institute at Tilburg University, the Netherlands. She is the associate editor of the *Journal of the European Economic Association* and the *Economic Journal*.

Garry Schinasi is an adviser to the International Monetary Fund (IMF). He is on a one-year sabbatical from the IMF writing a monograph on financial stability issues. He was on the staff of the Board of Governors of the US Federal Reserve System from 1979 to 1989, after which he joined the staff of the IMF. In 1997, he was appointed chief of the Capital Markets and Financial Studies Division in the IMF's research department and codirected the IMF's annual *International Capital Markets Report*. In August 2001, he was appointed chief of the Financial Stability Division in the International Capital Markets Department and coproduced the IMF's Global Financial Stability Report. He has published articles in *The Review of Economic Studies, Journal of Economic Theory, Journal of International Money and Finance*, and other academic and policy journals. His recent research has focused on systemic risks in international financial markets, the linkages between monetary and financial stability, and the relevance of asset prices in the formulation of monetary and financial policies.

Edwin M. Truman, senior fellow, was assistant secretary of the US Treasury for international affairs (1998–2000). He was staff director of the Division of International Finance of the Board of Governors of the Federal Reserve System (1987–98) and director of the division from 1977 to 1987. From 1983 to 1998, he was one of three economists on the staff of the Federal Open Market Committee. He has been a member of numerous international groups working on international economic and financial issues, including the Financial Stability Forum's Working Group on Highly Leveraged Institutions (1999–2000), the G-22 Working Party on Transparency and Accountability (1998), the G-10-sponsored Working Party on Financial Stability in Emerging Market Economies (1996–97), the G-10 Working Group on the Resolution of Sovereign Liquidity Crises (1995–96), and the G-7 Working Group on Exchange Market Intervention (1982–83). He has published on international monetary economics, international debt problems, economic development, and European economic integration. He is the author of *Inflation Targeting in the World Economy* (2003).

Index

impact of growth rates on, 8
issues, 54–55
supply-, demand-side policies, 55
government bonds, 112
European, 186–88, 187*n*
Gramm-Leach-Bliley Act, 120
Greece, 24
stock market correlations with France, 108*f*
stock market correlations with US, 109*f*
Greenspan, Alan, 51
on fiscal consolidation, 139
on inflation targeting, 69
on US current account deficit, 50
view of dollar's global role, 62
Group of Eight (G-8), 48, 84
Group of Five (G-5), 74*n*, 84
Group of Seven (G-7), 9, 10, 28, 48
Agenda for Growth, 41–42, 55, 64
and exchange rate flexibility, 53
formation of, 84
and a G-2, 8
G-20 replacement of, 10, 73–74, 84
members, 73*n*
policy coordination role, 42
"Telephone Communiqué," 57
Group of Ten (G-10), 74
Group of Three (G-3), 68, 69*n*
Group of Twenty (G-20), 8, 10, 42, 48
increasing the importance, role of, 74
members, 73*n*
as a replacement for G-7, 10, 73–74, 84
Group of Two (G-2), 33
case for, 7–8, 28, 36–38
concern over, 42
for finance, 36–38, 45
goals of, 36
political acceptance of, 37
positive impact on US, Europe, 37–38
growth rates
gaps between US and eurozone, 8
Hungary, 9
financial status of, 61

IIF. *See* Institute of International Finance
IMF. *See* International Monetary Fund
India, 73, 84
Indonesia, 84
inflation targeting, 69*n*, 83
benefits of, 68–69
cost-pull factors, 6
demand-push factors, 6
impact on exchange rates, 10
under Taylor rule, 79–80
Institute of International Finance (IIF)
current account, capital flow estimates, 59
interbank market, 188
interest rates
areawide, 153
crowding out, 159, 160
and euro-dollar exchange rate, 3

in Europe, 159
long term, determinants of, 160, 160*t*
international currency. *See also* common currency
criteria for, 25
definition of, 62–63
and financial market superiority, 32
importance of size, 32
plausibility of two, 63
and relation to global output, 32
selection of, 63*n*
International Monetary Fund Executive Board
consolidating European seats on, 84–85
EU representation, 72–73, 72*n*
International Monetary Fund (IMF), 48
Articles of Agreement, 84
crisis intervention packages, 79
and exchange rate flexibility, 54
impact of convergence, 4, 4*n*
International Monetary and Financial
Committee, 48, 74, 85
involvement in EU issues, 61
quotas, 60, 72–73, 72*n*, 73*n*
role of, 9
view of US current account deficit, GDP, 51–52,
51*n*–52*n*
Ireland, 131
countercyclical response of fiscal stance, 129*t*
economic performance of, 144*f*, 145
government bonds, 187
inflation rate, 184
stock market correlations with France, 108*f*
stock market correlations with US, 109*f*
Issing, Otmar
on global adjustment, growth, 54
on stock market declines, 51*n*
on US deficit, 51–52
Italy, 16, 70, 84
Agenda for Growth, 64
bond market, 112
countercyclical response of fiscal stance, 129*t*,
130, 133*f*
debt, 134, 135
debt-to-GDP ratios, 134*f*
determinants of interest rates, 160*t*
economic performance of, 144*f*, 145–47
and eurozone membership, 147, 147*n*
expansionary consolidation, 146
fiscal strength, 17
government bonds, 186
interest rates, investments, 146*f*, 159*n*
macroeconomic performance, 147*f*
motivation for eurozone membership, 144
stock market correlations with France, 107, 108*f*
stock market correlations with US, 109*f*

Japan, 36, 37, 49*n*, 53
1997 tax increases, 124*n*
countercyclical response of fiscal stance, 129*t*
debt, 138*n*
failure to modernize, 33

reserve requirements, 88–89
Rubinomics, 132
    characteristics of, 16
    in the eurozone, 124–25, 143, 159
Russia, 84, 173

Save Social Security First, 162, 164
Schmidt, Helmut, 32
Schröder, Gerhard, 41
security markets, obstacles to, 13
September 11 terrorist attacks
    and ECB financial market support, 31
SGP. *See* Stability and Growth Pact
"Shared Sacrifice," 18, 19, 162, 164
    vs. "Starve the Beast," 165
Single European Act, 141
single monetary policy
    and money market integration, 89
South Africa, 73
South Korea, 36, 84
    growth estimates for, 102f
Spain, 24, 84
    countercyclical response of fiscal stance, 129t
    determinants of interest rates, 160t
    government bonds, 186, 187
    stock market correlations with France, 107, 108f
    stock market correlations with US, 109f
Spearman correlation, 136
spillovers, 64, 64n, 65
Stability and Growth Pact (SGP), 7, 16, 17, 29, 34,
    55, 79, 123. *See also* Maastricht Treaty
    and countercyclical responses, 157–58, 169
    country violations of, 124, 126, 143
    effect on stabilization policy, 127–30
    impact on EMU countries, 157–58
    impact on euro, eurozone, 143
    and impact on euro fiscal stability, 17
    impact on eurozone fiscal policy, 130
    problems with, 125–27, 143
    purposes, 125
    shortcomings of, 18, 154
    viability of rules, 141
Standard & Poor's
    decline, recovery of, 51n
"Starve the Beast," 18–19, 161, 162–63
    evaluation of, 164
    vs. "Shared Sacrifice," 165
sterilized intervention, 36
stock market
    correlation of eurozone and US, 13–14
    integration, euro's impact on, 107–09
structural reform
    and cross-border payoffs, 64, 65
Sweden, 49n
    countercyclical response of fiscal stance, 129t
    economic performance of, 144f
    government bonds, 187n
    and nonadoption of euro, 72
Switzerland, 49n

Taylor rule, 79, 80
Toronto Summit, 65
tort reform, 55
trade
    impact of euro on, 19, 23–24
    US-Europe cooperation, 33
trade flows
    impact on euro, 104–05
    impact on financial integration, 104, 110
trade integration
    progress in EU, 173
transaction costs, 4
    reduction of, 19
Treaty of Rome, 71
Trichet, Jean-Claude, 52
Turkey, 59n

United Kingdom. *See also* pound
    Agenda for Growth, 64
    countercyclical response of fiscal stance, 129t
    economic performance of, 144f
    and euro area membership, 70
    government bonds, 187n
    growth estimates for, 102f
    interest rates, 160t
    and nonadoption of euro, 29, 72
    role in global economy, 71
    stock market correlations with EU countries,
    108n
United States. *See also* dollar
    Agenda for Growth, 64
    approach to monetary policy, 83
    attitude toward a unified Europe, 82–83
    bilateral trade balances with EU, 53n
    budget deficit, spending, 163, 163f
    budget forecasts, 165–66, 166f
    budget rules, 142
    capital accounts, 2
    corporate, government scandals, 51n
    countercyclical response of fiscal stance, 129t,
    130, 136f
    "cut taxes and spend," 161
    debt, 159
    debt and deficit problems, 34–35
    economy, 3–4, 31, 49, 49n, 175
    expansionary consolidation, 161
    external adjustment, 50, 52, 53, 54–55, 56–58
    external deficits, 10, 54
    financial integration with eurozone, 109
    financial supervision, 15, 119–20
    fiscal expansion, 140
    fiscal policy, 12n, 158, 167–68, 168t
    GDP, IMF view of, 51n–52n
    growth, 101, 102f, 175
    interest rates, 160, 160t
    international debt, 50n
    monetary policy and exchange dollar value,
    57n
    productivity, 49, 49n

Other Publications from the Institute for International Economics

POLICY BRIEFS

* = out of print

The Economics of Global Warming
William R. Cline/*June 1992*   ISBN 0-88132-132-X
US Taxation of International Income: Blueprint
for Reform*   Gary Clyde Hufbauer, assisted
by Joanna M. van Rooij
October 1992   ISBN 0-88132-134-6
Who's Bashing Whom? Trade Conflict in High-
Technology Industries   Laura D'Andrea Tyson
November 1992   ISBN 0-88132-106-0
Korea in the World Economy*   Il SaKong
January 1993   ISBN 0-88132-183-4
Pacific Dynamism and the International
Economic System*
C. Fred Bergsten and Marcus Noland, editors
May 1993   ISBN 0-88132-196-6
Economic Consequences of Soviet Disintegration*
John Williamson, editor
May 1993   ISBN 0-88132-190-7
Reconcilable Differences? United States-Japan
Economic Conflict*
C. Fred Bergsten and Marcus Noland
June 1993   ISBN 0-88132-129-X
Does Foreign Exchange Intervention Work?
Kathryn M. Dominguez and Jeffrey A. Frankel
September 1993   ISBN 0-88132-104-4
Sizing Up U.S. Export Disincentives*
J. David Richardson
September 1993   ISBN 0-88132-107-9
NAFTA: An Assessment
Gary Clyde Hufbauer and Jeffrey J. Schott/*rev. ed.*
October 1993   ISBN 0-88132-199-0
Adjusting to Volatile Energy Prices
Philip K. Verleger, Jr.
November 1993   ISBN 0-88132-069-2
The Political Economy of Policy Reform
John Williamson, editor
January 1994   ISBN 0-88132-195-8
Measuring the Costs of Protection
in the United States
Gary Clyde Hufbauer and Kimberly Ann Elliott
January 1994   ISBN 0-88132-108-7
The Dynamics of Korean Economic Development*
Cho Soon/*March 1994*   ISBN 0-88132-162-1
Reviving the European Union*
C. Randall Henning, Eduard Hochreiter, and
Gary Clyde Hufbauer, editors
April 1994   ISBN 0-88132-208-3
China in the World Economy   Nicholas R. Lardy
April 1994   ISBN 0-88132-200-8
Greening the GATT: Trade, Environment, and
the Future   Daniel C. Esty
July 1994   ISBN 0-88132-205-9
Western Hemisphere Economic Integration*
Gary Clyde Hufbauer and Jeffrey J. Schott
July 1994   ISBN 0-88132-159-1
Currencies and Politics in the United States,
Germany, and Japan   C. Randall Henning
September 1994   ISBN 0-88132-127-3

Estimating Equilibrium Exchange Rates
John Williamson, editor
September 1994   ISBN 0-88132-076-5
Managing the World Economy: Fifty Years After
Bretton Woods   Peter B. Kenen, editor
September 1994   ISBN 0-88132-212-1
Reciprocity and Retaliation in U.S. Trade Policy
Thomas O. Bayard and Kimberly Ann Elliott
September 1994   ISBN 0-88132-084-6
The Uruguay Round: An Assessment*
Jeffrey J. Schott, assisted by Johanna W. Buurman
November 1994   ISBN 0-88132-206-7
Measuring the Costs of Protection in Japan*
Yoko Sazanami, Shujiro Urata, and Hiroki Kawai
January 1995   ISBN 0-88132-211-3
Foreign Direct Investment in the United States,
3d ed., Edward M. Graham and Paul R. Krugman
January 1995   ISBN 0-88132-204-0
The Political Economy of Korea-United States
Cooperation*
C. Fred Bergsten and Il SaKong, editors
February 1995   ISBN 0-88132-213-X
International Debt Reexamined*   William R. Cline
February 1995   ISBN 0-88132-083-8
American Trade Politics, 3d ed., I. M. Destler
April 1995   ISBN 0-88132-215-6
Managing Official Export Credits: The Quest for
a Global Regime*   John E. Ray
July 1995   ISBN 0-88132-207-5
Asia Pacific Fusion: Japan's Role in APEC*
Yoichi Funabashi
October 1995   ISBN 0-88132-224-5
Korea-United States Cooperation in the New
World Order*
C. Fred Bergsten and Il SaKong, editors
February 1996   ISBN 0-88132-226-1
Why Exports Really Matter!*   ISBN 0-88132-221-0
Why Exports Matter More!*   ISBN 0-88132-229-6
J. David Richardson and Karin Rindal
July 1995; February 1996
Global Corporations and National Governments
Edward M. Graham
May 1996   ISBN 0-88132-111-7
Global Economic Leadership and the Group of
Seven   C. Fred Bergsten and C. Randall Henning
May 1996   ISBN 0-88132-218-0
The Trading System After the Uruguay Round*
John Whalley and Colleen Hamilton
July 1996   ISBN 0-88132-131-1
Private Capital Flows to Emerging Markets After
the Mexican Crisis*   Guillermo A. Calvo,
Morris Goldstein, and Eduard Hochreiter
September 1996   ISBN 0-88132-232-6
The Crawling Band as an Exchange Rate Regime:
Lessons from Chile, Colombia, and Israel
John Williamson
September 1996   ISBN 0-88132-231-8

Flying High: Liberalizing Civil Aviation in the Asia Pacific*
Gary Clyde Hufbauer and Christopher Findlay
November 1996   ISBN 0-88132-227-X

Measuring the Costs of Visible Protection in Korea*   Namdoo Kim
November 1996   ISBN 0-88132-236-9

The World Trading System: Challenges Ahead
Jeffrey J. Schott
December 1996   ISBN 0-88132-235-0

Has Globalization Gone Too Far?   Dani Rodrik
March 1997   ISBN cloth 0-88132-243-1

Korea-United States Economic Relationship*
C. Fred Bergsten and Il SaKong, editors
March 1997   ISBN 0-88132-240-7

Summitry in the Americas: A Progress Report
Richard E. Feinberg
April 1997   ISBN 0-88132-242-3

Corruption and the Global Economy
Kimberly Ann Elliott
June 1997   ISBN 0-88132-233-4

Regional Trading Blocs in the World Economic System   Jeffrey A. Frankel
October 1997   ISBN 0-88132-202-4

Sustaining the Asia Pacific Miracle: Environmental Protection and Economic Integration   Andre Dua and Daniel C. Esty
October 1997   ISBN 0-88132-250-4

Trade and Income Distribution   William R. Cline
November 1997   ISBN 0-88132-216-4

Global Competition Policy
Edward M. Graham and J. David Richardson
December 1997   ISBN 0-88132-166-4

Unfinished Business: Telecommunications after the Uruguay Round
Gary Clyde Hufbauer and Erika Wada
December 1997   ISBN 0-88132-257-1

Financial Services Liberalization in the WTO
Wendy Dobson and Pierre Jacquet
June 1998   ISBN 0-88132-254-7

Restoring Japan's Economic Growth
Adam S. Posen
September 1998   ISBN 0-88132-262-8

Measuring the Costs of Protection in China
Zhang Shuguang, Zhang Yansheng, and Wan Zhongxin
November 1998   ISBN 0-88132-247-4

Foreign Direct Investment and Development: The New Policy Agenda for Developing Countries and Economies in Transition
Theodore H. Moran
December 1998   ISBN 0-88132-258-X

Behind the Open Door: Foreign Enterprises in the Chinese Marketplace
Daniel H. Rosen
January 1999   ISBN 0-88132-263-6

Toward A New International Financial Architecture: A Practical Post-Asia Agenda
Barry Eichengreen
February 1999   ISBN 0-88132-270-9

Is the U.S. Trade Deficit Sustainable?
Catherine L. Mann
September 1999   ISBN 0-88132-265-2

Safeguarding Prosperity in a Global Financial System: The Future International Financial Architecture, Independent Task Force Report Sponsored by the Council on Foreign Relations
Morris Goldstein, Project Director
October 1999   ISBN 0-88132-287-3

Avoiding the Apocalypse: The Future of the Two Koreas   Marcus Noland
June 2000   ISBN 0-88132-278-4

Assessing Financial Vulnerability: An Early Warning System for Emerging Markets
Morris Goldstein, Graciela Kaminsky, and Carmen Reinhart
June 2000   ISBN 0-88132-237-7

Global Electronic Commerce: A Policy Primer
Catherine L. Mann, Sue E. Eckert, and Sarah Cleeland Knight
July 2000   ISBN 0-88132-274-1

The WTO after Seattle   Jeffrey J. Schott, editor
July 2000   ISBN 0-88132-290-3

Intellectual Property Rights in the Global Economy   Keith E. Maskus
August 2000   ISBN 0-88132-282-2

The Political Economy of the Asian Financial Crisis   Stephan Haggard
August 2000   ISBN 0-88132-283-0

Transforming Foreign Aid: United States Assistance in the 21st Century   Carol Lancaster
August 2000   ISBN 0-88132-291-1

Fighting the Wrong Enemy: Antiglobal Activists and Multinational Enterprises   Edward M.Graham
September 2000   ISBN 0-88132-272-5

Globalization and the Perceptions of American Workers
Kenneth F. Scheve and Matthew J. Slaughter
March 2001   ISBN 0-88132-295-4

World Capital Markets: Challenge to the G-10
Wendy Dobson and Gary Clyde Hufbauer, assisted by Hyun Koo Cho
May 2001   ISBN 0-88132-301-2

Prospects for Free Trade in the Americas
Jeffrey J. Schott/*August 2001*   ISBN 0-88132-275-X

Toward a North American Community: Lessons from the Old World for the New
Robert A. Pastor/*August 2001*   ISBN 0-88132-328-4

Measuring the Costs of Protection in Europe: European Commercial Policy in the 2000s
Patrick A. Messerlin
September 2001   ISBN 0-88132-273-3

**Australia, New Zealand,
and Papua New Guinea**
D.A. Information Services
648 Whitehorse Road
Mitcham, Victoria 3132, Australia
tel: 61-3-9210-7777
fax: 61-3-9210-7788
email: service@adadirect.com.au
www.dadirect.com.au

United Kingdom and Europe
(including Russia and Turkey)
The Eurospan Group
3 Henrietta Street, Covent Garden
London WC2E 8LU England
tel: 44-20-7240-0856
fax: 44-20-7379-0609
www.eurospan.co.uk

Japan and the Republic of Korea
United Publishers Services Ltd.
1-32-5, Higashi-shinagawa,
Shinagawa-ku, Tokyo 140-0002 JAPAN
tel: 81-3-5479-7251
fax: 81-3-5479-7307
info@ups.co.jp
**For trade accounts only.
Individuals will find IIE books in
leading Tokyo bookstores.**

Canada
Renouf Bookstore
5369 Canotek Road, Unit 1
Ottawa, Ontario KIJ 9J3, Canada
tel: 613-745-2665
fax: 613-745-7660
www.renoufbooks.com

India, Bangladesh, Nepal, and Sri Lanka
Viva Books Pvt.
Mr. Vinod Vasishtha
4325/3, Ansari Rd.
Daryaganj, New Delhi-110002
India
tel: 91-11-327-9280
fax: 91-11-326-7224
email: vinod.viva@gndel.globalnet. ems.vsnl.
net.in

Southeast Asia (Brunei, Burma, Cambodia,
Malaysia, Indonesia,
the Philippines, Singapore, Thailand
Taiwan, and Vietnam)
APAC Publishers Services
70 Bedemeer Road #05-03
Hiap Huat House
Singapore 339940
tel: 65-684-47333
fax: 65-674-78916

**Visit our Web site at:
www.iie.com
E-mail orders to:
orders@iie.com**